Practical Risk Management for the CIO

Mark Scherling

CRC Press
Taylor & Francis Group
Boca Raton London New York

CRC Press is an imprint of the
Taylor & Francis Group, an **informa** business

AN AUERBACH BOOK

CRC Press
Taylor & Francis Group
6000 Broken Sound Parkway NW, Suite 300
Boca Raton, FL 33487-2742

First issued in paperback 2018

© 2011 by Taylor & Francis Group, LLC
CRC Press is an imprint of Taylor & Francis Group, an Informa business

No claim to original U.S. Government works

ISBN-13: 978-1-4398-5653-6 (hbk)
ISBN-13: 978-1-138-37449-2 (pbk)

Library of Congress Cataloging-in-Publication Data

Scherling, Mark.
    Practical risk management for the CIO / Mark Scherling.
        p. cm.
    Includes bibliographical references and index.
    ISBN 978-1-4398-5653-6 (hbk. : alk. paper)
    1. Data protection. 2. Risk management. 3. Information technology--Security measures. 4. Computer networks--Security measures. 5. Chief information officers. I. Title.

HF5548.37.S34 2011
658.4'78--dc23   2011017505

Visit the Taylor & Francis Web site at
http://www.taylorandfrancis.com

and the CRC Press Web site at
http://www.crcpress.com

Contents

PART III LIABILITIES MANAGEMENT

Preface

Information is the lifeblood of any organization. Without good information, poor decisions are made, risks are not recognized and communicated, and valuable information is lost or stolen. Cyber risks are increasing, and these risks are seriously impacting organizations. Without good information risk management, customer trust and loyalties as well as the organization's reputation and brand are at risk. In taking a more holistic approach to information risk management, we encompass the risks to service delivery, information management, as well as information protection. Chief Information Officers (CIOs) are tasked with delivering information to the organization. In essence, this means making sure the right information is available to the right person at the right time to enable people to do their jobs and make good decisions. It also means making sure the wrong information is not being given to the wrong person at the wrong time, thereby increasing risks to the organization.

It is time for CIOs to relook at how they are organized and realign with what is important to the business. CIOs deliver information to the business. Good information is what is important to the business. Any Chief Executive Officer (CEO) or executive will tell you that without good information they cannot make good decisions. This means that information must be findable, managed, protected, and available. Risks to information must be managed and mitigated. The costs of mismanagement or ignoring risks are huge. Fines, noncompliance, breaches, loss of trust, loss of reputation, loss of key personnel, and perhaps jail time can occur if risks are ignored. CIOs must better improve the management of risks to their information. This book gives the reader some solid foundations for improving information risk management.

Acknowledgments

Many people encouraged me to write this book. Although I will miss a few names, I would like to acknowledge a few who really helped me. To

Robin Wakefield, who has helped me in many of my thoughts, especially some of the more radical ones.

Michael Legary, who was so enthusiastic about my book that he read it forward and backward.

Richard Mandy, who kept me thinking out-of-the-box.

Richard Hakim, who helped edit some key sections.

Shayne Fynes, who encouraged me to write it and said that he would be the first one to buy my book.

Joe Gollner, who helped me with the information management.

My wife Gerry, who tolerated my rants and raves about Microsoft Word®, formatting documents, and some other things about word processing software. She gave me time to write this book.

My brother Gary Scherling, who is a Project Manager and helped write the section on Project Management.

Some of my friends John, Mike, and Caner, and to my colleagues in the British Columbia (BC) Government, who encouraged me to write this book.

About the Author

Mark Scherling, CISSP, CRM, has been working in IT for over 30 years. For the past four years, he has been managing information security and privacy for the Justice Sector in the Government of British Columbia (Canada). Prior to the Justice Sector, he managed the Information Security Investigations Unit for the entire BC government. He has designed and implemented public key infrastructure (PKI) and security solutions for numerous clients.

He is considered a Subject Matter Expert in Risk Management and Information Security by the Information Systems Audit and Control Association (ISACA). He contributed to the Risk IT Framework and Certification in Risk and Information Systems (CRISC), a new ISACA Certification. He is viewed as a Security and Risk Management Expert by many people within and associated with the Government of British Columbia.

His background includes sales, marketing, and information management. In the mid-1990s, he was instrumental in developing and implementing the Canadian Department of National Defence Intranet or the DIN. He has significant experience in information and knowledge management. He combines this expertise with information protection to create an information risk management strategy for Chief Information Officers (CIOs).

He has been part of the evolution of information technology (IT) from Digital Equipment's Vaxes and PDP11s to mobile computing, the Internet, and cloud computing. The interconnected world we now live in holds exciting promise to link people, computers, applications, and information. There are risks when we link everything together and share information. Organizations are always trying to reduce costs and improve customer relations. Mark has been involved in information security for over 13 years and has oriented his approach from simple information security to risk management strategies. As the Internet continues to evolve, so evolves information security and risk management. The reality is that we need better ways of managing risks to our information and services. His approach takes a more holistic approach to risks, considering not just liabilities but also service delivery because information is one of our most important assets.

1

INTRODUCTION

Why Risk Management?

The purpose of this book is to help Chief Information Officers (CIOs), Chief Information Security Officers (CISOs), Chief Risk Officers (CROs), Information Management/Information Technology (IM/IT) Security Professionals, and IM/IT Managers deal with IM/IT risks. IM/IT risks are not all about information security. The CIO must deliver IM/IT services to enable the business to run effectively. The CIO must also protect information to prevent it from being lost or stolen. The CIO walks on the edge of a sword, balancing *service delivery* on one side and *liabilities* on the other. Straying too far on either side will result in failure, and that failure may be catastrophic.

We have been managing risk from the time we left the trees to modern times. Our risk model is still based on primal instincts (fight or flight). It was very simple and our choices were simple. We made the choice to eat, get eaten, or run away. We had to decide if the tiger was smiling because its belly was full or because it saw us as the next meal. We still use that same habitual way of thinking to deal with today's "tigers," and we can be led to make less than optimal decisions.

At a basic instinct level, our risk management skills are not well suited to making risk decisions in the complex environment in which we live today. If you consider a medium-sized network of 4,000 devices with routers, switches, servers, workstations, and printers, about 6.9 billion electronic events are generated every working day. Now think about which of those events could affect you or your organization in a negative way. How about in a positive way? We need tools, processes, and methodologies to help us make informed decisions when managing risks, especially information and IT risks.

With the advent of the Internet we now have a single worldwide network or, as Kevin Kelly from *Wired Magazine* describes it, "The

Machine." The Machine is composed of billions of computers, routers, switches, and mobile devices, all with a view into this network. And with this single network we have ways of doing amazing things. We can communicate around the world. People can read what is going on across the planet almost at the moment an event is happening. Think about some of the events that have occurred over the past decade and we knew about it the minute it was happening. We see pictures of disasters within minutes of the disaster happening. People have digitized this world into The Machine. And it will become far more connected. And the risks? If you don't keep up, you will fall behind and become a have-not. If you keep up, you pay the price of evolving faster than your people can evolve. You end up with technology that is too sophisticated to be understood. You end up with too many events happening. And you cannot make good decisions without good information.

We are in a war zone and we do not know it. The war zone is cyberspace. The events that happen in cyberspace happen a million times faster than events in real-time. The events happen all over the world and it is a global economy. Because we are all connected, we also are connected to people with criminal intent. Those people are intent on stealing your money, information, and anything of value. The world market for information is in the trillions of dollars. And it does not matter how it was gotten—the market is there for information.

Today the biggest risk in cyberspace is misunderstanding. According to the Internet Security Alliance (ISA) and the American National Standards Institute (ANSI) report entitled "The Financial Management of Cyber Risk," most executives wait until they are compromised to put a reactive plan in place. Waiting until after the problem has occurred damages reputations and costs more money. Reactive plans are too late. It is the proverbial "closing the gate after the horses are gone." According to the Ponemon Institute, the average incident cost to an organization rose from $4.5 million in 2005 to $6.65 million in 2009 for a security breach involving credit cards. And we cannot estimate the damage to reputation—not to mention the theft of intellectual property that has cost billions of dollars. It has cost companies dearly.

Risk management is something we do every day. We manage risks as we walk across a street or drive down the highway. On an individual basis, we manage risks fairly well, although we always hear stories about people who do not think about the risks and manage to hurt themselves or worse because they did something stupid. At an organizational level, we do not manage risks well. This is due to the complexity of organizations and systems. At some levels, we manage risks fairly well. However, as we have seen in many of the failures of organizations, risk was not managed well. *Risk management* is ad hoc management at best.

We have not formalized risk management in most organizations. The closest we come to enterprise risk management is the auditors and the board. In some organizations there is the recognition that risk must be managed at the corporate level and executives must be aware of risks in making key business decisions. In those organizations, there is an audit advisory committee that advises the board and directors on business risks. These are key business decisions that change the way an organization conducts business. Typically, these are focused on *rewarded risks*, which are risks associated with investments that create value for shareholders. What is missing is the incorporation of operational risks into these key business decisions. As indicated by a number of studies, operational failures can cause significant losses. In reality, risk management is still very much fragmented and managed within business lines and geographic boundaries.

Even more fragmented are risks associated with IM/IT. The reality is that we are all heavily invested in cyberspace. We do business in cyberspace because it reduces our costs. We do business in cyberspace because our partners and customers do business there. We use Web sites to provide information to our customers, our partners, and our competitors. We use the Web to inform, transact, and communicate. We do not manage the risks associated with cyberspace as business risks. Cyberspace is an enterprisewide risk management issue. It should be at the board. It should have a strategic, cross-organization focus.

Cyberspace has both rewarded risks and unrewarded risks (the organization is compelled to invest in security to prevent data loss or meet compliance). The requirement is to recognize that cyberspace risks are both horizontal across the organization and vertical within business units.

Risk management is an integral oversight function to help organizations avoid or mitigate situations or events that can harm individuals, groups, or the organization. Risk management is not just about organizational harm, but is also about how services are delivered. Risk management does not reduce risks; it measures and reports risks.

It is really simple why you manage risks:

- To reduce or mitigate liabilities
- To improve or maintain service delivery

Information risk management is about getting the right information to the right person at the right time while preventing the wrong information from getting to the wrong person at the wrong time. And what we are seeing is that information risk management is still considered a technical issue to be dealt with by IM or IT staff. According to the ISA-ANSI publication *The Financial Management of Cyber Risk* most enterprises categorize information security as a technical or operational issue to be managed by the IT department. This misinformation is being fed by outdated corporate structures and the lack of an overall strategy dealing with information risk management.

In the ISA-ANSI publication, they indicate that the Chief Financial Officer (CFO) as opposed to the CIO or CISO should be the most logical person to lead enterprise risk management, including information risk management. The problem is one of education and time. To properly inform a CFO, they need to have some background in IM/IT to understand some of the nuisances that make up information technology. Because of the complexity, there is no single person who has that understanding. That is why we must automate risk management to allow the information to be presented in a meaningful way. The Federal Information Security Management Act (FISMA), which was passed in 2002, is now looking toward continuous monitoring or near-real-time risk management so that on a real-time basis, senior executives understand the security state of their information systems.

We need to consider risk management starting at the top. We have all heard of enterprise risk management (ERM). ERM is usually practiced at the board or executive level in making strategic decisions. At the enterprise level, risk management as defined by ISO 31000 (2009) enables an organization to

- Increase the likelihood of achieving objectives;
- Improve the identification of opportunities and threats;

- Encourage proactive management;
- Comply with legal and regulatory requirements;
- Improve governance;
- Improve controls;
- Better allocate and use resources for risk mitigation;
- Reduce losses and the impact of risks to objectives;
- Improve loss prevention and incident management; and
- Improve organizational resilience.

Information risk management is a part of ERM. Information risk management is about managing the risks to your information. As described by the ISA-ANSI report on the financial management of cyber risk, information risks must be considered at the corporate level and not left to IT. Balancing the availability of information with the right level of access controls to prevent the wrong information from going to the wrong person is important. Understanding the balance between controls and access is critical.

Whether an order is processed, a credit card is used, information is transmitted to a truck to move goods, or a machine executes a set of instructions to complete a job, some information is processed and a transaction occurs. It does not matter if it is a banking transaction, an order transaction, or a manufacturing transaction. There are steps taken to complete the transaction. Getting the right information to the right person* at the right time will result in successful completion of the transaction. Getting the wrong information to the wrong person at the wrong time may result in a failed transaction. Worse yet, getting the wrong information to the wrong person at the wrong time represents a liability.

So what do we mean by *right information*? How about the *wrong information*? It depends. The right information means something different to every person. We can define right information as information with relevance to a situation or a decision. The information could have positive or negative relevance. Usually we associate right information with making decisions, and with the right information we hope we are making good decisions. Wrong information has a negative context. We can associate wrong information with making

---

* Person will be used to describe entities because a person could be a human being, an application, or a system.

Figure 1.1   Balance delivery with liability.

poor or bad decisions. And in some context, the information could be good information; but in the wrong hands, such as theft of credit card information, it will represent a liability. We also need to consider that incorrect information will definitely lead to bad decisions. This means that in terms of risk management, we have to manage our information better or else we will make bad decisions based on poor information (Figure 1.1).

Today, much of risk management is very fragmented in organizations. We are still wrestling with IM/IT as a service and information security as a means of preventing liabilities relating to our electronic service delivery. Often, information security is separated from operations and the business is further separated from IT operations. Applications further divide the organization into lines of business, and the expectation that IM/IT can handle all aspects of information service delivery is often misplaced. Risks tend to be managed locally and not globally, causing further fragmentation. Because we are connected to the Internet and we have such a dependency on computers, we need to reconsider risk management both from a horizontal (or enterprise) perspective and from a vertical (or business line) perspective. Access to one system in one business area may give someone access to all systems across the organization, and that someone may not be a person you want. We have heard about credit card theft, personal information theft, and intellectual property theft, and it is all happening now on our systems. As we continue to get more connected, have more dependencies on computers, and add social networks to our corporate capabilities, our liabilities will increase and our service delivery will become more complex.

So what liabilities are we most concerned with?

How do we manage and improve service delivery?

Risks must be put into terms that everyone understands. For an executive managing hundreds of millions of dollars, risk must be in terms of dollars that impact their desired outcome, such as a product, service, or program. What does risk mean to their budget? If a risk represents 10% of their budget when the risk is realized, how much will the executive spend mitigating the risk? On the other hand, if a risk represents less than 1% of their budget, they are less likely to spend a lot of dollars mitigating the risk. And we have to recognize that measuring risk and doing mitigation is not the end. Risks are always changing, and we are in a very complex world. We run very complex systems and have very complex processes. We have to expect that even minor risks that we usually might ignore can cause a major or catastrophic event.

The perfect storm that almost happened was Three Mile Island, a nuclear facility in the eastern United States. The accident started at 4:00 a.m. on Wednesday, March 28, 1979, with a failure in the nonnuclear secondary system. A second failure in the primary system was caused by a stuck-open valve. Compounding these failures were the inaction of plant operators in recognizing the situation as a loss of coolant. Additional factors were inadequate training and human failures such as industrial design errors. The investigation uncovered a series of events that, by themselves, were not significant. However, the combination of all the events caused a partial core meltdown in one of the reactors. The lessons learned showed how groups of people react and make decisions under stress.

This led, in 1984, to Charles Perrow describing "system accidents" as having two main characteristics: interactive complexity and tight coupling. Once an organization reaches a certain size there is a lot more complexity and uncertainty to deal with as there are more people, systems, applications, networks, end-point devices, and information. The chances of small coincidental accidents causing significant impacts increase. The complexity of The Machine is beyond our comprehension. With billions of devices and billions of messages occurring daily, we cannot predict with any certainty that events in cyberspace will not affect us. And with social networks becoming the norm, we have much more open communications and many more ways of being attacked.

Our resources are limited. Our budgets are limited. Our time is limited. Each year, more is demanded from CIOs. Each year, it is not enough to just run an IT organization; there must be more value back to the organization. We need an overall approach to managing both service delivery and liabilities. How do we make sure that the right information gets to the right person at the right time while preventing the wrong information from going to the wrong person at the wrong time? We start by defining what we mean by *liabilities* (Chapter 2) and *service delivery* (Chapter 3).

2

LIABILITY

There are many liabilities to consider. Fire, earthquakes, floods, typhoons, and hurricanes are all natural disasters that can impact your business. We need to consider these events in business continuity and disaster recovery scenarios. These events are random, may occur in your tenure, or may miss your operations altogether. We all know about Hurricane Katrina on August 23, 2005, which caused massive damage in New Orleans, Louisiana. Hurricane Katrina was one of the most costly hurricanes and one of the five deadliest. At least 1,836 people lost their lives and total damage was $81 billion. The need for *business continuity* and *disaster recovery* to manage these types of disasters is critical to the survival of organizations. Basic risk mitigation strategies that include business continuity planning and disaster recovery planning must be considered in any IM/IT organization.

As a CIO, you manage information and infrastructure. One of the organization's most important assets is information. When misused, it may become a liability. Figure 2.1 shows the magnitude of costs for three different scenarios involving the inappropriate use of information.

1. *Personal data disclosed or stolen:* Disclosure of personal data is well known and has very specific costs associated with it. Credit cards are a primary example.
2. *Intellectual property disclosed or stolen:* Theft of intellectual property has been known to bankrupt companies.
3. *Wrong decision made:* The third is not getting the right information at the right time and making the wrong decision. Less attention is paid to the wrong information at the wrong time because these are mistakes made by executives, engineers, scientists, and presidents, and nobody wants these mistakes in the public eye. When they are, there is a lot of public attention and it is mostly negative.

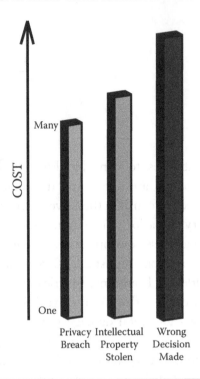

Figure 2.1   Magnitude of cost of liabilities.

Our primary goal is to prevent these scenarios from happening. If they happen, our secondary objective is to reduce the impact. We discuss these three scenarios in more detail.

Personal Data Disclosed or Stolen

Personal data is a form of money on the Internet. Over 100 million Americans have reported personal identity theft in the form of a credit card being stolen. According to the 2009 Data Breach Report by Verizon, personal data associated with a credit card has plummeted in value from a market high of $10 to $16 per magnetic stripe record to a low of $0.50 per record. This means that criminals are focusing their attention on other forms of personal data, such as personal identification numbers (PINs) as well as the associated credit and debit account information. It also means that criminals are focusing their attacks on corporations and organizations where the information is concentrated. The Ponemon Institute Study of 2006 determined that the cost per customer may be as high as \$182, with an average cost per corporation of \$4.8 million. This includes direct and indirect costs such as legal expenses, communications with customers, re-issuance of credit cards, stock price drop in publicly traded companies, external auditors, and civil suits.

Personal data is the focus of the Data Security Standard (DSS), Payment Card Industry (PCI), and Health Insurance Portability and Accountability Act (HIPAA), as well as California SB 1386 and numerous other state laws. Personal data is the focus of many other governments around the world, mostly in Europe and North America. In the United Kingdom there are several acts that pertain to proper management of personal data, including the Freedom of Information Act and the Data Protection Act. In Canada there is the Personal Information Protection and Electronic Documents Act (PIPEDA), as well as provincial legislation such as the Freedom of Information and Protection of Privacy Act (FOIPPA) in British Columbia.

We have seen numerous examples of breaches. One of the very first major Internet breaches occurred on July 20, 2005, when John Perry, President and CEO of CardSystems Solutions Inc., released a written statement to the U.S. Congress regarding a security breach that was discovered on May 22, 2005. The security breach was an unauthorized script placed on an Internet-facing application server that searched for and captured credit card records containing cardholder name, account number, expiry date, and Card Verification Value (CVV) code (information contained in the magnetic stripe on the back of a credit card). A total of 263,000 records were copied and sent outside the company. This was a small event by today's standards.

In 2009, the Data Breach Report by Verizon reported that the 90 confirmed breaches investigated in 2008 had 285 million compromised records, a 1,000% increase since 2005. Interestingly, the reported breaches had some similarities: 81% were not PCI compliant, 83% of attacks were not highly difficult, 87% were considered avoidable through simple or intermediate controls, and 99.9% of records were compromised from servers and applications. The bottom line is that most of these were preventable. In his Research Briefing, George Westerman said, "Many firms fall into patterns where one type of risk (most commonly availability) is prioritized over others."

The fact that 81% of the companies where the breaches occurred were not PCI compliant means that at some point in time, there was a failure in business or IT operations that led to noncompliance. If 87% of these compromises were considered avoidable, that means that some simple process was not being followed, such as a server being patched or an application not tested for vulnerabilities after an upgrade.

There is a price to pay if you sacrifice the proper management of risk to maintain availability.

The CIO's job is clear. If you are dealing with payment transactions, especially credit cards, you need to be PCI compliant as well as mitigate any risks to your payment transactions to avoid fraud. Better yet, your risk management program should be holistic and consider all other compliance requirements to meet regulatory, legislative, or industry standards.

Prevent the wrong information from getting to the wrong person at the wrong time.

Intellectual Property Lost or Stolen

In 1997, an American consortium was ranked at the top of the world's stock market value. Its value of $220 billion exceeded large conglomerates such as General Electric ($170 billion) and Nippon Telegraph and Telephone ($94 billion). It was the combination of two recent upstart companies known as Wintel. Wintel consisted of Microsoft and Intel. Microsoft stock traded at ten times its book value, which meant that 90% of its value is intangible. The intangible value is *intellectual capital,* which is the sum of human capital and structural capital that Leif Edvinsson described in his book entitled *Intellectual Capital.*

In 2002, Microsoft had a market capitalization of $250 billion, with tangible assets valued at less than $70 billion. The intellectual capital of Microsoft was valued at over $180 billion; this included technology, patents, brands, and human knowledge. We know that Microsoft has some very proprietary code in the form of applications and operating systems. This proprietary code is very well protected and considered *intellectual property* (IP) by Microsoft.

> Intellectual property (IP) refers to creations of the mind: inventions, literary and artistic works, and symbols, names, images, and designs used in commerce.
>
> **—World Intellectual Property Organization**

Loss of IP can bankrupt a company. IP is also a consideration for governments and not just within the private sector. For example, within government, pending legislation can be worth millions of dollars. Contract awards can be worth millions or, in some cases (e.g., very large contracts), billions of dollars. Leakage of information in criminal cases can result in criminals walking away free. IP information has very high value and in some cases people are willing to kill to get that information; the cost of leakage can be counted in lives. The U.S. military and its defense contractors know this very well. In a PowerPoint briefing "Killing with Keyboards," defense contractor Raytheon presented a powerful message about data leakage and its potential cost. Even the smallest piece of information may be the last piece of the puzzle to give your competitor or, in the case of defense contractors, enemy agents who will spend millions to get critical information. One of the problems is that people do not think it could be they who leak critical information.

A Ponemon Institute study published on February 23, 2009, and entitled "Data Loss Risks During Downsizing," indicated that 59% of employees who leave or are asked to leave are stealing company data. The study goes on to say that 67% of respondents used their former company's information to leverage a new job and a similar number of respondents plan to use the information in their new jobs. Some examples follow:

- "Rio Tinto Employees Arrested for Stealing Secrets," Reuters, July 9, 2009
- "Ex-Boeing Engineer Chung Guilty of Stealing Secrets," Bloomberg.com, July 16, 2009

- "Goldman Sachs Worker Arrested for 'Stealing Secrets,'" Timesonline, July 7, 2009
- "Worker Accused of Stealing Secrets," Daily Herald, April 3, 2008

Not to mention the professionals who have stolen secrets either through social engineering or directly. Ira Winkler, ex–National Security Agency (NSA) security expert, has described how he penetrates top-secret installations using very simple techniques such as fake IDs and by smooth-talking receptionists and security guards to allow him access.

At the other end of the spectrum are the many cases about illegal use of intellectual property (IP) in technologies. According to an article from Reuters entitled "Espionage and Property Theft Triggers Call to Suspend Israeli Access to U.S. Market" (April 21, 2009), Israel's weak protection of intellectual property rights has cost American companies billions of dollars. This is indicative of many foreign governments that may publicly condone such actions but privately fund activities that help their own corporations and government-owned organizations. The article goes on to describe how American intellectual property from U.S. weapons systems has been incorporated into Israeli-manufactured systems. The article also says that this occurs not only in the weapons industry but also in the pharmaceutical industry.

On the business side, there was a court decision involving a small Canadian company i4i and Microsoft; the court awarded i4i $290 million and an injunction that "prohibits Microsoft from selling or importing to the United States any Microsoft Word products that have the capability of opening .XML, .DOCX or DOCM files (XML files) containing custom XML." The impact on Microsoft is significant as Microsoft Office sales accounted for 90% of the $18.9 billion generated by the company's Microsoft Business Division. Microsoft appealed.

The fact is that people will try to use whatever they can to get ahead. Preventing theft of IP is a key part of the CIO's job.

Prevent the wrong information getting to the wrong person at the wrong time.

Wrong Decisions Made

One of the most misunderstood but perhaps the most common risk is getting the wrong information at the wrong time and making the wrong decision. There are a lot of instances where the wrong information leads to a wrong decision. Weapons of mass destruction in Iraq led to a decision. Whether it was right or wrong is an opinion. The decision cost trillions of dollars and thousands of lives.

Some great examples of wrong decisions are military blunders.

- The French were defeated easily by Germany in May 1940 in ten days of fighting. The reason: The Maginot Line. The Maginot Line was one of the most fortified lines in history. It consumed something like 40% of France's military spending in the years leading up to the war. The money would have been better spent modernizing the French army, navy, and especially the air force. The Germans had learned from World War I and simply went around the line through Belgium, rendering it useless.
- The famous invasion at the Bay of Pigs in 1961 was another example of a military blunder. The Inspector General's report released in February 1998 concluded that ignorance, incompetence, and arrogance on the part of the CIA were responsible. The direct consequences of the Bay of Pigs was a major embarrassment for President Kennedy and the CIA, as well as setting the stage for a confrontation between the United States and the Soviet Union in the missile crisis that brought the world to the brink of nuclear war.

There are many examples of wrong decisions in the corporate world. The Enron scandal in 2001 is a classic case of inappropriate decisions being made and the cover-up going sideways. The high-risk accounting practices not only brought the energy giant Enron to bankruptcy but caused one of the largest accounting, auditing, and consultancy firms (i.e., Arthur Andersen) to fail. The Enron scandal brought about the Sarbanes-Oxley Act in 2002. This act brought about huge changes in reporting and severe penalties for any breaches in compliance and added significant costs to organizations. Interestingly enough, before its fall, Enron was lauded for its sophisticated financial risk management tools.

American International Group, Inc. (AIG), one of the world's largest insurers, was taken over by the U.S. Government in 2008 in an $85 billion bailout. On February 28, 2008, AIG announced its 2007 earnings of $6.20 billion, or $2.39 per share; its stock closed at $50.15 per share. Less than seven months later, AIG was on the verge of bankruptcy and AIG's stock was trading at less than $1.00 per share. The collapse of the housing market in the United States no doubt contributed to the failure; however, AIG was leveraged beyond what it could manage and effectively needed a massive bailout to continue operations or go into bankruptcy.

As for IT projects, there have been major failures. Ford Motor Company's efforts to implement a purchasing system over four years at a cost of $400 million ended when they abandoned the new system and went back to their old system. J Sainsbury PLC in the United Kingdom scrapped a supply chain system after it was deployed and cost $527 million. McDonald's attempted to develop an information purchasing system but ultimately abandoned the project after spending $170 million. As a CIO, you may not have seen any project failures of this magnitude, but have seen some failures. We further discuss project risks in Chapter 12.

The objective of the CIO is very clear. What information is needed to make good decisions? How do you make sure the information is there?

Provide the right information to the right person at the right time.

Liability Risks

Liability risks for information are very real. Numerous court cases have rewarded those who are prepared and punished those who are not prepared. This means having the right information at the right time. Liability risks can be thought of in terms of

- *Compliance reporting requirements.* There are a number of different compliance and regulatory reporting requirements for organizations. For example, Sarbanes-Oxley (or SOX) section 302 has a requirement that the signing officers certify that they are responsible for establishing and maintaining internal controls over financial reporting. The U.S. Securities and Exchange Commission (SEC) interpreted the intention of section 302 as "disclosure controls and procedures." Under section 404, management is required to produce an internal control report as part of each annual Exchange Act report.

- *E-discovery requirements.* When an organization is hit with litigation, all information required for the litigation must be preserved. This includes paper, electronic, and any other media that relates to the litigation.
- *Uncontrolled information release causing harm.* When information is lost, stolen, or accidentally or intentionally released, there is the potential that this uncontrolled release of information might result in harm to the organization or individuals. Harm could be in the form of loss in reputation, liability, physical harm, or financial.
- *Decision support.* Getting the wrong information, insufficient information, or too much information can lead to making the wrong decisions. Getting the right information at the right time to the right people will generally increased the probability of making good decisions.
- *Health and safety.* Getting the wrong information could cause health and safety issues. Mislabeling of dangerous chemicals is a good example.
- *Damage to reputation.* Reputations are fragile at best. In negative situations, the wrong information released at the wrong time could seriously damage reputation.

In any event, the wrong information accessed by the wrong person at the wrong time could create an exposure. That exposure could turn into a loss or an event that brings harm to the organization or a person. The liability of the exposure depends on the value of the information. When we determine the value of the information, we need to consider all aspects, not just the financial implications. Loss or inappropriate disclosure of information could result in significant harm to an individual, including death. In most cases when we are dealing with corporations, financial losses are considered.

Liability risks should be considered in terms of the impact on the confidentiality, integrity, and availability of information. A fourth consideration—nonrepudiation or identity proofing—is fast becoming a concern for major organizations. Although it is not showing up yet as a major consideration in information security, there is significant liability in terms of fraud when we consider electronic misrepresentation. Financial institutions are now recognizing that nonrepudiation is very important in the electronic world. As a cartoon by Peter Steiner in the *New Yorker* described: "On the Internet nobody knows you're a dog." We do not know if the person we are dealing with is real, has the appropriate credentials, or is a criminal spoofing an identity. Having better assurance that the individual or organization is properly represented as we continue to advance more business electronically will reduce our risks. Nonrepudiation can be thought of in terms of access controls. Who is accessing what information at what time? Do you know?

An important part of liabilities is communicating what this means to an executive who is managing hundreds of millions of dollars. If the risk or exposure has a major impact on their budget, then they will pay attention. If it is a small exposure, they are not really interested. Their interpretation of the risk is almost as important as the right communication about the risk. We discuss risk management profiling as a means of identifying how people manage risks in Chapter 6.

3

SERVICE DELIVERY

An important part of any CIO's job is to make sure that the systems deliver what is needed by the business to operate effectively. On-line businesses like e-Bay mean that uptime is measured in five nines (99.999%). Where downtime costs money means that the highest requirement is availability. In some cases, the delivery of services means sacrificing security for the moment, such as in companies like FedEx and UPS. The requirement for making sure the package is delivered on time is the most important part of their business. Synchronizing vehicles to make delivery must be managed. More effective synchronization means greater cost effectiveness and improved customer satisfaction.

In essence, we are talking about getting the right information at the right time to the right person so they can do their job. It does not matter what job, from trucking goods to financial transactions to nuclear power stations. It is all about the information necessary to do the job. And we depend more on computers as an integral part of the increasing complexity of our jobs.

As we shift from a paper-based paradigm to an electronic paradigm, we will increasingly depend on systems being operational most of the time. Right now when systems are unavailable, we can still shuffle paper. In the future as the paper gatherers (baby boomers) slowly retire and the Gen X and Millennium generations take over, we will see less and less paper and more and more information that is only electronic. When information is only electronic, the systems must be operational. If all you have is a tablet or iPad™, then information being unavailable means that you cannot get your work done. IT will need to become a utility service just like electricity.

Using an example of a trucking company, we can quickly see that the information needed is around scheduling and load. If we cannot measure the time well, the resources are not available to load or unload the truck. If we cannot measure the time well, the truck may be idle for a period of time, thereby costing money. There is a direct correlation between time and money in the trucking business. And this means coordinating resources. The better the coordination, the better the return on the resources—meaning that if we provide the right information to the right people at the right time, we will get a synchronized dance of resources that optimize the resources. That is what investors want to hear.

There are many other scenarios that we can use to underline the importance of getting the right information to the right person at the right time. Let's take a look at financial services. Processing loans is a risky business at the best of times. We know from the 2008 market meltdown that the banks had a number of highly leveraged loans. The questions that should be answered are about getting the right information to the right person at the right time. Did the risk managers get the right information, or did they get the wrong information? By wrong, was the information complete? Was the information totally wrong? Was the information factual, calculated, estimated, or an opinion?

So how does that apply to you? What information is required to complete the processing of your business? As a CIO, you may deal with a number of lines of business. Each line of business processes information. The process may be transaction or information centric.

Transaction Centric

Transaction processing consists of multiple independent and distinct operations or tasks that are linked together in some way to form a single process or workflow. These operations or tasks are interdependent, and a complete transaction means that all operations are completed successfully or the transaction is rolled back to a known consistent state. A simple example is a banking transaction where a customer wants to move $500 from a checking account to a savings account. The transaction involves two basic operations: the first operation removes or debits the checking account and the second operation adds or credits the savings account. Both operations must be successful or the transaction is rolled back to the original state.

A more complex example is Wal-Mart's Supply Chain Management. Wal-Mart takes the retail business inventory management to an extreme where the suppliers are involved in the transaction. Not only do transactions manage the inventory at Wal-Mart but they also notify the supplier when an item is purchased. That way, Wal-Mart manages inventory as a just-in-time process to deliver goods when needed to restock the shelves.

Once the transaction is complete, the information from the transaction is available to be used in other ways. Information from the transaction is used to know inventory levels. Information from the transaction tracks revenues and sales and is used to determine marketing efforts. Information from the transaction can be used for customer reporting and relationship management, to identify problems, and to determine if there are inappropriate actions being taken (such as fraud).

Information Centric

Peter Drucker coined the term *knowledge worker*, and we can associate information-centric processes with knowledge workers. These include lawyers, physicians, financial workers, government workers, and researchers. According to a McKinsey Quarterly Report, in industries like financial services, legal, health care, high tech, pharmaceuticals, government, media, and entertainment, over 25% of workers are now knowledge workers—or, as they termed it, "professionals." Computers have become essential in producing work in some form, including research, forms processing, account management, transactions, policies, case management, customer relationship management, manufacturing, and just about any place where there is automation of equipment. Anywhere that there is complexity, a computer is used to help human operators and, in many cases, customers get the information they need.

For the CIO, up to 40% of your information may be in an unstructured format; that is, not in a database. Unstructured information refers to documents such as spreadsheets, presentations, Microsoft Word, PDFs, photos, or pictures, such as drawings. In some cases, the information is written on paper and has been imaged. Most CIOs focus on the structured information in databases and fail to properly manage their unstructured information. We discuss information management in another section.

Risks to Service Delivery

As you know, the most important risk to service delivery is the availability of systems. A system consists of one or more applications, data or information (may be a database or documents), infrastructure (servers, workstations, mobile devices, network, etc.), and the people to manage and maintain the system. There are other risks, such as people not having the appropriate skills, knowledge, experience, or education to support the system.

We also know about denial-of-service attacks on systems and networks. Any impact on availability must be considered when determining risks. We also must consider inappropriate* access to confidential or secret information as well as inappropriate modification. That is why controls must consider the capability of logging actions so we can determine who did what and when.

Make sure the right information gets to the right person at the right time.

Risks to the CIO

CIOs are under pressure to deliver services in the most cost-effective manner. Focusing on just service delivery of existing systems is a mistake. Many organizations are pursuing more aggressive agendas, and the CIO must be engaged with the business to enable business to more effectively deliver its services. There is a balance between managing risks to service delivery and presenting opportunities for business enablement. The evaluation and assessment of new technologies must be done to determine if the new technology will present an opportunity for the business. This must be balanced against the risk of the failure of a new technology to deliver expected results. The CIO must pick the right moment to deliver a new technology: too early and the technology may not be mature enough to support the business; too late and the competition may already be ahead in adopting the technology.

---

* Inappropriate access may be authorized or unauthorized. Someone with authorization taking an inappropriate action such as stealing information must be considered.

PART I
PRINCIPLES AND CONCEPTS

4

OVERVIEW

The number-one job of the CIO is to deliver information services to the business. That means making sure the systems deliver the right information to the right person at the right time. Having stated the obvious, we should examine principles, concepts, and some approaches that may help to ensure that services are delivered effectively.

What do we mean by *risk management*? Doug Hubbard, in his book entitled *The Failure of Risk Management*, defined risk management as

> The identification, assessment, and prioritization of risks followed by coordinated and economical application of resources to minimize, monitor, and control the probability and/or impact of unfortunate events. (2009)

Douglas Landoll, in his book entitled *The Security Risk Assessment Handbook*, defined risk management as

> The process of understanding, mitigating and controlling risk through risk assessment, risk mitigation, operational security and testing. (2006)

In practical terms, risk management is *preventing bad things from happening*. From an information perspective, it means preventing the wrong information from getting to the wrong person at the wrong time.

Risks can be defined in many ways. The approach we take in this book is to divide risks into categories that are related to information management (Table 4.1).

Market Risks

Although it may seem obvious, the effect of the global economy on organizations is significant. There may be a lag in the impact on business as one market undergoes a downturn. However, the interdependencies

Table 4.1   Categories of Risk

CATEGORY OF RISKS	DESCRIPTION
Market	Organizations must be aware of what is happening globally in terms of markets and economies
Budget	If there is an increase or decrease in budget, this will have an impact on the management of service delivery and liabilities
People	The most vulnerable and most volatile risks are people, both inside and outside the organization
	People are a risk to information disclosure, modification, and deletion, as well as operational, control, and detection
Technology	Failure of technology is a risk to availability
Operational	Failures within operations are risks to confidentiality, integrity, and availability
Information	Failures in information are risks to confidentiality, integrity, and availability
Control	Failures in controls are risks to confidentiality, integrity and availability.
Detection	Failures in detection are risks to confidentiality, fraud, and availability
Opportunity	Failure in opportunities are risks to the business

of our economies have a ripple effect. The 2008 impact of the housing meltdown and the financial crunch in the United States did not have a major impact until 2009 on the British Columbia (BC) government. In 2009, the BC government downsized its staff, curtailed spending, and initiated significant controls on expenditures.

Some interesting questions to ask when we look at information and markets for your information follow:

- Is there a market demand for the personal information that we hold?
- Is there a market demand for the IP information that we hold?
- Is there a market demand for the information pertaining to the processes that we use to be competitive?

Budget Risks

An increase or decrease in your budget has an effect on the amount of work that you can accomplish. A decrease will have a direct effect on your ability to deliver services. Losing budget usually means losing people or investment opportunities. It is most critical that you plan for the worst and plan for the best so that you have a strategy to move quickly in either case.

People Risks

People are your biggest risks. As described in *The Visible Ops Handbook*, 80% of outages are caused by people. According to a study by International Data Group, the majority of breaches (52%) result from accidental leaks and vulnerabilities. In their book entitled *The Accountant's Handbook of Fraud & Commercial Crime*, Bologna et al. went even further regarding fraud and people. They felt that personal honesty primarily depends on the situation. That is, many people are only honest if they do not think they can get away with being dishonest. If you think about it from an ethics perspective, 10% of people are ethical and 10% are not ethical. That leaves about 80% of the people who are either ethical or unethical depending on the situation. This means that in a given situation, up to 90% of people could be unethical (Figure 4.1). This explains the mob mentality and why riots make average law-abiding citizens sometime take criminal actions. Although these percentages are not definitive, the surest way to be victimized is to exclusively rely on the honesty of individuals.

We always "trust" people we work with. However, it is often these people who make mistakes or take advantage of a situation to do something wrong. Your procedures should include controls to reduce the risk of a person making a mistake that causes an outage or commits a fraudulent act.

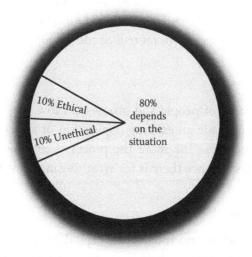

Figure 4.1 View of ethical behavior.

Table 4.2   Uptime Requirements

UPTIME REQUIREMENT (PERCENT)	DOWNTIME (HOURS) PER YEAR	COST OF DOWNTIME/OUTAGE	COST OF REDUNDANCY
99.999	0.1	?	?
99.99	1	?	?
99.9	9	?	?
99.7	26	?	?

Technology Risks

We all know that there will be failures in technology. There are so many interconnected components to our electronic infrastructure that there are bound to be equipment failures.

Equipment failures can be overcome to a certain degree by redundancy in technology and operations centers. A cost analysis should be conducted to determine what downtime can be afforded and the cost of buying and maintaining the infrastructure necessary to maintain a level of availability acceptable to the business. This can equate to the business accepting 99.9% instead of 99.999% in terms of availability (Table 4.2). Typically for most businesses, the cost/benefit analysis indicates that business losses for short outages versus the cost of increasing the availability by 0.099% are not warranted.

There is also the failure to adopt new technology at the right time. This includes new applications; new workstations, PDAs, and laptops; and network devices, firewalls, databases, and software as a service (SaaS). Do you move to cloud computing? Does this give your company a competitive advantage? Does it reduce costs? Does it reduce outages?

Operational Risks

Operations consist of people and processes. How you implement an application or upgrade an existing application or system depends on people and processes. The more the processes are documented and followed, the less chance there is for error causing downtime.

Information Risks

Personal information and intellectual capital are your most precious assets. Risk of disclosure, theft, loss, or unauthorized (or unintentional) modification must be managed.

Control Risks

Controls are used to manage operations and prevent bad things from happening. Controls should be automated where practical and monitored.

Detection Risks

Detection is auditing and monitoring. A review of access, network traffic, server logs, application logs, and security tools should be periodically performed. The period of time and the intensity between reviews is determined by your risk culture and appetite thresholds. The more risk averse, the shorter the review period and the higher the intensity of the review. Detection includes the ability to monitor the health of systems to determine when capacity is about to be exceeded so you can take the appropriate actions to reduce the possibility of an outage.

Risk Treatment

One of the biggest mistakes that organizations make is trying to only manage risks locally in a global environment. If you are connected to the Internet, you are connected globally. A single failure in your technology, operations, or people can result in a breach or outage. A breach may be contained locally; however, if it becomes public, it must be managed corporately. Damage to your reputation is a key consideration in mitigating or treating risks. The objective of risk management is loss prevention. Once a risk has been realized, the objective is to mitigate or reduce the impact of the event.

Risk treatment can be managed in four ways:

1. Avoid the risk.
2. Accept the risk.
3. Transfer the risk.
4. Mitigate the risk (to an acceptable level).

The first risk treatment is simple. If you can avoid the risk, you avoid the risk. This means the risk is unacceptable and there are no other methods of managing the risks.

The second risk treatment is that you accept the risk and the consequences. In terms of insurance, it means you are self-insured. Governments are typically self-insured. They indemnify for any damages, losses, or expenses that occur. In terms of house or car insurance, the amount that you pay up front is your deductible. When you are making a claim, you pay your deductible first and this is a form of self-insurance against small losses. In most cases, the larger the deductible, the lower the payments because you are taking more responsibility for the initial amount being claimed in an event. You should consider self-insurance as a means of managing your risks for smaller events. For larger events, you need to consider blending some form of insurance with self-insurance. Your CFO will most likely be the person who manages this level of insurance. You need to provide the CFO with the appropriate advice.

The third risk treatment is to transfer the risk or get someone else to own the risk. That is what insurance is about: for a fee, you get some form of indemnification against some risks. House and car insurance are good examples. You can also transfer operational risk through outsourcing to a service provider who will take responsibility for your operations. This is a contractual obligation and has service-level agreements (or SLAs).

The fourth risk treatment is to mitigate the risk to an acceptable level. From a liability perspective, we install firewalls, use anti-virus software, and educate users to prevent the wrong information from going to the wrong person at the wrong time. PCI, Sarbanes-Oxley (SOX), NIST 800-53, and HIPPA are all about measuring how we manage preventing the wrong information going to the wrong person at the wrong time.

One more thing! Information has value. The value is determined by the organization. The value is also determined by the market. It is not only intellectual property (or IP) but all the information used by the organization, including processes, procedures, policies, documentation, and records. As many people have come to understand, email records are a major concern and managing the life cycle of records is critical, especially when it comes to litigation and e-discovery. There have been more than a few instances where improper management of records has cost organizations millions of dollars. We will spend some time discussing information and how you can manage it all the time, making sure the right information gets to the right person at the right time and preventing the wrong information from getting to the wrong person at the wrong time.

5

BASIC CONCEPTS, PRINCIPLES, AND PRACTICES

The number-one priority of the CIO is service delivery. It is making sure the right information is available to the right person at the right time. Anything that affects service delivery must be considered a risk; this means an impact on the availability, confidentiality, or integrity of the information necessary for business transactions. We start with some risk management concepts, delve into risk management principles and information security principles, and finish with information management principles. We also include an approach to determine if the information is being presented as a fact, calculation, estimation, or a guess. Finally we discuss metrics and best practices.

Concepts

- *Confidence* is a firm belief or trust.
- *Confidence level* is described in statistics as how sure you can be. It is normally expressed as a percentage. It is how much you trust the information.
- *Confidence interval* is described in statistics as the plus or minus (±) reported in figures such as poll results. It is the range of probabilities of a result. A confidence interval of 4 indicates that if you have a confidence level of 90% ± 4%, it means the answer could be as low as 86% (90 − 4) or as high as 94% (90 + 4). This gives you some latitude in how much you trust the information.
- *Risk* can be defined as "the threat or probability that an action or event will adversely or beneficially affect an organization's ability to achieve its objectives." Risks are typically known or identified.
- *Risk management profile* can be described as how an individual manages the risks or amount of exposure physically,

emotionally, financially, or politically that an individual is willing to undertake. Individuals have different risk appetites and tolerances. A risk appetite is the amount of risk an individual will undertake. Risk tolerance is the individual's acceptable variation relative to the amount of risk.

- *Risk appetite* is described in Committee of Sponsoring Organizations of the Treadway Commission (COSO) ERM and ISO 31000 as the broad amount of risk an organization is willing to accept in pursuit of its goals, objectives, mission, or vision.
- *Risk tolerance* is described in COSO ERM and ISO 31000 as the acceptable variation relative to the achievement of an organizational objective (typically measured using the same units as those used to measure the related objective).
- *Risk culture* is described as the underlying risk management philosophy that organizations have based on individual risk management philosophies. Typically the risk culture is dictated from the top but can be different in organizational units, depending on the individuals.
- *Uncertainty* is described as the possibility of an event happening. Uncertainty is about unknown risks.

Risk IT Framework Principles

The ISACA Risk IT Framework, which is based on Control Objectives for Information and related Technology (COBIT), describes a number of principles. These principles are based on COSO ERM principles. We describe them here.

- *Always connect to business objectives.* IT risks are treated as business risks. IT supports business outcomes, and IT risks should be expressed as the impact they can have on reaching these outcomes. IT risk management is a business enabler.
- *Align the management of IT-related business risk with overall ERM,* if ERM is implemented in the organization. IT risks are managed at an enterprise level and incorporated into overall ERM.
- *Balance the costs and benefits of managing IT risks.* IT risks are prioritized and addressed in line with overall risk appetite and tolerance (risk culture).

- *Promote fair and open communication of IT risk.* IT risks are translated and communicated into relevant and understandable business terms.
- *Establish the right tone from the top while defining and enforcing personal accountability for operating within acceptable and well-defined tolerance levels.* The right people are engaged in IT risk management. IT risks decisions are made by authorized people with the focus on business management.
- *Effective management of IT risk is a continuous process and part of daily activities.* IT risks continue to evolve and the management of these risks must evolve with the changes. Consistency in risk management practices, assessment, and processes is key in managing risks.

ISO 31000 Risk Management Principles

Risks exist in every organization. The risk of failure or loss sometimes creates inertia in making decisions. Risk management cannot be based on gut decisions. As much as possible, decisions must be based on facts or calculations. Risk management is a decision-making methodology that considers as many factors as possible. ISO 31000 has defined a set of principles for risk management that organizations should comply with at all levels. The ISO 31000:2009 risk principles are as follows:

- *Risk management creates and protects value.* Risk management contributes to the demonstrable achievement of objectives and improvement of performance in, for example, human health and safety, security, legal and regulatory compliance, public acceptance, environmental protection, product quality, project management, efficiency in operations, governance, and reputation.
- *Risk management is an integral part of all organizational processes.* Risk management is not a stand-alone activity that is separate from the main activities and processes of the organization. Risk management is part of the responsibilities of management and an integral part of all organizational processes, including strategic planning and all project and change management processes.

- *Risk management is part of decision making.* Risk management helps decision makers make informed choices, prioritize actions, and distinguish among alternative courses of action.
- *Risk management explicitly addresses uncertainty.* Risk management explicitly takes into account uncertainty, the nature of that uncertainty, and how it can be addressed.
- *Risk management is systematic, structured, and timely.* A systematic, timely, and structured approach to risk management contributes to efficiency and to consistent, comparable, and reliable results.
- *Risk management is based on the best available information.* The inputs to the process of managing risk are based on information sources such as historical data, experience, stakeholder feedback, observation, forecasts, and expert judgment. However, decision makers should inform themselves of, and should take into account, any limitations of the data or modeling used or the possibility of divergence among experts.
- *Risk management is tailored.* Risk management is aligned with the organization's external and internal context and risk profile.
- *Risk management takes human and cultural factors into account.* Risk management recognizes the capabilities, perceptions, and intentions of external and internal people who can facilitate or hinder achievement of the organization's objectives.
- *Risk management is transparent and inclusive.* Appropriate and timely involvement of stakeholders and, in particular, decision makers at all levels of the organization ensures that risk management remains relevant and up-to-date. Involvement also allows stakeholders to be properly represented and to have their views taken into account in determining risk criteria.
- *Risk management is dynamic, iterative, and responsive to change.* Risk management continually senses and responds to change. As external and internal events occur, context and knowledge change, monitoring and review of risks take place, new risks emerge, some change, and others disappear.
- *Risk management facilitates continual improvement of the organization.* Organizations should develop and implement strate-

gies to improve their risk management maturity alongside all other aspects of their organization.

There are six principles defined by the ISACA Risk IT Framework and eleven principles defined by ISO 31000. Here are a few more risk management principles developed by this author; they are outside the Risk IT Framework and ISO 31000 but may be useful for a CIO.

Other Risk Management Principles

One of the foundations of good risk management is being able to calculate with reasonable confidence the probability and magnitude of the consequences from the realization of a risk or uncertainty. We must recognize that, at best, there is a measure of error in our best calculations. There are too many factors to consider, as evidenced by accidents such as Three Mile Island and BP's devastating Deepwater Horizon oil platform explosion and subsequent oil leak. We cannot always do worst-case scenarios and have plans in place to deal with these scenarios. These accidents or "black swans" are so improbable and occur with such infrequency that we cannot develop comprehensive plans and contingencies to handle every possible black swan. However, we can have good incident response capabilities that can handle the majority of situations. Hence, the following principles must be considered.

- *Inexact science: Risk management is an inexact science.*
  - Rationale: Risk equals the possibility of loss. Loss is usually financial but in some cases could be far greater in terms of loss of life, freedom, and country. We can determine the probability that a risk may cause a loss. We cannot predict or determine with any certainty that a loss will occur, when it will occur, or the exact size or scope of that loss.
  - Example: In his book entitled *The Black Swan*, Nassim Taleb (2007) described how a casino protected itself from known risks such as cheating gamblers but could not predict that events outside its sophisticated models would cause them significant losses.
  - Comments: Risk management has been practiced in the financial and insurance industries for centuries. Early

Mediterranean sailing merchants took out loans to fund shipments and paid an additional sum to guarantee the cancellation of the loan should the shipment be lost. Separate insurance contracts were invented in Genoa in the fourteenth century. Project managers practice risk management in managing projects. Information risk management is very new, and the ability to predict risks is evolving. Expect risk management to start with estimates and, as information becomes more available, to become more factual and calculation based (i.e., losses such as credit card record theft are known per record cost and we can calculate the costs of a security breach involving the theft of credit card records).

- *Risk culture: Every organization has a risk culture that affects how decisions are made.*
  - Rationale: Risk taking and risk aversion are proportional to the number of people involved and the size of the organization: the larger the organization, the more risk averse. Typically in larger organizations, rules, policies, and committees dictate decisions.
  - Example: The risk culture within most government organizations is conservative. In most cases, the risk culture determines the risk appetite.
  - Comments: Determining the risk culture of your organization is very important in understanding how decisions are made. When the BC government implemented intrusion prevention systems at the Internet gateways, the network folks were very reluctant to install them in-line for fear that the systems might cause slow-downs or disruption of service. Eventually, the intrusion prevention systems were accepted and proved very valuable in preventing worm and virus infections. The risk culture of the organization was very much risk averse and acceptance of change proceeded very slowly.
- *Logical: Risk management must be based on facts and calculations.*
  - Rationale: Decisions about risk must be based on facts and calculations. Our own biases and values sometimes skew our decisions the wrong way. As much as possible, risk

mitigation decisions should be based on facts and calculations. This means we base our decisions on computational trust; that is, we calculate our risks based on facts and calculations—not on our gut feelings.

- Example: When a financial institution gives a loan to an individual, that institution calculates the risks based on financial information received from the individual. The institution bases its risks on whether the individual's track record is good for loan repayments, as well as other assets that may be used as collateral in case the loan is defaulted.
- Comments: Risk management is not an exact science. We need to seriously look at how we manage risks and base more of our decisions on facts and calculations rather than opinions, guesses, and estimations. Our gut decisions are emotional and not based on logic and may lead us into trouble. As discussed further in Chapter 6 we need to start calculating our risk decisions, including ranges, as opposed to making decisions based on gut instinct.

- *Continuous monitoring: Risk management must be continuously monitored as change is continuous.*
  - Rationale: Risks evolve and we must continuously monitor our mitigation strategies to evolve with those risks.
  - Example: Internet threats have evolved since MafiaBoy first performed a denial-of-service attack against eBay and Amazon. The technology has also evolved and there is more information being managed (or not managed properly) electronically. As new threats evolve, we need to identify mechanisms to mitigate our vulnerabilities to these threats.
  - Comments: Like information security and application development, risk management is evolving. Risk management is a process, not a solution. The desired outcome is to mitigate losses to a sustainable level.
- *Practical: Risk mitigation must be practical.*
  - Rationale: The cost of risk mitigation must be commensurate with the value of the asset being protected. Any proposed risk mitigation must be practical and not duplicate existing controls. The total cost of mitigation must

be considered, including changes to existing controls, procedures, and personnel.

- Example: Risk mitigation can be accomplished in any or a combination of these three ways: acceptance, transfer, or reduction to an acceptable level. The cost of mitigation should not exceed the value of the loss. The analogy is building a $1,000 barn to house a $100 horse.
- Comments: Risk management and mitigation must be practical. It should be included in daily operations. Your strategy must include significant investments in education and awareness at all levels. One of our biggest problems is the "not me" syndrome. I can do whatever I want because the "I am the boss, expert, or whatever" excuse is used. Not following proper procedures will inevitably lead to a breach or outage.

Summary: Risk Management and Risk IT Principles

There are eleven risk management principles from the ISO 31000, six principles from the Risk IT Framework, along with these last five principles, which are more practical or common sense, in this author's opinion. It is not expected that every organization adopt these as their principles for risk management. What is expected is that as part of your review, you will consider all these principles in developing your own risk management strategy.

From a CIO perspective, you should consider the following principles in managing IT risks:

1. Always connected to business objectives
2. Integral part of organizational processes
3. Aligned with enterprise risk management: IT risk has both enterprise and business line components
4. Practical: Risk management is based on a balance between cost and benefits
5. Inexact science: Risk management is based on estimates, best information, and human interpretation (make sure you have understood where your information is coming from and who is presenting the information)

6. Tone from the top: Must always reflect the bottom line and messaging must come from the top to emphasize risk management

IT risk management should be automated and have the appropriate resources assigned to monitoring. In cyberspace, events happen in milliseconds. Risk changes in seconds. We do not know that the threat or vulnerability has changed unless we are monitoring. A review of risks must be done periodically and the information constantly updated.

Information Security Principles

Information security should be based on a set of principles. The Generally Accepted System Information Security Principles (GAISP) can be used to provide high-level assurances that information security is properly founded in industry-accepted security principles. These principles address the following properties of information:

- *Confidentiality:* Characteristic of information being disclosed only to authorized persons, entities, and processes at authorized times and in an authorized manner.
- *Integrity:* Characteristic of information being accurate and complete and the information system's preservation of accuracy and completeness.
- *Availability:* Characteristic of information and supporting information systems being accessible and usable on a timely basis in the required manner.

These principles provide general governance-level guidance to establish and maintain the security of information. These principles set the tone for information security within an organization. GAISP does go further and defines some broadly functional principles such as security policies, education and awareness, and access controls; these are described in the following section.

Accountability Principle

- *Information security accountability and responsibility must be clearly defined and acknowledged.*

- Rationale: Accountability characterizes the ability to audit the actions of all parties and processes that interact with information. Roles and responsibilities are clearly defined, identified, and authorized at a level commensurate with the sensitivity and criticality of the information. The relationship among all parties, processes, and information must clearly be defined, documented, and acknowledged by all parties. All parties have responsibilities for which they are held accountable.
- Example: Information logs should be controlled and monitored with an accompanying audit log to report any modification, addition, or deletion to information assets. Logs should report the user or process that performs the actions.
- Comments: Job descriptions should include accountability for information security.

Awareness Principle

- *To foster confidence in information systems, owners, providers and users of information systems, and other parties should readily be able, consistent with maintaining security, to gain appropriate knowledge of and be informed about the existence and general extent of measures, practices, and procedures for the security of information systems.*
  - Rationale: This principle applies between and within organizations. Awareness of information security principles, standards, conventions, and mechanisms enhances and enables controls and can help to mitigate threats. Awareness of threats and their significance also increases user acceptance of controls. Without user awareness of the necessity for particular controls, users can pose a risk to information by ignoring, bypassing, or overcoming existing control mechanisms.
  - Example: The security mechanism of wearing identification badges is weakened if not exhaustively enforced. If unidentified individuals go unchallenged, vulnerability is introduced to the system. (If every user, authorized or

unauthorized, is made aware of the organization's position on unauthorized use and its potential consequences [e.g., via a log-on banner], some misuse can be avoided.)
- Comments: Make sure you have an education and awareness component in your information security program. Try to keep it high level and focus on key messages such as identification badges, not leaving doors open, escorting visitors, and email etiquette.

Ethics Principle

- *Information systems and security of information systems should be provided and used in such a manner that the rights and legitimate interests of others are respected.*
  - Rationale: Information systems pervade our societies and cultures. Rules and expectations are evolving with regard to the appropriate provision and use of information systems and the security of information. Use of information and information systems should match the expectations established by social norms and obligations.
  - Example: Some organizations have developed a Code of Ethical Conduct that outlines for all employees a set of actions, behaviors, and conduct guidelines with respect to information security and information use. The code sets forth expectations for conduct that may not be illegal but may be contrary to an organization's policy or belief. Behavior outside the bounds of the code would be considered unethical.
  - Comments: It is important to establish a code of ethics in your organization so people know what is expected. Your human resources group should be involved.

Multidisciplinary Principle

- *Measures, practices, and procedures for the security of information systems should take into account and address all relevant considerations and viewpoints, including technical, administrative, organizational, operational, commercial, educational, and legal.*

- Rationale: Information security is achieved by the combined efforts of information owners, users, custodians, and information security personnel. Decisions made with due consideration for all relevant viewpoints and technical capabilities can enhance information security and receive better acceptance.
- Example: When developing contingency plans, organizations can establish a contingency planning team of information owners, representatives from facilities management, technology management, and other functional areas in order to better identify the various expectations and viewpoints from across the organization and other recognized parties.
- Comments: Many aspects of information security can be embedded into technical operations. Consider separation of duties when assigning tasks to operations and manage due diligence as a separate oversight function.

Proportionality Principle

- *Security levels, costs, measures, practices, and procedures should be appropriate and proportional to the value of and degree of reliance on the information systems and to the severity, probability, and extent of potential harm, as the requirements for security vary depending upon the particular information systems.*
  - Rationale: Security controls should be commensurate with the value of the information assets and the vulnerability. Consider the value, sensitivity, and criticality of the information, as well as the probability, frequency, and severity of direct and indirect harm or loss. This principle recognizes the value of approaches to information security risk management, ranging from prevention to acceptance.
  - Example: Some organizations determine information security measures based on an examination of the risks, associated threats, vulnerabilities, loss exposure, and risk mitigation through cost/benefit analysis using a risk management framework.

- Comments: Consider information life-cycle management as a key component of proportionality. As some information ages, it typically loses value. A key and sensitive report that has critical information may not be so sensitive next year. The objective is to make sure you are not overprotecting information that no longer has value to the organization.

Integration Principle

- *Measures, practices, and procedures for the security of information systems should be coordinated and integrated with each other and with other measures, practices, and procedures of the organization so as to create a coherent system of security.*
  - Rationale: Many breaches of information security involve the compromise of more than one safeguard. The most effective control measures are components of an integrated system of controls. Information security is most efficient when planned, managed, and coordinated throughout the organization's system of controls and the life of the information asset.
  - Example: Accounts and accesses may be properly controlled when the information owner selects the right type and level of access for users, informs system managers of which users need accounts, and promptly informs them of changes. If one control in the system of controls is compromised, other controls can provide a safety net to limit or prevent the loss.
  - Comments: Oversight of all security will prevent or reduce the risk that a single control will be compromised and lead to a loss or disclosure of information. A defense-in-depth strategy will mitigate or reduce your risks.

Timeliness Principle

- *All accountable parties should act in a timely, coordinated manner to prevent or respond to breaches of and threats to the security of information and information systems.*

- Rationale: Organizations should be capable of swift coordination and action to enable threat event prevention or mitigation. This principle recognizes the need for the public and private sectors to jointly establish mechanisms and procedures for rapid and effective threat event reporting and handling. Access to threat event history could support effective response to threat events and may help to prevent future incidents.
- Example: An organization with access to timely threat and vulnerability information can make prompt decisions that will prevent or mitigate an incident. Expertise can be brought to bear on a problem, for example, the introduction of a virus on an internal network, if it is rapidly reported to an organization's incident handling team.
- Comments: Incident response procedures should not be limited to one aspect of information security. Procedures should be generic enough to manage any type of attack or compromise. Make sure you include escalation procedures for legal advice as well as law enforcement.

Assessment Principle

- *The security of information systems should be assessed periodically, as information systems and the requirements for their security vary over time.*
  - Rationale: Information and the requirements for its security vary over time. Risks to the information, its value, and the probability, frequency, and severity of direct and indirect harm/loss should undergo periodic assessment. Periodic assessment identifies and measures the variances from available and established security measures and controls, such as those articulated here in the GAISP, and the risk associated with such variances. Periodic assessment enables accountable parties to make informed information risk management decisions whether to accept, mitigate, or transfer the identified risks with due consideration for cost effectiveness.

- Example: Listed below are events that may trigger the need for a security assessment:
  - A significant change to the information system
  - A significant change in the information or its value
  - A significant change in the technology
  - A significant change to the threats or vulnerabilities
  - A significant change to available safeguards
  - A significant change in the user profiles
  - A significant change in the potential loss of the system
  - A significant change to the organization/enterprise
  - A predetermined length of time since the last assessment
- Comments: Most often, the problem is communication of changes from technical operations or the business to information security. Periodic audit of logs should form a significant part of good information security practices.

Equity Principle

- *Management shall respect the rights and dignity of individuals when setting policy and when selecting, implementing, and enforcing security measures.*
  - Rationale: Information security measures implemented by an organization should not infringe upon the obligations, rights, and needs of legitimate users, owners, and others affected by the information when exercised within the legitimate parameters of the mission objectives.
  - Example: Individual privacy should be protected. A system administrator may need access to private information for problem diagnosis and resolution only.
  - Comments: The challenges of respecting people's privacy while maintaining information security is not to be underestimated, especially when your administrators have access to a lot of personal information. Security policies should reflect the rights of individuals in dealing with operational issues with technologies such as email and instant messaging.

Information Management Principles

Information management is an area of growing concern. Many organizations do not have good information management. Many of our information management policies, practices, and processes are based on a paper paradigm. Although I have heard a number of records officers in government talk about electronic information, they still work in a paper world. It is prevalent in many organizations where email is printed and preserved. The reality is that we are in an electronic world and need to make the dramatic leap to managing information electronically. This becomes more pronounced when litigation hits an organization and they start scrambling to find all the relevant information. Here are a few information management principles.

Value

- *Information has value.*
  - Rationale: Information may be intellectual property, procedures, personal, medical, historical, business, military, research, formulas, pictures, movies, etc. The level of protection must be commensurate with the value. You do not protect a $100 horse with a $1,000 fence.
  - Example: Credit card information has significant value to organized crime. Read any report on organized crime and many of the criminals have turned to credit card theft and fraud. Although the per card information value has dropped, there is still a huge market for credit card information.
  - Comments: Thefts of IP and personal information are mostly financially motivated crimes. Even industrial espionage by other countries has financial motivation. With the Internet you can steal sensitive information from another country without leaving home. Information may also have negative value if it is kept too long.

Life Cycle

- *Information has a life cycle.*
  - Rationale: Typically, information is active for a short period of time and then becomes stale. Determining

when information becomes stale or reduced in value is critical to managing the life cycle. Information should not be kept forever unless it has value. Proper life-cycle management of all information includes archiving and disposition.

- Example: During e-discovery, information is very valuable and must be managed and accessible to multiple parties. After the case has been resolved, the information is archived and not as valuable.

- Comments: Life-cycle management of information is very important in managing multiple copies and versions of the same document. Ideally, a single copy of the final document should be retained and managed. All other copies should be destroyed. Information must be destroyed at the end of its life cycle or it may start accruing negative value.

Reuse

- *Information may be reused many times.*
  - Rationale: Sensitive data may be reused in multiple reports, spreadsheets, and presentations, therefore presenting the problem of multiple copies, in multiple formats, in multiple places. Even worse is that the wrong data may be reused many times, thereby creating misinformation and incorrect decisions.
  - Example: Some studies and reports are often referred to many times to lend credence to a business case. In the case of MafiaBoy and his denial-of-service attacks, the information was reused many times to justify the purchase of equipment to mitigate such attacks.
  - Comments: Although similar to the proliferation principle, the reuse principle focuses more on secondary and tertiary usage of information. It also underlines the fact that wrong information can also be reused. There are a lot of urban myths propagated and sometimes used to make decisions. Care must be exercised to determine if the information is true.

Proliferates Quickly

- *Information proliferates quickly and is hard to contain.*
  - Rationale: E-discovery searches often uncover many copies of the same information—or worse, different versions of the same information with added comments from different people with different perspectives.
  - Example: Email is a great example of how information is proliferated and how copying different people can create problems in containment.
  - Comments: Electronic information will proliferate throughout an organization and beyond. New tools for sharing information make containment even more difficult. Social networks, instant messaging, and email are all ways information is distributed. I know of instances where very sensitive information was left on printers and copies given to the press.

Dependencies

- *Information has dependencies on technologies.*
  - Rationale: Electronic information depends on the technology that created it. If the information is created on a proprietary technology, you need to consider moving it to a nonproprietary format. Information should not be kept in proprietary formats. Electronic information may not be readable after a period of time. The format may not be supported and this must be considered in managing information over long periods of time. If the technology becomes obsolete, the information may be rendered unreadable.
  - Example: 8-inch disks, 5.25-inch floppy drives, AES Micom Word Processing. These technologies still may exist but are increasingly becoming very hard and expensive to find and maintain.
  - Comments: As much as possible, move to open source formats such as XML and maintain an upgrade program for equipment to refresh equipment and transfer the information.

Principles

Principles are a key foundation of any risk management program. Whether you use ISO 31000 or develop your own, the key is that a risk management program be based on principles. There are many different principles that you can put into your policies and practices. Privacy principles are included in Appendix A. There are a lot of similarities in the principle statements, and there are interrelationships between different principles that need to be understood. For example, the fact that electronic information proliferates quickly and is hard to contain is well known. Linking it with data loss prevention or digital rights management will set a good foundation for managing sensitive information. Principles are the foundation for any policies. In the end, we recreate policies and practices as technology evolves. No one could have predicted the rise of social networks. Now we have to deal with them in our workplace as more people accept this as part of their daily lives.

No matter what business you are in, you have to deal with some basic principles:

- There will always be people.
- There will always be infrastructure.
- There will always be intellectual capital.
- There will always be processes.
- There will always be customers or clients—whatever you call the people who use your services or buy your products.

In other words, you will always have a product (goods and/or services) to give, sell, or provide; processes to deliver the product; and projects to enhance the product or processes. And these are all linked by IT.

6

RISK ASSESSMENT, ANALYSIS, AND PROCEDURES

What are your risks? Are your risks primarily with people? In most cases, people cause risks based on the decisions that they make. Whether the disclosure of sensitive information was caused by an accident, a series of accidents, or deliberate actions of a person still means the information was disclosed. Preventing the disclosure is what we are trying to do with risk management. Our first step is to perform a risk assessment. In any risk assessment, we make assumptions and deal with constraints. The accuracy of our risk assessment depends on whether we can trust the information being presented. How much we can trust that information depends on whether it is fact, calculated, estimated, or guessed. In most cases today, we do not know how much trust we can put in the information. This next section deals with some of that trust and how we can improve on our ability to add more confidence into our decision-making processes.

Making Decisions: Fact or Fiction? How Do You Decide?

In their book entitled *Hard Facts,* Jeffrey Pfeffer and Robert Sutton (2006) discussed *evidence-based management.* Their interest in evidence-based management was inspired and guided by evidence-based medicine management. While evidence-based management is far from being totally embraced, the newer generation of doctors and teaching hospitals are adopting this approach and taking these best results to bedsides. Their research indicated that many successful companies such as Cisco, Intel, and Harrah's have adopted this approach.

> Evidence-based medicine and evidence-based management require a mind-set with two critical components: first, willingness to put aside belief and conventional wisdom—the dangerous half-truths that many

embrace—and instead hear and act on the facts; second, unrelenting commitment to gather the facts and information necessary to make more informed and intelligent decisions, and to keep pace with new evidence and use the new facts to update practices. (Pfeffer and Sutton, 2006)

Adopting evidence-based management does take a fundamental shift in thinking because the reality is that many decisions are made on guesses, opinions, and so-called expert advice. Yet if we look at getting the wrong information to the wrong person at the wrong time, we see the potential for liability and poor decisions. So how do you adopt an approach that will start you in the right direction? By asking the right questions, Jonathan Koomcy, in his book entitled *Turning Numbers into Knowledge*, discusses verifying information. Chapter 15 in that book describes how guesses can become facts; where estimation became a fact used by the U.S. Department of Energy Information Administration. In Chapter 19 he noted that facts are interpreted by a person's values and this may distort the facts. So how do you distinguish between facts, calculations, guesses, and estimations? How is that affected by the values of the person presenting this information?

It was pointed out to me that many decisions are made based on limited information. We need to recognize that we cannot have all the information available to make the best decision and that in a given situation where time is of the essence, we make decisions based on the information present. There also may be a personal agenda for the person providing the information that could reduce the amount of information and bias the information. One can always point out that the order to engage in a war with Iraq was based on misinformation regarding weapons of mass destruction. We do not know why, who, or any other detail about the individual's agenda for giving this information to the president but we know now that it led to a decision to invade Iraq. Similarly, as a CIO you are given information and you need to determine if the information is based on facts, calculations, estimations, or guesses and if there are agendas at play.

An approach that you can deploy is to determine your confidence level in the information being presented to you to make decisions. This approach provides a way to make informed decisions. When making decisions, we look at factors such as who or what is presenting the information, the timeliness of the information, the relevance of the information, and the situation.

Confidence Ranking Process

Often, you are presented with information for which you do not know the source, do not know how much trust you can put into the information or the source, and/or do not know the value of the information. In short, you are relying on the person presenting the information to give you the right information at the right time to make the best decision you can.

The following process in Figure 6.1 will help you ask simple questions to understand the information being presented to you. It is a simple process where you need to understand what information is being presented to you and how much you can trust that information. Basically, you should be determining if the information is factual, a calculation, an estimation, or a guess (someone's opinion or bias). The more factual or calculated the information, the higher the trust, the higher the confidence level, and the smaller the confidence interval. If information cannot be verified by a third party, then you need to consider reducing your confidence level or how much you trust the information.

What you are looking for is to determine if the information being presented to you consists of facts, calculations, estimations, or guesses. Table 6.1 provides you with how you could view the type of information presented with a confidence level and a confidence interval. Basically you have to trust the information and the source of the information to establish a confidence level and what interval you could depend on the information. A simple formula could be derived from this where you sum the information based on the type of information and your confidence level and come up with "computational trust." You have removed, to some degree, your gut instinct if you compute a trust level. You also have to consider the risk culture of the organization and the risk tolerance of the executive by considering the return on investment (ROI).

- A *fact* is anything known to be true or to really have happened. (Example: World War II happened from 1939 to 1945

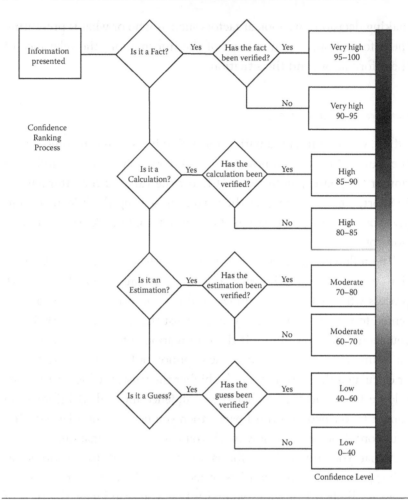

Figure 6.1 Confidence ranking process.

Table 6.1 Confidence Level and Interval

TYPE OF INFORMATION	CONFIDENCE LEVEL	CONFIDENCE INTERVAL
Fact	Very High 90–100%	5
Calculation	High 80–90%	10
Estimation	Moderate 60–80%	20
Guess	Low–Moderate 0–60%	40

is a fact.) We can verify this information and it is known to
be true.

- A *calculation* is a result found by adding, subtracting, multi-
plying, or dividing. (Example: 2 + 2 = 4.)
- An *estimation* is a judgment or opinion about how many, how
much, or how good. (Example: This firewall works very well.)
- A *guess* is forming an opinion on what one thinks is likely without really knowing for certain. (Example: I think it may rain.)

Facts Facts can be distorted by values and misinterpretations. Unless
the fact can be verified, you need to be careful about assuming that it is
a fact. In his book entitled *Turning Numbers into Knowledge,* Jonathan
Koomey cautioned that when technical people make a choice that
is portrayed as logical, rational, and objective, they are still making
a value judgment. When evaluating options, you need to consider
that a fact may have a value element as you make your decision. An
example is technology decisions: the more a person has examined a
specific technology, has met with the sales team, has rationalized the
solution, is more comfortable with being able to implement the solution, and has reduced his options, the more value judgment has been
placed on the decision. Public and other expert opinions often sway
advice. In the 1970s and 1980s, one piece of advice when people were
buying information technology was that you could never be fired
for selecting IBM. That was a theme that IBM unofficially touted
to reduce competition. It was not a fact but many buyers took that
advice as fact. As a person selling digital equipment, it was frustrating for me to come up against that mindset knowing that I had a
superior technology.

When making decisions, you need to consider that the information
presented to you may be value laden. Using Table 6.1, if the information being presented to you is a fact, then the confidence level would
be ranked as Very High (90% to 100%). If the fact has been verified
by a second or third person, then you can apply a smaller confidence
interval; otherwise, you may want to increase the confidence interval.
This means if the information has been verified, then your confidence
interval could be ±2%. If it cannot be verified, then you may want to
increase your confidence interval to ±5%.

Calculations   Calculation errors can introduce a lot of problems. Pharmacists make a lot of calculations every day in prescriptions. In fact, in a study conducted by the Ontario College of Pharmacists, 53% (80 of 150) of teaching hospital doctors were unable to correctly calculate how many milligrams of lignocaine were in a 10-milliliter ampoule of 1% solution. We know that a significant number of deaths in hospitals have been attributed to inaccurate prescriptions. When presented with some numbers, you should be able to estimate, at least to some magnitude, if the calculations are correct. Beware of complexity. Analysts like to create elaborate models and it is difficult for you to determine if the calculations used by the model are correct. You need to ask the questions and simplify the model to some easily explainable calculation, especially if you are presenting this to executives. They do not have time to understand all the differences, and you do not want to be coming back explaining that there were errors in the model or calculations. Remember that the wrong information to the wrong person at the wrong time still leads to poor decisions.

Estimations   Estimations can be useful in helping make decisions as long as you can put some level of confidence in the estimation. *Project management* is a prime example of using estimations to determine how long a project will take and how many resources are needed. Unless the project is a repeat, it is difficult to estimate the level of work required. IT projects have a reputation for not being delivered on time and on budget. We had been rolling out two-factor authentication within the Justice Sector for the BC government. It was originally thought that this could be done within three years. The reality was that it would take longer. There were too many dependencies that made successful completion of the project in three years doubtful. You will find more information about managing risky projects in Chapter 6.

Guesses   Guesses should be scrutinized carefully. Some people have a very convincing way of presenting guesses. They may have significant interest in a specific outcome and a value-laden guess can make for wrong decisions.

When we were looking at cost cutting, I was asked my opinion if we should cut the Justice Sector Data Terminal Services (DTS) servers and move to the basic corporate DTS. The Director of Operations did not see any problem with turning off the Justice Sector DTS servers and moving over to the Corporate DTS servers, and in his opinion there were no risks. I was not sure and asked one of my security analysts to look into this. It turned out that several of our applications specifically used the Justice Sector DTS servers and our firewalls were set up to allow only these servers access to these fairly sensitive applications. If we proceeded with turning off these servers, we would have removed access to some critical applications and caused downtime and frustration for the users. Asking some questions gave us the right answers and established the facts. With the right information being presented to the right person at the right time, we prevented downtime and could determine if there were other ways to proceed.

Information can be of many different types. The level of confidence or trust you put into the information must be considered. When we view information, we have certain biases. These biases can be based on prior information, direction from above, business requirements, legal requirements, compliance requirements, culture, misinformation, and other people's agendas. Remember that the wrong information at the wrong time can lead to a poor decision.

> Without the right information, you're just another person with an opinion.

> **—Tracy O'Rourke, CEO of Allen-Bradley**

Let's work through a few samples to help us understand how the process works and how we can separate facts from estimations and guesses. Earlier we used the example of how the Germans easily defeated the French in 1940 by going around the Maginot Line. The real fact is that the line was not only between the German–French border but extended all the way between the French and Belgium borders to the coast. The Germans actually attacked the line at one point in Belgium and, once penetrated, the Maginot Line was rendered useless.

The second point is that the French thinking did not adapt to newer warfare. They thought that the war would be fought the same way as World War I; that is, trench warfare. The Maginot Line reflected that thinking. The Germans, on the other hand, developed new techniques and, using armored divisions, quickly rolled across the French countryside, meeting little resistance. The fact that the French used most of their military budget in setting up and maintaining the Maginot Line is a perfect example of getting the wrong information to the wrong person at the wrong time, making poor decisions. So the questions that you may want to ask include where is technology going, and should I be investigating how we can use that technology to improve our business?

Here is another example of how to distinguish between facts and someone's value-laden information. In 2001, the government of British Columbia had initiated a project to pilot Public Key Infrastructure (PKI). When I joined in 2002, one of my tasks was to assess the pilot project and determine what we should do: proceed with full implementation or close the pilot. I carefully looked at the information being presented to me by my technical team. They were very eager to continue with the pilot and expand it into a production model. One of the first questions I asked was, "Is there a business need for PKI?" The pilot was being used by a very small number of employees within the Ministry of Finance specifically to protect budget information prior to the government's release of the budget each year. However, they were not funding the project. When I asked one of the directors of finance if they would fund the project, they answered no. So although the technical team had told me that there was a business need, their information was very much based on their biases: the technology was cool, and their desire to keep the pilot going, they felt important. The fact was that there was no business need, so I shut down the PKI pilot, saving us approximately $50,000.

It is our beliefs that hold sway over what we believe as truths. These beliefs often bias or color our knowledge of what is fact and what is fiction. Nicholas Copernicus (1473–1543) changed the thinking of the Western world with his great work entitled "De Revolutionibus," which asserted that the Earth rotated on its axis once daily and traveled around the sun once yearly. This went directly against the existing beliefs that the Earth was a fixed, inert, immobile mass located at the center of the universe and all celestial bodies, including the sun, revolved around it. Galileo and Giordano Bruno embraced the Copernican theory and, as a result, suffered much personal injury at the hands of the church inquisitors. During the Roman Inquisition (1542–1860), Bruno was tried, condemned, and burned at the stake in

1600 for such blasphemy. Galileo was forced on his knees to renounce all belief in Copernican theories. We now know better.

We will always be swayed by beliefs. The information we receive and process will be filtered by these beliefs. It is why we find it difficult to accept that our trusted church-going colleague was stealing money from the company. Our colleague was trusted and exhibited all the mannerisms of trust. It is why our internal gut system fails us. It is why we need to really look at the facts and not trust opinions, guesses, or estimations.

When a project is budgeted at $1 million and the project costs start to exceed the budget by 50%, we are never sure how it could have exceeded the budget by so much. The answer is that we went on estimates and thought these were fact. The project would cost $1 million if all conditions and risks were met. The reality is that we are not good at IM/IT estimates. Why? We do not understand the complexities. The building industry has been building structures for thousands of years. They have established standards. We know with reasonable certainty that the plumbing or electrical will meet specifications based on using these standards. There are always complications but these pale in comparison to information systems. The code is developed by programmers who do not program to a standard. The million or so lines of code interact in unspecified ways. Microsoft does a very good job of finding bugs in code. However, they cannot test every permutation of how the code reacts in every way. When you have 50 million lines of code, you can expect to have 1% of the code with some sort of error condition (not necessarily a bug but an unexpected condition that arises when the code is executed). That means about 50,000 lines of code could have conditions that may cause an error. It is why Microsoft is constantly patching software as these conditions arise.

One caution is that we also need to consider new ideas that may be revolutionary and not something we can understand or have any prior knowledge. In their book entitled *Hard Facts*, Jeffrey Pfeffer and Robert Sutton (2006) made the point that leaders need to figure out when and how to get out of the way. In any organization, there are a lot of very intelligent people working and some are very creative. These people may see something that is innovative and can make a difference in some aspect of the business. The difficult part is figuring out how much risk you want to take in promoting their idea. That is where the organization's risk culture requires an understanding of what impact that idea would have on a business area or within IT.

Risk Management Starts with the Individual

Why is it important that we consider how individuals manage risks? People manage risk differently. Some individuals are very aggressive in taking risks while others are very conservative. This affects the way they deal with risks in an organization. The collapse of Barings Bank in 1995 was caused by a single trader who managed to hide losses totaling 827 million British Pounds (GPB). In January 2008, a rogue trader cost French bank Societe Generale 4.9 billion Euros ($7.1 billion U.S.). These are spectacular failures in risk management; however, there are many more cases where organizations and even countries have ended up in financial ruin due to a single individual. The fact that we do not consider risk management profiles as part of our hiring practices is leaving a gap in our risk analysis of our most important asset—people.

The financial market has been describing investment philosophies for the handling of risks for investing for years. People have different philosophies for managing investment risks. When you sit down with a financial advisor or investment broker, the first thing they want to know is your investment philosophy. In his book entitled *Risk is a Four Letter Word*, George Hartman (1994) described a personal investment philosophy. A personal investment philosophy determines the amount of risk a person will take when investing his or her money. A set of questions is used to determine the investment risk profile. These questions usually consider age, gender, income, risk tolerance, as well as risk appetite. An investment strategy is described as *conservative*, *moderate*, *balanced growth*, or *aggressive* (see Figure 6.2). This determines the person's investment strategy; that is, how much risk a person is willing to take when investing.

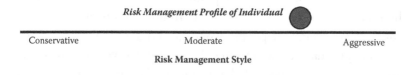

Figure 6.2 Risk management profile of individual.

Insurance companies use actuaries to profile drivers and, based on the number of accidents, age of the driver, and gender, consider young male drivers a higher risk, and hence higher insurance rates. Insurance companies also use risk analysis to determine residential and commercial insurance. There are higher risk areas for crime, fire, earthquake, and flood.

Meyers-Briggs is a psychometric questionnaire designed to measure psychological preferences in how people perceive the world and make decisions. Psychological preferences are described in four pairs, or *dichotomies*. The dichotomies can be described as introversion or extroversion, sensing or intuition, thinking or feeling, and judging or perception. Each person can be described as having four of these preferences. Meyers-Briggs has been described as one of the most trusted personality assessment tools available today. Similarly, each person has a risk management profile.

A risk management profile can be described as how an individual manages risks and is shown in Figure 6.2. Each person has a risk management style. The style may be that the person is very aggressive in taking risks or very conservative. Risk is the amount of exposure—physically, emotionally, financially, or politically—that an individual is willing to undertake. Individuals have different risk appetites and tolerances. A risk appetite is the amount of risk an individual will undertake. Risk tolerance is the individual's acceptable variation relative to the amount of risk.

In their book entitled *The Accountant's Handbook of Fraud & Commercial Crime*, Bologna et al. describe personal integrity. They give the unflattering picture that 20% of people are honest, 20% are dishonest, and 60% are either honest or dishonest, depending on the situation. That means that up to 80% of your staff could be dishonest if an opportunity presented itself to them. So when staff skim funds from tills, take small amounts from cash boxes, pass bad checks, or take company property, they are being dishonest based on the situation. They do not think they will be caught. It should be noted that most of the inappropriate activities are perpetrated by employees, administrators, and power users. Most of these are the small-time thefts; however, insiders already have access to sensitive information and it is easy to defeat manual controls or high-level audits. Make sure you consider the larger ones where CFOs or other executives are embezzling funds, as executives often have rights to override controls.

Understanding individual risk management profiles is critical in discovering risks to the organization. As we continue to evolve our risk management capabilities, we also need to consider hiring practices to make sure we get the right person with the right aptitude for the right role. We can no longer assume that a criminal record check or a financial background check will give us the necessary information we need to determine if the individual we are hiring is the right fit for the role. Keep in mind that a criminal record check and a financial background check are point-in-time checks. If the person does not have a conviction or has a conviction in another jurisdiction, nothing may show in the criminal record check.

The story about Robert Hanssen, the FBI agent who spied for the Soviet Union and Russian Intelligence Services for 22 years, tells us about trust and risk management profiling. Hanssen was arrested on February 18, 2001, and charged with selling American secrets to Russia for more than $1.4 million. His motive was money.

Hanssen was a devout Catholic, father of six, and a regular attendee at daily 6:30 a.m. mass for more than a decade. His family life and his Catholic involvement hid his double life very well. He was even put in charge of finding all known and rumored penetrations of the FBI in order to find the man who had betrayed Martynov and Motorin, who were KGB agents secretly working for the FBI. Ironically, that meant he was looking for himself. Hanssen was reported by other agents a number of times but no actions were taken until his brother-in-law recommended to the bureau that Hanssen be investigated. From there he was finally arrested. Interestingly, one of the smoking guns was his PDA, where he kept his information about his contacts and activities.

The question that begs to be asked here is how did he manage to evade arrest for so long? His family and religious activities were good cover for his spying, and it would be hard to think of him as anything but trusted. If there were some sort of screening process that did risk management profiling and continuous control monitoring, would the FBI have caught him sooner? I think the answer is yes.

In 2009 in an information privacy breach in British Columbia, Richard Ernest Wainwright, a supervisor in the youth and special-needs office of the Ministry of Children and Family Development, had over 1,400 personal records at his house. Wainwright had a criminal record for credit card fraud and counterfeiting offenses and used false identity documents in the name of Richard Ernest Perran to get his government job. The case, however, raised questions about how Wainwright avoided pre-employment checks. A criminal record check against the name Richard Perran would not have revealed that he was Richard Wainwright and that he changed his name. However, a good risk management profile may have determined that Richard Perran was a risk to the organization in his role. His role allowed him access to sensitive personal information. By either denying him employment or adding a level of controls, the BC government could have avoided the situation entirely.

Not all risks can be identified and covered. Not all situations can be appropriately controlled to limit losses. But by identifying potential risks and using the appropriate controls, we can limit our liabilities and potential losses. If we can improve the process of identifying the people who could create more risk, we can change the controls and reduce the risks. By taking some preventive steps up front, such as identifying risk management profiles, we can determine the best role and responsibilities for the person.

Taking a view from the top, new CEOs often reset direction in an organization to align with the board and the CEO's vision. The vision may be taking the organization into a more aggressive position to gain market share from competitors. The individual risk management profile of the new CEO may not be the same as the risk management profile of other executives. In other words, the other executives who cannot share the same vision will be replaced.

Managing Risky People

People are often promoted into roles that they cannot handle. The most glaring example is a very capable technical person being given a manager role or, even worse, a director role when they have no managerial experience. The expectation is that the person will continue to perform in their technical role as well as take on management responsibilities. We will continue to repeat this pattern until we learn that people cannot expect to be good managers without experience. In his book entitled *Managers Not MBAs*, Henry Mintzberg discussed how organizations hire MBAs directly out of school and the expectation is set that the MBA can perform as a manager.

"Management is where art and craft and science meet," and most MBA programs are simply "training in analytical skills for analytical jobs … like investment banking and consulting." Whatever you do, don't confuse an MBA with a license to manage. "If people want to be managers, there's a better route to it: get into an industry, know it, prove yourself, get promoted into a managerial position—and then, go to a program that uses managerial experience explicitly—not other people's cases, but your own experience." (Henry Mintzberg, 2005)

Another example of people being promoted into roles that demand different skills are consultants. Consultants often perform an advisory role to a CEO or CIO. In that role, they often recommend industry standards, best practices, and business strategies that may have worked previously in other organizations. Sometimes the CIO has an opening or creates an opening and hires the consultant into the organization. Because of the higher salary or earnings that the consultant had prior to joining the organization, the CIO will place the consultant in a director or executive position. The consultant may have some managerial experience or some implementation experience but most likely not. Yet the consultant is expected to manage people. I have experienced the consultant being hired into an IT director position and not being able to change from his consultancy role to an IT director role. The result as described to me by one of the business directors was confusion and duplication of work. The IT director was unable to let go of his strengths and focus on supporting his staff.

There is another scenario that really requires risk management and identifying the individual's risk management profile. In their book entitled *Snakes in Suits*, authors Paul Babiak and Robert Hare (2006) described psychopathic behavior and how disruptive it can be to teams and the workplace.

Using a variety of influence tactics, the psychopaths manipulate their network of one-on-one personal bonds to gather information they could use to advance their own career, derail the careers of rivals, or enlist technical support when the company makes demands on them (to actually do their job). Specifically, their game plan involved manipulating communication networks to enhance their own reputation, to disparage others, and to create conflict and rivalries among organization members, thereby keeping them from sharing information that might uncover the deceit. (Babiak and Hare, 2006)

Psychopathic behavior is very difficult to spot. A psychopath is very skillful at lying and manipulating, often to the detriment of their patron, whom they often replace. We cannot go around labeling people as psychopathic, but it is good to be aware. Just remember that you need to understand that there are personal motives and behaviors behind decisions and conversations. Make sure you look at the facts and get third-party involvement.

There are no magic bullets for managing risky people. It takes a lot of work. Key steps will help you identify those individuals, such as a risk management profile to determine if the person is risk averse or risk aggressive. Good human resources practices will always support making good decisions about hiring a person. Routine investigations about their background, reference checks, financial checks, and even technical and school checks will help reduce the risk of having someone with psychopathic behaviors or with the wrong skill sets in a role in which they cannot hope to be successful.

We have to understand that people are your biggest risk. Most people in the IT industry are knowledge workers. Knowledge workers have the ability to transfer their assets (knowledge and experience) from one organization to another with relative ease. Knowledge workers bind their loyalties to a person, mission, or belief until they lose faith or it no longer suits their needs. Typically, money is a motivator for knowledge workers. They demand to be paid well but are not totally motivated by cash. If, on the other hand, they feel that they are not getting enough money, the effect is quite dramatic. There are two other very powerful motivators: challenge and peer respect.

Knowledge workers are almost totally consumed by challenge and respect. The best are a ship of knowledge adrift in a sea of buyers. They dock at someone's island because it gives them challenge, respect, and money. You do not manage knowledge workers. You provide them with challenges and respect and pay handsomely for their knowledge, not the hours they work. You cannot control knowledge workers. You can control the environment and give them the incentives to produce results.

These are the people who work for you. They could be working for your competitor next week. Organizations are no longer loyal to their employees. Knowledge workers are no longer loyal to the organization. This is business risk. Who are the key workers in your organization that you depend on for operations, development, projects, and any other aspect of IT? If they were to leave today, what are your contingency plans? Do you have succession planning? Do you know what information they will take with them?

Risk Management Profiling and Risk Culture

The Risk IT Framework from ISACA discusses some essential elements of risk governance. Risk appetite is described in COSO as the amount of risk a company or other entity will accept in pursuit of objectives. Individuals can cause aberrations in the risk appetite based on a situation. These aberrations could be attributed to a misalignment of the risk culture of an organization. Risk culture is described as the behavior toward taking risks and the behavior toward following policies. In both situations where the banks were put at risk by individuals, the individual traders exceeded the risk appetite of the banks by taking excessive risks and circumventing policies. The question is: How do you spot the aberrations in individuals who are taking excessive risks and not following policies?

Aggregating individual risk management profiles can be useful in helping to understand the risk culture of the organization. An individual risk management profile is useful for determining if the person is the right person for the given roles and responsibilities. When you start to look at many individual risk management profiles, you start to see a pattern as shown in Figure 6.3. In the case of the individual, the risk profile of that person is moderately aggressive. In the case of many different risk management profiles, the patterns indicate that the organization has a risk management profile that is moderately aggressive. We could say that the risk culture of the organization is moderately aggressive. So what does that mean? We could argue that organizations have their own life cycle and the risk culture reflects that life cycle. In the beginning, an organization

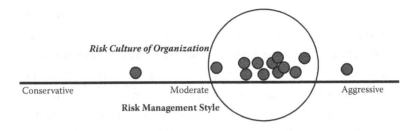

Figure 6.3 Risk culture of an organization.

starts with an aggressive risk culture to gain market share. This is to enable cash flow and establish a return on investment for shareholders. This aggressive risk culture continues until an organization reaches a certain size and complexity dynamics start to take over. The larger the organization, the more complex, and the risk culture becomes more conservative.

In his book entitled *Complex Organizations*, Charles Perrow (1986) described how most organizations today are, in fact, bureaucratic. Bureaucracy adds to complexity by adding hierarchies.

Organizations are mostly based on a military-style structure: command and control. These hierarchical structures have been around for 10,000 years. It is difficult to change this into a customer-focused structure.

Measuring Risks or Uncertainty

In his book entitled *How to Measure Anything*, Douglas Hubbard (2007) talked about measuring risks and uncertainty. He defined uncertainty, risk, and their measurements as follows:

- *Uncertainty:* The lack of complete certainty; that is, more than one possibility.
- *Measurement of uncertainty:* A set of probabilities assigned to a set of possibilities.
- *Risk:* A state of uncertainty where some of the possibilities involve a loss or other undesired outcome.
- *Measurement of risk:* A set of possibilities, each with quantified probabilities and quantified losses.

I would take that one step further and define risk and uncertainty differently.

- *Risk is based on probability.* Risk management is managing/ reducing the probability of a known risk that may cause an impact. We have known risks and can do some form of risk mitigation: reduce, accept, or self-insure; avoid; transfer (insurance); or some combination thereof. We know that a building can have fires so we install sprinklers as a risk miti- gation strategy. It reduces the potential impact and probability that a fire will cause major damage. We also identify risks of low probability and have generalized plans to deal with them. An example is a meteor hitting a building. Although there is a low probability of occurrence, we should have generalized strategies to handle very diverse but low-probability events.
- *Uncertainty is based on possibility.* There is a possibility that something could happen that could have an impact. These are unknown risks. We have not identified them as risks and have no mitigation strategies.

There should be a higher degree of certainty if we are measuring risks. In terms of IM/IT, we are not very good at measuring risks. We often make decisions based on value-laden information or someone's guesses or estimates. Even facts can have biased information attached. To reduce the reliance on value-laden information and guesses or esti- mates, there is a need to look at facts and calculations. Even experts have biases and set value standards that can skew the results.

In his book entitled *Super Crunchers*, Ian Ayres (2007) talked about data mining and formulas making data-based decisions.

- Rental companies and insurers are refusing service to peo- ple with poor credit scores because data mining tells them that credit scores correlate with a higher likelihood of hav- ing an accident.
- Wine connoisseurs are having their taste buds adjusted by a simple formula using rainfall and growing season length. That is, the accuracy of the formula is astonishingly more accurate than that of the wine critics.
- The sport of baseball has been turned upside down by a for- mula to better measure a hitter's contribution to runs created. The old method was to send out scouts to high school and col-

lege games to watch kids play ball and determine if this one kid was going to be the next Mickey Mantle or Babe Ruth.

The point of all of this is that there is uncertainty in measurement due to subjectivity of the measurer. In his book entitled *The Drunkard's Walk*, Leonard Mlodinow (2008) described how researchers have influenced control groups in various ways and have determined that people are fooled by labels, price, or color. In blind taste tests where food coloring was added to the same white wine to make it appear a rosé, expert testers were fooled by the fake rosé into perceiving that the fake rosé was sweeter. In other tests, the researchers switched labels on bottles. The bottles were labeled with prices $5, $10, $25, and $50. The reality was that it was the same wine in all the bottles. The testers were fooled by the labels. Nearly all the testers thought the $50 bottle was the best wine.

In the 1950s, a decision psychology researcher, Egon Brunswick, measured expert decisions statistically. His model, known as the Lens Model, considers how observers correctly or incorrectly interpret objective cues* to perceive reality. The Lens Model reduces the error of a person's (judge's) inconsistency from evaluations. Unfortunately, we do not always have the time to use models such as the above in making decisions. However, with a little practice we can reduce our confidence interval and increase our confidence level by asking questions about the information being presented to us using the confidence ranking process.

Measuring risk is not an exact science. The more we can use large numbers and calculate the probabilities, the more certainty we can have in the numbers. Scoping projects are always risky in terms of getting the cost right. For example, a project manager will tell you that a project will cost $500,000 to complete. What is her confidence in that number? How many projects of similar size and scope has she completed? If this is IT, the probability is that she may have completed one or maybe none. Her costs are mostly an estimate of the project. Her time frames are an estimate of the time frames. What degree of certainty do you need to determine project costs for your entire portfolio and how that

---

* A *cue* is a suggestion, hint, or signal and can have a probabilistic (uncertain) relation to the actual object; the same cue can signal several objects in the environment, and cues are often redundant.

may impact on your budget? If each project manager is off by 10% and you have twenty projects, how much of your budget will be impacted?

Risks are often measured using a scale such as High, Medium, and Low. These measurements are not quantifiable. That is, what is meant by high risk? Is this measurement based on probability or possibility? Is there an impact if the risk is realized? How much impact? What is impacted? Impacts must be quantifiable; that is, there must be some financial or other value associated with the impact of a risk. The impact measurement must be based on a fact, calculation, estimation, or guess. We must have a confidence level and associated confidence interval associated with the measurement of the impact.

We know that the experts can be wrong. We also know that a lot of money is spent convincing the experts and they have biases. You need better information to make better decisions. It starts with facts and calculations.

How to Measure Risks

When trying to measure risks, we need to have something that is quantifiable or else the risk is not measurable. When we talk about high risk and tell executives that everything is high risk, they tend to turn off. It's selling fear, uncertainty, and doubt (FUD). We know that at some point people become numbed by a repeated message and tend to start ignoring the message. As a CIO, which of the following messages would be more important to you?

> "Our ability to detect a large breach is a high risk to our organization."
>
> "According to a Ponemon Institute report on cyber crime, only 43% of respondents believe that their organization could detect a large breach involving more than 10,000 customer records. I do not believe we have the ability to detect a large breach in a timely manner."

Most reasonable people would take more notice of the second message. Both messages indicate a risk. The first does not give any information as to the extent of the risk. The second provides information that the risk involves 10,000 or more customer records. Information from a report indicated that 43% of respondents believed their organization could not detect a breach. And the person delivering the message is stating that the organization could not detect such a breach in a timely manner. I would expect that the person would have a proposal on how this risk could be mitigated, including how much it would cost, the time frame, etc.

So how do you measure risks? As reviewed previously, risk information must be based on facts and calculations as much as possible. Communicating the risk is sometimes more difficult than what we think. Douglas Hubbard, during his IT security measurement project for Veterans Affairs, described how he had to get consensus on a very simple question: "What do you mean, IT Security?" We often talk about impact, IT Security, improvements, value, and we think everyone is on the same page without considering that everyone looks at things differently based on their background, education, and experience.

Identify the Risk

The first step is to identify the risk. The risk could be in terms of service delivery, such as a risk of availability or a liability such as the risk of credit card information theft. Risks must always be put in terms that the business can understand. Using the credit card example, we would identify that we had gaps in our information protection that could allow a hacker to penetrate our defenses and gain access to our information. This would result in noncompliance with PCI data security standards and damage our reputation, cost us dollars in mitigating the effects, and potentially lose our customers and market share.

Consensus of the Risk

The next step is to get consensus on what the risk is. This means defining the risk and communicating that definition of risk to the people who need to be involved. We can use RACI as defined by COBIT to determine who should be involved in the effort. RACI means who is responsible, accountable, consulted, and informed. Using our example of credit card theft, we would identify who are the major players in managing credit card information and define the risk better. Knowing that the application protecting the credit card information is vulnerable to a Structured Query Language (SQL) injection attack is the first step in communicating the risk. Defining the risk in terms the business can understand will help improve the ability to get the appropriate level of funding to mitigate the risks. We know from our reading that the majority of credit card breaches that occurred and have been reported were compromised by SQL injection attacks. What we need is for everyone to agree that this is a risk.

Analysis of Risk

Once we have identified and gained consensus, we need to analyze the risk to get a better understanding of the risk. We need to get agreement on variables that will be used to calculate the risk. For a breach, the variables could be the number of customer records affected, productivity loss, cost of breach, etc.

For each variable, a range of answers should be provided. The answers should be numeric in value to give you upper and lower boundaries. For example, the number of customer records affected for a large security breach is 10,000 to 100,000.

Finally, the cost of a risk such as the cost of a breach can be calculated. Just remember that this must have a confidence level and a confidence interval; so, for the number of customers affected given that the cost of mitigation per customer is about $140, the cost of a breach would have a range from $1.4 million (10,000 customer records) to $14 million (100,000 customer records). We have fairly good confidence that this information is correct based on a few studies and reports of how much it costs to manage a breach per customer record. Our confidence level could be 90% with a confidence interval of 5%. What this really says is that a large breach could cost as much as $13 million and as low as $1.2 million. Our calculation has a 90% probability of being correct within ±5% error. Now you have a cost range of a risk using a breach as an example. Finally, determine what mitigation strategy you should adopt and how much money you should spend in proportion to the cost of the risk.

Using an example from government, we can look at how a risk assessment is done on a system. Prior to the system becoming operational, we had a cyber attack that compromised one of the servers. The remediation was quick; however, we needed higher assurances that the system was not at risk. A Threat Risk Assessment (TRA) was done on the system using the standard government risk assessment approach. This involved using a tool called Citicus™. The result was a report that indicated that the system had forty-seven risk areas, and nine of them were considered high risk. The executive was briefed on the report and asked the question, "Are my operations at risk?" Nobody could answer that question based on the information from the TRA.

I analyzed the situation and prepared a briefing note to help reduce the report to more meaningful information that would answer the question. Basically there were three conditions that needed controls to minimize effects on operations:

1. A breach in confidentiality, meaning that the disclosure of sensitive information may compromise operations.
2. A breach in integrity of the information, meaning that changing information in the system may compromise operations.
3. An extended outage of the system may affect operations.

The first two conditions were controlled through access management, meaning that only authorized persons could access the system. If an authorized person released or changed the information, there was very little that could be done to control that situation. Because most of the authorized people were working professionals whose lives were at risk, the probability of disclosure or tampering with information was low.

The third condition, an extended outage, had good physical controls that would prevent the system from sustained outages. There were two redundant sets of hardware geographically separated and a failover capability to maintain operations. Each site had appropriate power backup. The power grid was such that even a major event such as a powerful earthquake should not knock out both systems due to geographic separation. We then looked at the cyber threats to determine if there were risks that could affect both systems. We found that there were insufficient controls due to the configuration of the systems that had to allow port 80 to stay open to communicate with operational personnel. The system was key for coordinating multiple levels of government as well as private organization personnel. We concluded that if the attacker had the means and the motive, the systems could be affected and could be compromised, thus affecting operations. Because the system had already sustained a successful attack, we decided to put additional controls to limit a cyber attack. We determined that, based on the additional controls, the probability of an attack being successful was low.

We measured the impact of a compromise in confidentiality, integrity, or availability. The range was very large—from very little impact to catastrophic. Worst-case scenarios indicated that a breach could cause significant risk to public safety, meaning that people's lives could be at risk. The executive had to be sure.

If you are unsure how to determine impact or consequence of a risk, there is a table in Appendix C (Risk Impact Scales) with an explanation on how to use them. Here is an example risk registry (Table 6.2) for measuring the business risk and consequence of not doing information management at an organization. The organization had annual revenue of $40 million. I measured that a 10% impact on their annual revenue (or about $4 million) would represent a catastrophic consequence.

Let me step through some of the risks. The organization was in ongoing negotiations with third parties on some very sensitive issues. The organization would have to deliver on some commitments and if during the negotiations there was a breach in trust, it would create significant ongoing liabilities. The loss of reputation could be estimated at $4 million or more loss of revenue. Two key mitigation strategies were to make sure proper negotiation protocols were followed and to make sure sensitive negotiation information was not released jeopardizing the organization's position.

Another major risk was the unauthorized disclosure of sensitive information. In this case, these negotiations involved personal property and premature disclosure could result in confrontations that could place people at risk for harm. This was a public safety issue and we had to maintain proper security measures to keep this information from being leaked. I estimated the financial cost to be at least $400,000 but probably not more than $1 million. Using the scale gave the executive a sense of the magnitude of potential risk. It would not be catastrophic but would have a major financial impact.

Calculating how much you are at risk is not just the numbers but also a review of the controls in place to mitigate the risk. If the controls are sufficient, then you can just monitor the situation periodically to see if there are any changes. If the controls are insufficient, then you

Table 6.2 Risk and Impact

RISK & IMPACT	CONSEQUENCE	ESTIMATED RISK COST	RISK MITIGATION STRATEGIES
Misrepresentation at negotiations Loss of reputation	Catastrophic	$4 million+	Negotiation protocols followed Good information security for sensitive information and documents Knowledge management
Unauthorized disclosure of sensitive information (privacy breach, loss of reputation)	Major	$400,000	Good information security Good information security awareness and training Appropriate information security classification of information assets
Unauthorized disclosure of sensitive information (safety impact: public safety may be in jeopardy if inappropriate information is released at the wrong time)	Major	$400,000	Good information security Good information security awareness and training Appropriate information security classification of information assets
Missed delivery of obligations (reputation loss)	Major	$400,000	Improve tracking of obligations Agreements with all parties reviewed annually Content management strategy
Loss of knowledge (productivity loss)	Moderate	$40,000	Knowledge capture through video interviews Improved documentation of processes

need to examine what needs to be in place and the timing of implementing the controls. Several options (scenarios) should be reviewed, including short term, medium term, and long term. In the example above, a short-term strategy may be to deploy some sort of application firewall to minimize the possibility of an SQL injection attack on the application. A longer-term strategy would be to enforce secure coding standards for all applications in conformance with some standard such as Open Web Application Security Projects (OWASP).

Mitigate the Risk   If the controls are not sufficient, then the gap analysis performed in the previous step will help determine the next steps.

A proposal should be prepared, including annualized cost of mitigation. The mitigation strategy should determine how much residual risk is left and if that is acceptable. Keep in mind that there will always be some risk and we cannot reduce the risk to zero.

The business needs to assess the risk and determine what money should be allocated to mitigating the risks. If the impact of a risk is high enough and the potential for the risk to occur is high, then the business needs to respond. Linking risk to business outcomes will ensure that the risk is examined at the highest level and the decisions made will be made by the CEO or the board. One of the key considerations is that we all view risk differently. Our determination of the risk may be that the risk is very high; however, the CEO or board may consider the risk lower based on a number of other business priorities and risks.

Monitor the Risk   As part of your monitoring, you will have a control in place to allow you to monitor the risk to determine if the risk is increasing or decreasing. We often assume that controls are static and will protect us from a risk. We know that this is not true and risks are evolving; hackers and their methods of attack are a good example.

Reassess the Risk   Periodically, you should review identified risks to determine if your controls are sufficient and you have not changed processes or systems to reduce the effectiveness of the controls. An overall control strategy should be in place to manage risks holistically and not piece-meal. PCI is a good starting point, and blending all controls into one overall strategy is important. Use enterprise information security architecture such as Sherwood Applied Business Security Architecture (SABSA) to develop an overall control strategy. Continue to focus on the risks to the business and measure the impacts and consequences.

Performing a Risk Assessment

Every organization exists to provide value for its stakeholders. It does not matter if the organization is government, publicly traded, or private. There must be some value provided back to the stakeholders for the entity to exist. The purpose of risk management is to help manage the risks associated with providing that value. The value may be an improvement to business in the form of a process, program, infrastructure, or application. The purpose of a risk assessment is to determine the risks associated with providing that value.

In the case of IT, the value is associated with information. IT is about getting the right information to the right person at the right time so they can perform a task or make a better decision. In doing a risk assessment for IT, we need to consider the financial impact of the improvement to business as part of the risk assessment. This should be the first consideration of any project or improvement. Does this improvement add value to the organization? How much value? And what are the associated risks?

I have developed a simple methodology for performing risk assessments as seen in Figure 6.4. There are ten steps, and a lot of the risk assessment is done by group consensus. It is important that you get multiple inputs into a risk assessment from all stakeholders. I prefer using a team or committee to work in determining risks and impacts, rather than one individual, to get different perspectives on the risks and associated impacts. Throughout the risk assessment, you will see that there must be consensus built on every step. This is to ensure that the team is on the same page and that as many risks as possible are identified and analyzed. Another thing that is really important before, during, and after any risk assessment is to make sure you communicate and brief the sponsor(s). Some risk assessments can take weeks, and I have seen several assessments take months if the auditors are involved. Make sure that you keep the communications brief and salient. Sponsors want to know where they are spending their money and what value they are getting for that money.

A risk assessment should ask five basic questions:

1. What can go wrong?
2. How can it go wrong?
3. What is the possible impact?
4. What are the consequences of the impact?
5. Can we mitigate it?

The last question should be expanded to include mitigation strategies and solutions to reduce risks.

Risk Assessment Process Steps

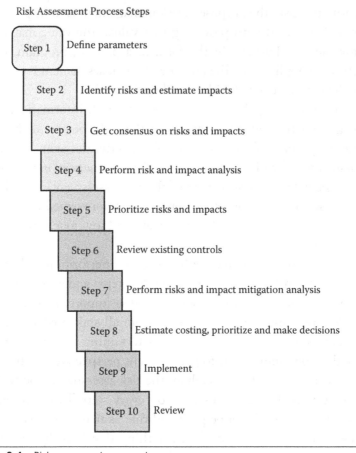

Figure 6.4   Risk assessment process steps.

I want to take some time here to differentiate among threat, risk, impact, and consequence. These are important concepts and we often confuse the terms. Let's start by defining each term:

- *Threat:* the potential for harm (can be natural, accidental, or intentional).
- *Risk:* the vulnerability to a threat.
- *Impact:* a forceful or dramatic effect (an effect is something produced by a cause).
- *Consequence:* the result of an effect.

There is a difference between an impact and a consequence. We have to put consequences in perspective of the organization or entity. In other words, a risk is a realized threat.

Taking a simple example, we can see the relationship between threat, risk, impact, and consequence. If your shoelace is untied and you trip, you could break your leg. If you are a dancer, you could lose your job.

THREAT	RISK	IMPACT	CONSEQUENCE
Shoelace untied	Tripping	Break leg	Loss of job

Another example using a cyber threat:

THREAT	RISK	IMPACT	CONSEQUENCE
Code exploitation	System compromised	Information stolen	Loss of reputation

The important point here is the business consequence. The technology threat, risk, and impact have little meaning unless there is a business consequence. Business consequences are why you are doing a risk assessment. If there is a major or catastrophic business consequence, then you need to consider risk mitigation.

A risk assessment is useful to an organization to help in accomplishing one or more of the following:

- Identify threats, vulnerabilities, and opportunities
- Improve controls
- Better allocate and use resources for risk treatment
- Improve operational efficiencies and effectiveness
- Improve loss prevention and incident management
- Reduce losses
- Enhance safety or health

In many cases, you do not have the in-house expertise or already have significant workload on your resources. This is where external consultants can be useful. They provide the extra capacity to enable your resources to work more effectively. Ideally, external consultants would be able to do the risk assessment. They typically would perform Steps 1 through 8, although it is expected that you should have a handle on the parameters from an enterprise risk management perspective. I view Step 1 as the most important step because it sets the tone, scope, time frames, and expectations of the risk assessment. Consultants can also be asked to come back for a review of the implementation to gain a third-party view of how well you implemented the solutions.

Team or Committee Selection

A cross-functional team or committee is necessary to help you determine risks, impacts, and consequences. There are some criteria for team selection that you should consider:

1. *Team size:* The optimum size of a team is five to nine persons. The size of the team can be related to the number of items we can retain in our short-term memory. Most people can remember five to nine items. For a team or committee, more team members means more diversity and less chance of gaining consensus or having all team members participate equally. The consultant or security person is a facilitator and may lead the discussion at points. Each person on the team may lead the discussion. Remember that participation is very important and you want to hear from all team members.
2. *Team composition:* You need a cross section of people to help facilitate discussion on risks. Representation should come from business, technical, operations, management, and security.
3. *Participation:* You need participation from all team members. The representative from management must not take over the meeting and agenda.

The goal of the team is to create a list of possible risks and identify impacts. There must be some thought of the consequences.

Step 1: Define Parameters

The first step in any risk assessment is to define the parameters. Parameters include

- *Enterprise risk management:* Is there a risk management strategy across the organization in place? If there is already an enterprise risk management program in place within the organization, how do you link this specific risk assessment to it?
- *Risk culture:* What is the risk culture of the organization? Is there a risk culture prevalent in the organization? Is the risk culture conservative or aggressive?
- *Risk appetite:* What is the risk appetite of the organization? Has a risk appetite been articulated for the organization?
- *Risk tolerance:* What is the risk tolerance of the organization?

Table 6.3 Categories of Risks

CATEGORY OF RISKS	DESCRIPTION
Market	Organizations must be aware of what is happening globally in terms of markets and economies.
Budget	If there is an increase or decrease in budget, this will have an impact on the management of service delivery and liabilities.
People	The most vulnerable and most volatile risks are people both inside and outside the organization. People are a risk to information disclosure, modification, and deletion, as well as operations, control, and detection.
Technology	Failure of technology is a risk to information availability, integrity, and confidentiality.
Operational	Failures within operations are risks to confidentiality, integrity, and availability.
Information	Failures in information are risks to wrong decisions and trust.
Control	Failures in controls are risks to confidentiality, integrity, and availability.
Detection	Failures in detection are risks to confidentiality, fraud, and availability.
Opportunity	Failures in opportunities are risks to the business.

- *Risk capacity:* What is the maximum risk that an organization will bear? Has the board or senior executives articulated the maximum risk the organization can handle?
- *Risk types:* What are the categories of risk that should be considered? The categories of risk in Table 6.3 should be considered in defining the parameters.

Taxonomy of Risk Types   If we are looking for consistency in risk assessments, it is important to have a common taxonomy of risks types. A taxonomy is the practice and science of classification according to relationships. The categories of risks as described in Table 6.3 are fairly broad. You may want to consider your own classification for risk or look at some standard risk types such as the one in Table 6.4 that is based on Standard and Poor's.

Based on agreement of risk categories or taxonomy, the risk assessment can be compared against other risk assessments and the information shared across the organization between business areas.

Scope, Time Frame, Complexity, and Stakeholders   The following questions should be answered about scope, time frame, complexity, stakeholders, dependencies, and other factors:

- What is the scope of this risk assessment?

Table 6.4 Taxonomy of Risk Types

ENVIRONMENTAL RISKS	FINANCIAL RISKS	SUPPLY RISKS	MANAGEMENT RISKS	OPERATIONAL RISKS
Business continuity	Capital availability	Commodity prices	Corporate governance	Compliance
Business market	Credit counterparty	Supply chain	Data and information security	Procedures
Environmental	Financial market	Partners	Employee health and safety	Processes
Liability lawsuits	Inflation	Suppliers	Intellectual property	Controls
Natural disaster/ weather	Interest rates		Labor disputes	Equipment
Pandemic	Liquidity		Labor skills shortage	Infrastructure
Physical damage	Currency value		M&A restructuring	Buildings
Political risk			Managing complexity	Vehicles
Regulatory/ legislative			Managing uncertainty	
Terrorism			Outsourcing	
			Project management	
			Reputation	
			Technology failure	

Source: Modified from Standard and Poor's Taxonomy of Risk Types.

- What is the time frame?
- What are other factors to consider?
- Are there any dependencies?
- How complex is the environment (organization)?
- Who are the stakeholders?

In most cases, a risk assessment is a project and has specific deliverables. In his book entitled *The Security Risk Assessment Handbook*, Douglas Landoll (2006) made the point that the risk assessment needs to have the scope, budget, and time frames established and agreed to by everyone. Organizations are very complex, and the challenge is limiting the scope of the risk assessment to very specific assets and controls. This is not the case for Enterprise Risk Management and the business objectives or goals of the organization. Enterprise Risk Management means the scope of a risk assessment dealing with Enterprise Risk Management is the organization and its goals and objectives. That is why scoping the risk assessment is very important.

In the BC government within the Justice Sector, we had developed a simple approach to TRAs for new applications. The scope was defined in three categories: small (project for new application was simple and not complex and there were no financial requirements); medium (project had some complexity and there were some financial requirements and/or personal information); and large (project was complex and there were financial requirements and/or personal information). I have provided a methodology for Project Risk Profiling that will help determine how much controls and monitoring should be placed and done for a project. This will help focus scarce resources on the higher risk projects and define more rigorous controls for those high-risk projects.

Overall, an environmental scan should be done to determine if there are any significant risks that need to be addressed or at least noted in the risk assessment. This includes market, business, operational, budget, financial, technology, and business objectives. For example, in 2010, the economic situation was static. There was little growth in the GDP. This meant that budgets were tight. In the BC government, there were still layoffs as government struggled to manage budgets. The effect of this was a concerned and desperate workforce that did not know if and when they would be affected by workforce adjustments. In that environment, there was a higher risk that some employees would do something inappropriate.

In the first step, you also need to identify the stakeholders. This is an important step as these stakeholders will form your committee or working group. In some instances, the stakeholder may assign or delegate that responsibility to another person. A committee or working group will provide input and decisions for the rest of the risk assessment. The committee should be cross-functional and include representation from business, audit, finance, IT, risk management, human resources, and policy to get different perspectives on risks.

As an example, we will use a project for knowledge and content management that I worked on for a small ministry. There were several environmental concerns that we had to consider:

1. *Budget constraints:* There was very little budget allocated for any project work and this was a new project.
2. *Government was under severe financial pressure:* The government was running a deficit.
3. *Key people were retiring:* Loss of their knowledge would have a negative effect on the long-term goals and objectives of the ministry.

In addition, the time frame for the project was short. The Deputy Minister considered this a high priority and he wanted the knowledge of key people captured prior to their retirement that year. So time was a major factor in deciding how we would proceed.

In considering environmental factors, you need to consider possible future impacts that may jeopardize the value of the asset you are assessing. If you are looking at a system and you anticipate it to have a life cycle of ten years, then you need to consider other factors in your risk assessment, such as time horizon; scenarios to determine what events could impact your application or system; and risk measure to determine if you are comparing the right exposure and benchmarking to set a point of comparison. One other aspect—and perhaps the most difficult to consider—what about a black swan? Is there some event that could cause a catastrophic failure? Just remember that in Three Mile Island and numerous other cases, there was a combination of small errors that caused the disaster and many of them were related to human error.

Also, the value of the asset should be considered. All assets have value. In many cases when we talk about information, there is a time value; that is, the asset may only have value for a certain amount of time. If you consider a corporation releasing the quarterly financial report, there is a value if the information is leaked prior to the reporting. This may be positive if the numbers are good and affect stock prices upward or negative if the numbers are bad and cause downward pressure on stock prices. Knowing this information may allow investors to buy or sell a position. Once the financial report is published, there may be further reactions. The time span of these reactions is typically measured in days as the stock market reacts to the report.

Using the Justice Sector as a different example of asset value, in criminal court cases the information used to prosecute the accused is very valuable, especially in gang-related or organized crime cases.

In particular, the Witness Protection Program has some of the most valuable information that, if disclosed to the wrong persons, could result in death or a witness being threatened. In other words, the witness will not testify.

The reason for including different examples is that not all information has a financial value. For most considerations, there is a dollar value attached to an asset. However, in a much larger context of countries, states, provinces, and territories, there are other considerations such as national security, public safety, and life and limb.

Step 2: Identify Risks and Impacts

Once the scope, time frames, and an overall environmental scan have been completed and a value put on the asset, the second step is to identify risks and impacts. This can be done in two ways: assign a person to come up with a list of risks and associated impacts, or get the committee to brainstorm or develop the risks and impacts as a group. I prefer using the committee as it gives different perspectives and allows for greater latitude of thought. Either way, the risks and impacts must be identified. The scale in Appendix C provides some guidance to provide some ideas as to categories of risks and magnitude of impacts. In the brainstorming session, you need to allow all ideas to come to the table and be considered. At this step, the idea is to identify the risks and to determine a relative magnitude of the impact if the risk was realized. Table 6.5 provides a partial list of risks and was developed looking at potential risks to implementing knowledge and content management at a government ministry. The ministry had an annual budget of $40 million. I estimated that a very large loss could represent about 10% of the annual budget. In this case, the loss

Table 6.5 Risk and Impact Ratings

RISK	IMPACT	CONSEQUENCE	ESTIMATED RISK COST
Misrepresentation at negotiations	Loss of reputation	Catastrophic	$4 million+
Unauthorized disclosure of sensitive information (privacy breach)	Loss of reputation	Major	$400,000
Unauthorized disclosure of sensitive information	Public safety	Major	$400,000
Loss of knowledge	Productivity loss	Moderate	$40,000

of reputation could cost the ministry $4 million or upward annually. Table 6.5 is meant to give you some idea as to how you could use the scale in Appendix C and identify the risks and impacts.

As Douglas Hubbard (2007, 2009) pointed out in his books (*The Failure of Risk Management* and *How to Measure Anything*), a scale does not provide an accurate measure of the impact of risk. However, risk management is an inexact science and in most cases management considers the magnitude of the consequence rather than exact dollars. The intent of using scales is to give a sense of magnitude of the impact and capture all identifiable risks. It will help later when risks are prioritized and further analysis is done. Then, for some of the risks we can perform more accurate calculations where practical. It makes sense if we are trying to determine how much mitigation effort is required to have better numbers.

At the end of Step 2 you should have a risk map identifying risks that will be used in the next few steps.

Step 3: Consensus of Risks and Impacts

Whether you decided to forego a committee or group session and provide the risks and impacts based on an experienced person, you need to gain consensus of the risks and impacts. This is a crucial step. More often than not, people are not thinking the same way about a particular risk. To get consensus on risks and impacts, you need to get everyone on the same page. This may take several meetings to accomplish, considering the different perspectives you have with the different functional areas represented on the committee. The intent of this step is to get agreement on the risks that will be analyzed and prioritized in detail. There is very little value in looking at a hundred risks or even tens of risks if the impact is not significant enough. These risks have been identified and should be monitored to determine if there are any changes. There is no magic number of risks that you could have for a given system, application, or asset. The objective is to agree on a specific number of risks that will be analyzed in detail.

Again using Table 6.5, Risk and Impact Ratings, we can have a discussion on the risks and associated impacts. Unauthorized disclosure could cause one of two risks: privacy breach if the information disclosed is personal or safety risk if the information disclosed is sensitive in terms of land being claimed. This may cause certain people to become hostile. This is our best guess at the moment and we will need to focus on these when we perform our analysis.

We included the loss of knowledge as a productivity loss and estimated that the impact was moderate, considering the cost of rework and research.

Step 4 Risks and Impacts Analysis

Further analysis of the risks and impacts must be done to really understand the risks, impacts, and consequences. In my way of thinking, a risk is something that has a probability of occurring; uncertainty is something that has a possibility of occurring. In looking at risks, we often include some things that are really uncertain or events that have a possibility of occurring. It does not mean that we dismiss these events. I have determined that it is better to group these uncertainties. So for events like a meteor hitting data center, an earthquake, a tornado, hurricane, or plane crash (the likelihood of a plane hitting your data center is extremely small even though we had 9/11 where three planes crashed into their targets and a fourth crashed in a field short of its target), you could group them into a category called *natural disasters* and use business continuity or disaster recovery planning to encompass your reaction strategies. All of the above could involve loss of life, loss of facilities, and loss of data.

Our analysis should look at the threats, risks, impacts, and consequences. We may go further and identify the effects of a consequence. In our example of the risks of not doing good information management, we identify the effects.

THREAT	RISK	IMPACT	CONSEQUENCE	EFFECT (COST)
Loss of information	Misrepresentation at negotiations	Loss of reputation	Catastrophic	Cost government additional $4 million per year

Make sure you understand the difference between a cause, risk, consequence, and effect. ISO 31000 does not differentiate between consequence and effect but looks at it from an outcome of an event affecting objectives. In a simple example below, we can look at the differences and produce better results.

CAUSE	RISK	CONSEQUENCE	EFFECT
Inconsistency in information	Failure in negotiations	Different agreements reached	Cost more money

Figure 6.5   Cause, risk, consequence, and effect.

If we take the risk example and look at loss of reputation, which is the first risk identified in Table 6.5, we can see that we thought it would be catastrophic for negotiations. In the project to set up a knowledge and content management capability for the ministry, we determined that if wrong information is being given to the wrong person at the wrong time, we could compromise negotiations. This could damage our reputation. If the information was not consistent, then it could lead to different agreements on the same thing. And the effect would be that the negotiations and settlements would cost more. The question that arises is how much damage could that have on negotiations? Consider that these negotiations are based on a Supreme Court decision that certain rights must be upheld; we needed to consider what a loss in reputation would mean for these negotiations. Looking at the time frame, we saw that negotiations took a long time. There were a few scenarios that we had to work out:

- How would a loss in reputation affect the time frame for future negotiations?
- How would a loss in reputation affect the value associated with each negotiation?

We had to consider that there were many negotiations to come; we had only successfully completed three. We concluded that a loss in reputation would cost the ministry in terms of time and value. Now the question was: How much?

To present our business case to the Deputy Minister, we had to put this risk in financial terms. There are five negotiation teams, each with eight to ten persons. If we extended the time frame for each negotiation by one year due to a loss in reputation, we could quantify the impact of the loss in terms of salary dollars. That would answer the impact of the first questions regarding extending the time frame due to a loss in reputation.

Five teams times ten persons times annual salary (average full-time employee cost averages $100,000 considering all aspects of salary, support, administration, computer, workspace, benefits) equals $5 million. And this is for each negotiation if there is a loss in reputation, which means a loss in trust.

The second question was more difficult to quantify. How many more dollars for each negotiation would it cost the ministry if there was a loss in reputation? Considering that there was a lot at stake in these negotiations (the total cost of the outcome for these negotiations could exceed $1 billion), we knew that there was an associated impact with a loss in reputation that would be in the millions of dollars. If we considered that with a loss in reputation each negotiation could cost $1 million, then if there were one hundred negotiations, we could have an impact of $100 million.

Our original assumption of this being a catastrophic risk was valid. The impact was much higher than we estimated. We had determined that the impact would exceed $4 million in annual costs and if the negotiation time frame was extended by one year, it would cost approximately $5 million in salaries alone. In addition, there was an estimated impact of $100 million. This was indeed catastrophic.

We knew that the impact of a loss in reputation would harm negotiations and now we could put this in a perspective of impact. Even if we were wrong by 10%, it was still a significant impact to the ministry.

The presentation of the information is important. I have shown several examples of different ways to show the impact, consequences, and effects of risks. The bottom line is that you should be able to project with reasonable certainty the effect or consequence; in other words, you should be able to calculate the consequences with a confidence level and interval that would allow the CFO to fully appreciate your concerns about the risk.

Step 5: Prioritize Risks and Impacts

Remember that cross-function committee from Step 1? Now is the time to engage that committee. You have determined the risks and evaluated the impacts. Now you must prioritize the risks and impacts. In the example we are using, it is fairly simple. The risk of a loss in reputation has the greatest impact. That would be your number-one priority. In some cases, as in our example, you have to make a decision on the number-two risk. In our example we are looking at two major risks, each having been estimated to have a $400,000 impact on our annual budget. This is where additional criteria must be considered. What is the likelihood of either risk occurring? Is there more risk of a privacy breach or an information breach involving public safety? To sort these two risks into priority number two and three, the key piece of information needed is the press's reaction. Will the press make a bigger issue of a privacy breach or an issue that puts the public at risk? This is where it is important to include someone from public affairs. Because public affairs deals with the press all the time, they will be able to determine which risk will have the larger impact. These are your subject matter experts when it comes to the press. If public affairs or marketing is not included in your committee, it would be prudent to get their advice on this matter. Negative press will damage reputation.

In many methodologies for risk assessment, likelihood is used to prioritize risks. We must be careful about using likelihood. As described for the confidence ranking process, most of these calculations are estimates at best and guesses at worst. If we take that into consideration, we end up with a wide margin of error. Using the Annualized Loss Expectancy (ALE) calculation, we can see why this might be a problem. Two numbers multiplied together determine the ALE:

$$ALE = SLE \times ARO$$

where SLE is the Single Loss Expectancy and ARO is the Annualized Rate of Occurrence.

You should have an accurate number for the SLE, which is derived from the Asset Value (AV; cost of asset or replacement*) times the Exposure Factor (EF; portion of asset value likely to be destroyed by a particular risk). ($SLE = AV \times EF$.)

Assuming that you are guessing at the SLE (not sure of asset value and exposure factor) and guessing at the ARO (how many times did

---

* Asset Value should also consider reputation loss, productivity loss, customer confidence, etc.

that occur or could occur), then you have introduced significant error into your calculations. As an example, let us assume you are guessing at the AV (unsure of the replacement cost or the loss of reputation, productivity, and inconvenience factor) so you place the AV at $10,000. You also do not know the EF (assuming this is a system and the event is a cyber attack that compromises the system, then the system is still left intact so there is no cost in replacing the hardware). You are now guessing that it will take two days to rebuild the system and you will need five people. So the exposure factor is 2 days × 5 persons = 10 person-days. Other aspects involve the function of the system. Is it used to process customer orders? Was there a big event about to happen and the system was critical? What information was on the system?

We have introduced significant errors into our equation, so the calculations can be ±40% compounded. The value you have calculated for SLE may have an error level of 80% based on two guesses. Then you are making a third guess about the ARO. Your compounded error level is now 120% based on three guesses. Unless you have facts or known calculations, you will end up with some erroneous results that can mislead you into making poor decisions.

We saw a catastrophic event occur in 2010 when a deep-sea oil platform exploded, caught fire, and sank, releasing millions of gallons of crude oil into the Gulf of Mexico. I would guess that BP did a risk assessment on the possibility of a catastrophic event occurring, such as an oil platform sinking. I am not sure of the actual risk assessment or the outcome but I would guess that the ARO was deemed very small; in other words, the event has a very low probability of occurring. As it turned out, they were wrong. The event will cost BP billions of dollars. During the first few weeks, BP lost 50% of its market value on the stock market, or about $85 billion. This type of event is known as a black swan, which is an event that is very improbable but has a catastrophic effect when it does occur.

Unless you are sure of your numbers, you must be careful about including likelihood in your calculations. I am more inclined to determine the impact and consequence. For example, we can state with certainty that there will be a cyber attack on your Internet-facing systems. What we cannot determine is if the attack will be successful and when. We can also predict with reasonable certainty that if you have known vulnerabilities on your systems, there is a high probability that these vulnerabilities will be exploited the longer they remain vulnerabilities exposed to the Internet.

I had a conversation with Roger Graves from Davion Systems, who make Risk Information and Assessment System (RIAS), a software risk assessment tool. He had an approach to using likelihood that made sense. Likelihood was derived from two parameters: probability and intervention difficulty. That way, you could assess the difficulty of intervention combined with the probability of an event happening. I know that each person has his or her own preferences, and putting the organization at risk because your estimation of probability or likelihood indicated the risk was very small and the consequences not large could create a black swan for your organization.

It is better to group your risks as much as possible to aggregate the potential impact and consequence. For example, a virus could infect a system. The virus could have a package that adds a Trojan and calls home. The Trojan could allow an attacker access to the system. The compromised system could be used to attack your servers. ... Your users could download a virus from the Internet or have a virus sent to them via email or instant messaging. Or it could be included in a document on a memory stick. These all can be grouped into one risk: system compromise. It is not the threat but the risk and the impact and consequence that must concern you. The consequence must always be expressed in business terms and it is best to use monetary terms.

At the end of Step 5 you should have a risk map identifying and prioritizing risks.

Step 6: Review Existing Controls

An asset or process typically has some controls already in place. In the event that it is a new application, there are already existing controls that may be used. As an example, consider putting in a new application for marketing to track and forecast sales. There should be an existing infrastructure in place as well as proper practices and procedures.

This should include

- Firewalls
- Security zones

- Intrusion prevention or protection
- Anti-virus
- Secure coding practices
- Patching and upgrading of OS and software
- Incident response
- Business continuity and disaster recovery

You should not have to re-create the entire infrastructure and the procedures. One of my biggest criticisms about TRAs is the inability to consider the existing infrastructure and processes. It seemed that every consultant started by stating the obvious, such as you need anti-virus, firewalls, security zones, etc. Or you need security education and awareness training. And the existing controls may be good enough or there may be gaps. That is what we are expecting from the consultants. Tell us the gaps and give us some remediation plans. That is why the next step is important.

Step 7: Risks and Impacts Mitigation Analysis

There will always be gaps between the ideal controls and the existing controls. In this step we do not focus on cost but try to develop scenarios of different mitigation strategies that will reduce risks and impacts. Now is a good time to look at existing controls to determine if they are still effective. In your risk assessment you are looking to answer the question: Can we mitigate the risk and impact? Much of the existing thinking is about threat management. Controls do not reduce threats. Controls reduce vulnerabilities to threats. There will always be threats. Now that you have identified risks and associated impacts, you need to consider what existing controls are in place and the effectiveness of these controls.

In the example case that considered loss of reputation as the biggest risk with the largest impact, we need to consider some mitigation strategies. We started by looking at the existing procedures. There were inconsistencies in the procedures that could cause damage to reputation. We also determined that consistency in information was a key consideration in causing damage to reputation. If the information being used is stale, out of date, or wrong, there could be some damage in using it. Considering that we were building a business case for implementing knowledge and content management, this was one of the key risks that we identified. We knew that if the risk was not mitigated by implementing better controls and developing a single source of truth (a repository for knowledge and content that contained corporate history, decisions, facts, and relevant information), this risk would become an event at some point in the future.

Step 8: Costing, Prioritization, and Decisions

Costing is a delicate art of determining the price we are willing to pay versus the impact of the risk. As previously discussed, there will always be gaps between what is ideal and what is acceptable. Many of us want a Ferrari; few of us can afford one. The question is how much can we afford? There may be several mitigation strategies that were developed in the previous step. For PCI compliance, you may want to install data loss prevention software. If your organization is only processing hundreds of payments per day and you have outsourced the processing to a bank, then this may be a bad idea. The cost of each mitigation strategy should be calculated in this step. In our sample case we did some preliminary costing of implementing a robust knowledge and content management solution. We included a lot of automation using tools like Text Analytics™ from SAS and Google's Search Application to help with finding, putting metadata on information, and organizing the information. We looked at using Oracle Universal Content Management™ or Alfresco's Content Management™ solution as our repository. We considered SharePoint™ but the cost per gigabyte of storage was very high compared to other server solutions. This will have to go to a Request for Proposal (RFP) but we needed a budget number to present in the business case. Preliminary estimates put the cost of development, integration, and implementation at $800,000. We also calculated ongoing maintenance costs and operational support of several hundred thousand dollars. This included training, new support positions, and ongoing software support.

In many cases you have developed multiple scenarios for mitigation and once you have costed these, you can prioritize based on cost and residual risk. There will always be residual risk. Just like you ranked risks and impacts, you will also rank the various solutions from the Cadillac to the bicycle. Each one has pros and cons.

Make sure you determine appropriate metrics for each solution. This means looking at what you proposed, your estimate of the risk mitigation, and what impact on a business outcome you expect will occur.

Then you will ask for a decision based on the risk mitigation, the requirements, and what the impact is on the business outcomes. Either the risks are accepted, mitigated, or transferred.

Step 9: Implementation

Implement the mitigation solutions as selected in Step 8. Assuming you have more than one mitigation solution, you should consider setting up individual projects for each solution. Avoid any suggestion that these can all be done together as a mega-project. The objective is to demonstrate progress in mitigating risks. Each project should be less than six months for implementation. Prior to implementation you should benchmark the existing situation to establish a baseline. This baseline will provide a starting point for the effectiveness of your controls.

Step 10: Review

Establish a review of the risks and impacts as well as the mitigation solutions. Were the mitigation solutions effective in reducing the risks? Were the necessary controls in place? Did you miss something?

In Step 9 you established the metrics and hopefully a baseline of the situation prior to implementing the controls. The review should benchmark the baseline as the starting point and look at the new or upgraded controls to determine if the controls are effective. The review should be done shortly (within three months of implementing the solution(s)). You want to measure if the solution is effective.

A review should be carried out periodically to determine if the controls are effective in managing the risks. In the world of information management and cyberspace, things change in an instant. Your current controls for managing vulnerabilities may be outdated by new threats and vulnerabilities that arise tomorrow. Continuous monitoring of the controls and logs must be done. A review is only a short and small window of time into the constantly changing environment of cyberspace. It still helps to have a formal review process set up. The problem with most organizations is that there are no formal review processes, and it is only when an event occurs or the auditors come knocking that a review is done. A periodic review will go a long way toward establishing good practices for regulatory or PCI compliance.

7
METRICS

Metrics are difficult to present in a meaningful manner. What are you measuring? What does this metric mean? To the executive? To the staff? How do you make people responsible for a metric? Does the metric include compliance or regulatory reporting? The bottom line is that metrics are meaningless unless they are tied to business outcomes. If the metric does not reflect a success or failure of the business in achieving a desired outcome, then there may be no point in reporting that metric. In *The Visible Ops Handbook*, from the Information Technology Processing Institute (ITPI) Behr, Kim, and Spafford (2004–2005) used Mean Time to Repair (MTTR) and Mean Time Between Failures (MTBF) as a metric that measures the uptime of systems. Measuring the uptime of systems is part of the metric. The real metric that should be measured is the impact on service delivery that should be measured. This means the recovery of the service back to full production, not just the recovery of the server or application back into production. An outage of the infrastructure could be a router, server, or a workstation. It could be a virus or a denial-of-service attack. The point is that until the business is back in full production, the impact is still being felt even if the infrastructure is back to full operations.

So what metrics can you use? Metrics must be measured vertically (outcomes) and horizontally (outputs). Linkage between an output (MTTR) and an outcome (5% improvement in profit margin) is the challenge. Keep in mind that executives are measured on outcomes, and their success in achieving that outcome is directly linked to your success. Your success is to make sure your outputs affect their outcomes in a positive way.

Metrics are useful if they provide the right information at the right time to the right person to make the right decisions. That is, metrics should have the following characteristics:

- *Metrics must have value:* Measuring IT performance does not necessarily mean something to an executive. A metric should provide information to make decisions. In the example of MTTR, the value of measuring MTTR is to be able to determine if there is a problem with the frequency and time to fix systems. The shorter the MTTR, the better. Putting the MTTR metric into business impact will have some relevance to the executive in terms of lost productivity, lost sales, and lost customers.

- *Metrics must be relevant:* As you move up the food chain, the metric loses relevance to individuals. The measured outcome of a division has little meaning to an accounting clerk who is processing payments. The metrics must be measured to be relevant to individuals. Linkages between metrics are important. Using MTTR, the individuals responsible for infrastructure, application, and network can relate to making sure the uptime is as high as possible. Using business impact in terms of lost productivity, lost sales will link MTTR to the business executive in terms that they can understand. Metrics must be repeatable. You must measure the same thing repeatedly. If you measure outputs and outcomes, you must measure them repeatedly to gain a sense of performance. Measuring the performance of IT systems like MTTR must be consistently measured using the same metrics (hours of lost productivity, hours of lost sales).

- *Metrics must be measured over time:* To determine changes—positive or negative—metrics must be measured periodically and over time. Taking one measurement is a way to establish a baseline. Measuring the same thing over a period of time gives performance metrics and shows patterns.

User Experienced Metrics

On my first day back to work after an extended absence, I started up my laptop. It appeared to be loading some patches, so I waited. It cycled through a couple of times before I realized it was in an infinite loop. So I called the help desk. "Oh" they said, "you have a known problem and the system has to be re-imaged." The technician came

Table 7.1   User Experience

USER EXPERIENCE	HOURS WASTED
Day 1: No computer no productivity	8
Day 2: No computer, no productivity	8
Day 10: System crashed, rebooted	1
Day 11: System crashed, rebooted	1
Day 12: System crashed, rebooted	1
Day 13: System had blue screen, had to restart multiple times	1

over and started the re-imaging process (an all-day process). On day 2, I came in early to get caught up. The re-image had failed; I called the help desk and the technician came back and restarted the re-imaging of the laptop.

My user experience was not good (Table 7.1). It cost the government 20 hours of lost productivity. It cost the government two call-outs to the vendor to fix the problem. My satisfaction was very low, off the scales. Our help desk response: "No, I cannot get you another computer."

I have often heard that the servers were up 99.7% or the network was up 99.6%. What I have not heard is what the user experiences. While each IT component is reporting 99% uptime, the user is typically experiencing far less uptime. As a matter of fact, the user may only be experiencing 90% uptime. This is due to the aggregation of outage times. Although each component reports a 1% outage, the actual outage to the user is far greater. It is similar to compounding interest, where each additional outage time is compounded. This cumulative effect is a result of the user having to do the following almost every time there is an outage:

- Re-authenticate to the system, server, application, and/or database
- Remember what they were doing prior to the outage
- Re-enter or rework the last known entry
- Get back into full production

Uptime metrics are important to measure as they indicate what time each component is available but do not reflect true downtime that the user experienced during each outage (Figure 7.1). For a component outage that lasts ten minutes, you should double the time for the user.

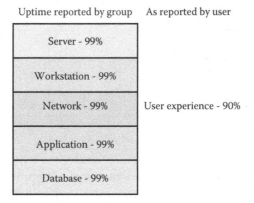

Figure 7.1   Reporting uptime and user experience.

One of the directors at Corrections pointed out that for an outage, his staff might have significant difficulties in returning to full production because they may be in the middle of a crisis dealing with some difficult situation that completely takes their attention from completing a report into the application. Having to log back in and rework a report after dealing with a crisis may mean lost information. This could jeopardize the safety of other staff, especially if the report dealt with a critical incident. The point is that users may be more than inconvenienced by an outage than what is reported. One can look at the IT Infrastructure Library (ITIL®) and how it describes availability:

> Availability is a measure of an IT service and not just individual components. Each IT component needs to be examined individually to assess its impact on overall availability of the IT service.

We can calculate the cost as

User productivity loss + IT productivity loss + Other business losses

Losses are based on the hourly cost of each user, IT staff multiplied by the time of the outage. Outages focus your staff on reacting to a problem … aka unplanned work. It reduces your effectiveness as an organization.

In the case of customers to your Web site, outages may mean that they will not return or will use other methods of communicating with your organization. As we are all well aware, the Internet offers a less expensive model for service delivery. Companies such as Amazon have built their business models on delivering services cheaper and faster, using the Internet. So an outage of your Web site may mean that you lose customers. In the case of essential services like government, the customer may use more traditional methods of communicating with you, thereby increasing your overall cost of service delivery. Our focus must be on outcomes, and the reporting of metrics is not useful unless linked to business objectives.

8
BEST PRACTICES

Staff, vendors, and consultants often approach us with how an organization should perform according to best practices. I agree with the principle behind best practices; however, I do not agree that we need to have best practices for everything we do. There is a cost to performing to best practices and we have to measure our ROI and risks against the cost. It is really a risk management decision.

When the government CIO for the BC government was evaluating a cryptographic standard for the government, the technical folks considered using the best and most secure standard available. They selected 256-bit AES as the encryption standard. I, and several colleagues, argued against using 256 bit, stating emphatically that it was overkill and would require a large investment to change some of the existing equipment as well as some of our partners. We argued that 128 bit was more realistic and would not be compromised using existing technology for at least ten years. I verified that fact with the Chief Technical Officer (CTO) from Entrust, a leading vendor of security solutions.

Ignoring the protests and flaws in their thinking, the technologists at the CIO thought 256 bit was a best practice and would maximize protection. Things quickly came to a head when the BC government rolled out Windows Vista® with BitLocker™ using 256-bit encryption. As you may know, 256-bit encryption is computationally about four times slower than 128 bit. One of the criteria we were benchmarking Vista systems against the existing XP systems was performance, especially around start-up times. Using BitLocker to secure the disks meant the operating system had to decrypt the disks in order to launch successfully. To speed up performance, the operational engineers determined that changing the standard for encryption from 256 bit to 128 bit would significantly enhance performance during start-up. The government CIO agreed and lowered the cryptographic standard to 128 bit. This is the compromise between performance and security, and the lesson learned is that we must make sure we consider all the issues prior to establishing a standard.

When asked to consider best practices, we need to consider the number of person-hours required to develop, implement, and maintain a specific best practice. For the average person working 52 weeks a year (actually, many organizations provide vacation of two to four weeks on average) and working five days a week at eight hours per day means that, on average, a person-year is about 2,000 hours, excluding overtime. For each control we implement, there are hours required to manage that control. Take, for instance, firewalls. There are the basic operational requirements to configure and maintain the firewalls; there is the analysis for each access request (change in firewall rules to allow or deny access); finally, the change must be made for each firewall request. For the Justice Sector within the Province of British Columbia, we estimated that just managing the firewall requests took about 1,000 person-hours per year as each request had to be analyzed and implemented manually. This does not take into consideration the person-hours required to maintain the firewalls operationally. We instituted a change management process wherein most requests would be dealt with weekly in the Wednesday change window and limited exceptions to operational critical or business essential. We found that there were many more exceptions than anticipated as changes to routers or office moves caused denial-of-service for users accessing applications. We were dealing with over 6,000 staff members, over 400 locations, about 50 different business units, and over 100 applications, not counting our partners who also required access to critical applications.

It is important to consider best practices in reviewing your operations. Perhaps you can look at it differently. Best practices could be considered the most cost-effective way you can perform a task. This may not compare to a benchmark of best practices for the task. If you have unlimited funding and resources, then you can implement best practices. The reality is that we do not have unlimited funding. Take a practical approach and it will serve you better.

9

PRINCIPLES AND CONCEPTS

Section Summary

The focus in this chapter is on the concepts and principles that apply to risk management. In every organization there are multiple other factors to consider, such as HR, regulations, legislation, politics, and government. Each of these has risks and associated principles. The intent of this section is to help you look at specific risk management principles and both information management and information security risks. In my research I did not uncover any basic risk management principles. I have presented a few risk management principles similar to what the Organisation for Economic Co-operation and Development (OECD) has done for information security. I also present some principles for information management. However, I do not summarize or try to amalgamate these principles into an overriding set of principles. Each organization is unique in its culture, risk culture, risk profiles of the individuals, and its products, services, and outcome requirements.

People are your biggest strength and risk. If you consider that 80% of your people are honest, depending on the situation—and paradoxically 80% of your people could be dishonest, depending on the situation—then your biggest risk is people. As a friend of mine says, "Silicon does not fail much; carbon units fail many times." He is referring to the fact that the technology usually has high availability and that most mistakes or events are caused by human error. This is where policies, practices, and processes are the most important part of risk management. You must have good monitoring and audit of these practices and processes.

As humans, we often rely on our gut instinct. We trust people. We put too much faith in people. When we are presented with information, we often do not question if that information is true. To be more effective, we need to make sure we know if the information is true and that it does not reflect personal biases. Asking questions such as "Is this information a fact, a calculation, an estimation, or a guess?" will help us filter the information more carefully. Adding a confidence level and interval will make us less reliant on gut instinct and more reliant on computational trust. Computational trust is taking a calculated risk based on facts, calculations, estimates, and guesses and understanding what it may really mean. We view information differently; and if we cannot define what we mean by a risk, then we cannot get everyone on the same page or even in the same library.

In the end you should have a set of principles that guides your organization and, most importantly, your people. In any organization you must have policies, practices, and guidelines. Policies should be based on principles. Practices should be based on industry standards. Guidelines should be there if you cannot agree on a standard practice or policy to give direction to people.

Measuring risk is important. Making sure you measure it right is paramount. We can have all the metrics in the world but if the system is not functioning to provide the right information, then we have a problem. If you decide to measure risks, make sure your focus is on consequences to the business. Your risk assessments should provide you with key indicators of risks, impacts, and consequences. Furthermore, you should be able to aggregate your risk assessments to look across the organization to determine organizational (horizontal) risks and business-specific (vertical) risks. Grouping risks will allow you to add appropriate controls that are practical and cost effective. A simple example is anti-virus software. Buying multiple vendor products will definitely cost more than a single licensing agreement with a single vendor.

PART II
SERVICE
DELIVERY

The number-one job of the CIO is to make sure the right information is available to the right person at the right time. The number-two job of the CIO is to make sure the wrong information is not available to the wrong person at the wrong time. The focus of this section is *service delivery*. Service delivery is about ensuring that the right information is available to the right person at the right time to allow them to complete the task at hand. The task can be customer focused, done by a customer (self-service), or operational. A banking transaction is a good example of a transaction that can be performed by an employee or a customer. Organizations have turned to the Internet to provide customer services. When the service is outward or customer facing, there are more risks. The two biggest risks are (1) failure of the infrastructure, meaning network, systems, applications, and databases; and (2) compromise of information. In this section we deal with failure of the infrastructure and in Section III we discuss compromise.

When talking about getting the right information at the right time to the right person, we have to consider outcomes. What is the outcome that we want to accomplish? Organizations have specific outcomes that they want to achieve. These may be selling widgets, televisions, seats in airplanes, homes, vacations, aircraft, consulting services, beds in hospitals, or whatever outcome that the company has set out as its mandate. A government's outcomes are about services to its citizens. Each organization has a desired outcome, and we can generalize that outcomes are either profit or not-for-profit driven, or some combination. An outcome can be described as a business objective. To help us achieve that outcome, we have to manage the business objective. That is, we must have projects and processes that work to achieve an outcome. We can define these in broad terms:

- *Product management*—all the processes and projects related to a business objective to achieve a desired outcome.
- *Process management*—the measurement of processes to organize processes into the most effective delivery of services so processes are performing as expected.
- *Project management*—the processes related to organizing a specific set of tasks to achieve a measurable goal within a time period. Usually these are cost, schedule, quality, and function delivered.

There is a hierarchy that must be recognized. The number-one priority of an organization is product management or desired outcomes. Processes and projects must support product management. Processes should be designed to support product management. Projects should be changes to the business to help processes become more effective and products improve.

Our focus should be to support product management. Our processes and projects should support product management. We need to be in a position to help achieve the outcomes or business objectives. We need to be forward thinking and not just interested in maintaining the status quo. In his book entitled *Blindsided*, Jim Harris (2002) wrote about the phrase "Nothing fails like success." Once you have spent thousands or millions of dollars and countless person-hours on developing systems and structures, you are reluctant to change anything because of all the effort sunk into the status quo. We get caught in our own success. Only by continuously investing in new technologies, processes, and people will we be able to stay ahead and deliver the outcomes needed. Making the processes better for manufacturing horse buggy whips will not save the company when new technologies such as cars are introduced.

What is it going to take to thrive in the next decade? Considering that the world is awash with change and you have the wheel of the information ship, what do you need to do to avoid floundering on the rocks of competition? It takes people and skills. Is your organization structured the right way to be successful? Are you still dealing with a hierarchical structure and too much bureaucracy?

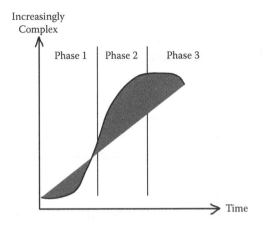

Figure II.1   Complexity of organization over time.

As a leader, you are always looking for advantages to help your organization get and stay ahead of the competition. Most organizations claim that their most important asset is people—yet their policies and procedures do very little to enhance that importance or give their people the ability to create that competitive advantage. Do you have the right skills? What type of organization is yours? George Land developed a "growth model" to help organizations understand and identify what stage of growth they are in. Land described these in three phases. In a simple graph as shown Figure II.1, he put "increasingly complex" on the vertical axis and "time" on the horizontal axis. He explained growth as a process of increasingly complex connections. He used a standard "S" curve or sigmoid to show the growth.

- Phase 1—Entrepreneurial stage:
  - Formative stage
  - Lots of trial and error
  - Informal culture
  - Few rules, procedures, or specialization
  - Close to customer
  - Trust the entrepreneur
  - Goal is to get out of Phase 1
- Phase 2—Production:
  - Focus on improving the efficiency and effectiveness of systems and structures
  - Replica pattern becomes highly organized and systematized

- Rapid growth
- Focus moves from external to internal (satisfy the boss and not the customer)
- Less sensitive to outside world
- Trust the system
- Command and control hierarchy
- Phase 3—Diversification:
    - Move from command and control hierarchy to trust-based developmental organization
    - Need to empower people
    - Need to trust people and allow them to grow
    - Focus moves from pleasing the boss to pleasing the employee
    - Employee closest to customer
    - Leaders must be fast learners

Ideally, an organization would move in a linear manner between phases. However, the reality is that organizations have different growth patterns and the "S" curve would represent typical organizations. Most organizations and institutions are in Phase 2. Most will face the difficult challenge of moving from a hierarchical organization where there is one boss to a flat organization where everyone is a leader. Hierarchical organizations are a 10,000-year-old norm. There are three values associated with hierarchical organizations:

1. The leader (boss) has all the answers.
2. The leader does not trust that people will do what is asked.
3. The leader must have control.

It used to be that information was given on a need-to-know basis. Information was very limited and only available to a few at the top. Information was jealously guarded. Things have changed. Information now flows freely in cyberspace. There is too much information. The world is becoming more complex. Things are changing fast; as a matter of fact, in cyberspace, things change at the speed of light. No one person has all the answers.

Employees are closest to the action. It is the front-line workers who interact with the customers. It is the employees who fix the systems and make sure they are operational. It is the employees who know the most about the databases, applications, and infrastructure. We have to trust the employees. And employees will make mistakes.

Larry Wilson, the founder of Wilson Learning, does a fascinating exercise on leadership with senior management teams. After stepping them through Land's growth model, he talks about it being okay to make mistakes as long as three conditions are met:

1. *The mistakes are made on purpose:* That is, the mistakes are made in an effort to carry out the organizations purpose or meet an outcome.
2. *People learn from mistakes:* Do not keep making the same mistake.
3. *People share their mistakes with others in the organization:* People learn from others' mistakes and do not repeat the mistake.

Charles Darwin said, "It is not the strongest species that survive, nor the most intelligent, but the ones most responsive to change." Can you move from a hierarchical organization to a developmental organization? The important question is: Can you let go of control? When you consider the level of expertise required for installing, configuring, and managing servers, even with considerable automation, you need to relinquish control and empower your staff to make decisions. In his book entitled *Complex Organizations*, Charles Perrow (1986) wrote about the discrepancy between the expertise of a subordinate and that of a superior. A manager or executive knows less about operations and systems than the people who work for her or him yet exercises authority over them. Talcott Parsons, in his analysis of Max Weber's (1978) *Economy and Society*, said that Weber confused two types of authority in his discussion: the authority that is based on technical competence and the authority based on the incumbency of a legally defined office based on a hierarchical organization.

We often make the mistake of assuming that academic qualifications are superior to experience. We are always impressed by those people who have a string of acronyms behind their names, as we equate that with expertise. I evaluated security architects for a supply arrangement for the BC government and found that a lot of the people who were applying had stated they had their Certified Information System Security Professional (CISSP) designation and yet when you looked at years of experience, they had one or two years. They had recently graduated from the university and according to the company, ISC^2 requirements did not meet the five years of experience required to obtain their certification. My experience in evaluating security architects taught me that we cannot place a lot of value on certification or on pieces of paper that show academic achievements. And in the large firms that hire these university graduates, the expectation is that they know more than the seasoned professionals. And these young graduates get hired into managerial positions and our expectation is that they can manage people when they have no experience.

A recent example of this occurred in my organization where they hired a bright young person who had a university degree and promoted him to a director role. He was technically competent but his lack of experience in managing people encumbered him to continue to be the expert and not empower his staff. He was always reviewing their work and was unable to make quick decisions. Needless to say, staff morale hit an all-time low and productivity dropped.

We have to relinquish control and empower our people. The more we empower, the faster we can respond to incidents and change. The flatter the organization, the faster the decisions are made. This is not to say that we do not influence or make key decisions, but we look more to our people to make operational decisions and present new ideas to support the goals and desired outcomes of the organization.

10

PRODUCT MANAGEMENT

Product management is about organizational outcomes. In most organizations there are one or more products or outcomes that are mission critical to the business. These products could be considered a portfolio similar to a financial portfolio of stocks, bonds, and cash. A financial portfolio is a blend of stocks, bonds, and cash depending on the risk appetite of the individual. Aggressive financial portfolios may have more stocks, whereas conservative financial portfolios may have more bonds. Product portfolios need a mix of products to help achieve a good return on investment to shareholders. The Boston Consulting Group developed a matrix model for product life-cycle marketing that can be extended to portfolio management. The matrix model had four quadrants, each representing different types of products that an organization may have. The products are assessed on two criteria: market growth rate (growth rate will require a higher investment in the product to compete) and relative market share (market share indicates the size of the organization's share in the market and assumes growth of earnings will be faster if the share is bigger). The quadrants are

- Stars: high market growth and high market share
- Cash Cows: low market growth and high market share
- Dogs: low market growth and low market share
- Problem Children: high market growth and low market share

Although this mostly applies to for-profit organizations and typically for larger corporations, it still has some applicability to thinking about your product portfolio. Even for not-for-profit or government institutions, there is some mixture of products and some driving forces that dictate the mixture of products or outcomes. For government, it is the citizen who votes for different products, such as health care, environmental concerns, oil prices, military spending, roads, infrastructure, and laws. Not-for-profit organizations have constituents who shape the products that they support. No matter what organization, there will be a portfolio of products to manage and there are certain considerations that must be made.

There must be governance, and this is normally the domain of the executive. The executive must decide on the portfolio mix. It is a risk management decision, and the decisions are critical to the success of the organization in delivering a return on investment to stakeholders. A logical starting point is to create product strategies for each product. This should include market, customers, approach, competition, product (or products, as it could be a line of different products), costs, and analysis. From there the second step is to look at budgets and resources. The third step is to look at each product to determine rewards, investment requirements, risks, and other factors.

Organizations must look at their goals to balance their portfolios. Some decisions must be made between risk versus reward, new product versus improving product, strategy versus tactical, market versus product line, short term versus long term, and risk appetite versus risk culture. These goals should be aligned with desired outcomes. To achieve desired outcomes, there are dependencies. One of the dependencies is having the right information at the right time so a person can complete a task. This means that the CIO must be in a position to ensure that the infrastructure is functioning as expected to achieve the desired outcome(s). There is a lot of buzz about IT alignment with business. There is often a disconnect between IT and business because the requirements are quite different. IT is about technology and the infrastructure needed for IT. Similar to building management where heating and cooling pipes, air conditioning, and physical alarms are important, there is a need to have the right IT infrastructure to support the business. This includes the technologies, applications, and databases, as well as the people, processes, and projects. When we get down to the bottom line, the CIO job is about making sure the right information is available to the right person at the right time to achieve business objectives. This is a very complex job. It involves significant dependencies on an IT infrastructure that may be fully within the purview of the CIO or have further dependencies on partners and other parties that may not have the same business objectives.

In today's environment, the infrastructure is very complex. Using multi-tiered architecture we typically have three or more servers, and with Service-Oriented Architecture (SOA) or cloud comput-ing we can have many more components. We also have the network with hundreds or thousands of routers and switches, not to mention firewalls, intrusion prevention systems, and unified threat manage-ment devices. A typical configuration may have over 4,000 devices and when you are dealing organization to organization, the complex-ity increases as each organization has its own set of servers, routers, switches, firewalls, desktops, laptops, and other hand-held devices. To put this into perspective, a network of 4,000 devices generates about 80,000 unique electronic events per second, or about 6.9 billion events per working day. This is just your network!

As you go beyond your network into the Internet, the complex-ity increases into the billions of devices. According to the Internet World Stats (www.internetworldstats.com), there were over 1.9 bil-lion Internet users as of June 30, 2010. Each user has one or more devices that allow them access to the Internet. Each of these devices is connected to other devices such as routers, switches, firewalls, and servers. If one of these is your customer or client, then the failure of a device represents an inability to get to your information to per-form whatever transaction they need to do with your organization. The Internet is outside your control. The customer devices are outside your control. What is within your control is what you have to manage to deliver the services for your organization. From a risk management perspective, you have to manage the risks according to your level of control. You can reduce these risks by duplication of infrastructure, offloading all or part of the infrastructure to a third party, or just accept the risk. The objective is to minimize outages that affect your service delivery.

When thinking about service delivery, we should not be limiting ourselves to the IT services we provide to our organization. We need to think beyond our services to the business objectives or outcomes that the organization expects to achieve. That puts things in perspec-tive to allow us to understand the impact of infrastructure outages on outcomes.

Figure 10.1 describes the impact of outages on service delivery. When talking about service delivery, we are talking about units pro-cessed over a period of time, whether it is the number of cases we can process in a year or the number of widgets being produced in a factory.

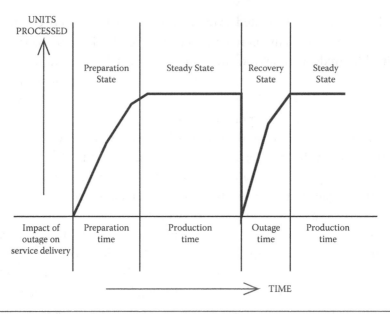

Figure 10.1 Impact of outage on service delivery.

We refer to production time as steady state; that is, the information is available to the person at the right time to perform their functions. On a typical workday, whatever the work being performed, a person needs time to prepare for production. It does not matter what the job is: the shorter the preparation time required, the faster they move into a steady state of production, producing or processing the maximum number of units. In terms of information systems, this means they can enter information into the system as quickly as possible to achieve maximum throughput. In the event that a system is unavailable, the steady state is disrupted. This means that while the system is unavailable, they cannot produce or process units. The recovery state means that the person requires time to get back into a steady state. This duration of time required for a person to return to steady state or full production is typically much longer than the system outage.

From the business perspective, downtime of systems represents a loss of production. This means the information is not available to the right person at the right time to process units. In the for-profit sector, that is a loss of revenue. For not-for-profit organizations and governments, it usually means nonproductive time. There is a cost associated with both sectors. In the Justice Sector, we often equate system or information unavailability with potential loss of life or public safety.

One of the managers responsible for desktop systems put it in this perspective: When a lawyer is presenting her case to the judge and her laptop has had six crashes in the past four days, she is not only focusing on presenting the information in the best way, but a part of her thought process is hoping the system does not crash again in the middle of her presentation. Judges have very little tolerance for equipment failures. It may mean the difference between convicting a criminal and the criminal walking away free.

Referring to Chapter 7, we must make sure we are dealing with outages in relationship to the user's experience and the business loss, including lost opportunities. We have to measure each outage in these terms as well as IT staff time to isolate and repair systems. In some cases, we need to make everyone aware of the consequences of failure; in the example above, allowing a criminal to go free would be putting the public at risk.

Using the example above about the lawyer presenting her case in court, we should step through the process of how to go about getting the information to produce an outcome. In the Justice Sector for the Province of British Columbia, there were a number of goals or outcomes that were articulated in the ministry's plan. Specific to criminal cases, there was the goal of reducing the median time for concluding criminal cases (the median time is measured from the time the information is sworn in to the conclusion time). The goal in 2008–2009 was to achieve a median time to conclude of 80 days. This does not mean that all court cases must be concluded in 80 days. There are some very complex cases and these may take years to gather evidence and present in court. The objective was to process most criminal cases as quickly as possible, and the median of 80 days was chosen to represent most cases, not the extremes. The median actually measured for 2008–2009 was 85 days, meaning the Ministry of Attorney General did not achieve its result.

Lawyers have to determine if there is sufficient evidence for a prosecution to proceed. In a typical Canadian criminal case, police "solve the crime" and prepare the evidence to be presented to the Crown (criminal justice lawyers are referred to as the "Crown" in Canada). If there is sufficient evidence that the Crown thinks will result in a conviction, then the Crown proceeds with the case. Depending on the severity of the case, the Crown swears in the information and, depending on the severity of the crime or other circumstances, the accused is arrested. The accused appears before a judge who determines if the accused remains in custody, posts bond, or is released pending trial.

Lawyers must prepare information to be presented in court. In terms of IT and information management, this is where the CIO must enable better tools to help the lawyers prepare and manage this information. Considering that most Crown lawyers are dealing with several cases at a time, the better the tools, the better and quicker the lawyers can process the information and present their court cases. The information at this point in time is very sensitive and inappropriate disclosure could result in a mistrial.

Once the information has been prepared, it must be shared with the accused. This is known as e-disclosure. In most cases, the accused has hired a lawyer and the lawyer will review the information to prepare the defense. When an accused is in custody, he or she has the right to view this information. This puts additional pressure on IT systems. In one such case, the accused was given a laptop containing a hard drive with all the case information on the hard drive. The accused took apart the laptop and destroyed the hard drive, thinking that if he did this, there would be no evidence against him and therefore no case. As we all know, this was not the case and he was given the information on a DVD.

The judge must also have a copy of the information for court so that he or she can view the evidence. This information still has sensitivity and only certain people will have access to this information. This increases the complexity of managing information. You now have multiple copies of trial information and all must be protected. Once the information is presented in court, it becomes public. That is, anyone can look at the information presented in court.

At the time of writing this book, I was involved in trying to improve the tools and management of information. The objective was to improve the ability of lawyers to manage their information by providing them with better tools. We discuss more about that in the "Information Management" chapter (Chapter 16) of this book. The point of this example is to show that the CIO could help achieve the desired outcome of a median of 80 days from the time of swear-in to the conclusion of a criminal case. Through the use of technology, the CIO could streamline the management of the information and help Crown lawyers by giving them better tools for the e-disclosure process. We had realized that this replication of information was also causing problems for the Crown. In presenting information in court, lawyers must be able to present the information in its best format. This may mean using different viewers to handle some of the media, such as video monitoring tapes. See Chapter 16 for more on information management and how this can be done better.

The linking of IT to outcomes or product management is critical to the success of the organization. A 2008 Deloitte study of Information Security and Enterprise Risk documented that 65% of U.S. companies do not have a documented procedure or a person responsible for assessing cyber risk. And this is indicative of most organizations. IT is still not considered a risk at the enterprise level, and very little discussion occurs at the board or executive level about cyber risk and IT investments. As it happens, within the Ministry of Attorney General, the Executive Financial Officer (EFO, or the Chief Financial Officer as they are known in industry) is not involved in IT investments or information security risks. These were delegated down to a technical level. This reflects the results of the Deloitte study and confirms that boards and senior executives are not adequately involved in the governance of enterprise information security or IT investments.

This is further complicated in our funding models. Typically, funding is managed by vertical business units and not across the enterprise. As an example, within the BC government, we had a mainframe that had an outstanding vulnerability: the data in transit was not adequately protected. This was an ongoing concern identified by the auditors and for five years we sent a letter stating that we understood the concern and were still working on resolving it. I tried to put together a business case to address this concern by working with the various parties who had applications and sensitive information on the mainframe. Each party was very interested in solving this problem. Not one ministry would step forward to fund this initiative. And I could not get the ministries to do proportional funding. The model that was being used was simple. The first group that wanted the initiative completed paid. The shared services organization running the mainframe would not fund it. So it continued as an outstanding issue. The point of this discussion is that the funding model often does not take into consideration that the risks associated with IT are not considered at an enterprise level. Funding is usually a business line problem for IT although the risks of a poorly implemented solution may have a ripple effect. Loss of data or a privacy breach may impact the entire organization and put the organization at risk even though the application may be associated with a single business line.

Products You Deliver as a CIO

Most CIOs view their operations as service delivery. The question I have for CIOs is this: What is the product you deliver? There is the infrastructure. Without the infrastructure you could not deliver services. There are the applications and databases. Without applications and databases you could not deliver services. But what is the product that you are delivering to the business? What makes IT so valuable to the business? The answer is: *Information*. You deliver information to the business. That is what makes business run. Information is the lifeblood of an organization. Without it, everything grinds to a halt. Figure 10.2 represents how most CIOs utilize their budgets in IT.

Let's look at how these are allocated (Figure 10.2) and try to understand that if your most important asset is information and your most important function is to deliver that information to the business, then where should you be putting your focus? In other words, where should you allocate your budget and resources? Simply put,

- Infrastructure represents the transport and storage of data;
- Applications represent access and manipulation of data; and
- Data represents information and knowledge of the organization.

You need an infrastructure to view, transport, and store data. You need custom and commercial-off-the-shelf (COTS) applications to access and manipulate the data. The data need to be searchable, organized and findable, and protected and available.

When I look at how much money we were spending on IT in the Justice Sector and what portions were allocated to infrastructure, applications, and data, I found that we spent the majority of our dollars on infrastructure. Part of this was due to the lack of virtualization. Part of the infrastructure costs was tied up in individual servers— one server for one application. There was a lot of underutilization of

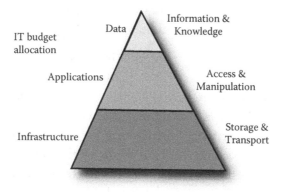

Figure 10.2 IM/IT budget.

servers. There also was a lot of duplication of data on servers. There are two aspects of data: structured and unstructured. Structured data is the data in databases. Unstructured data is the documents, emails, and other electronic information. Each of these contributes to increasing costs in infrastructure.

- *Structured data:* We store all our transaction in databases. We archive this data. What we do not do is life-cycle manage this data. The databases become huge and we need more storage space. The applications accessing this data slow down, so we need more performance and add more servers and larger servers. All these increase our infrastructure costs.
- *Unstructured data:* The BC government used shared file and print servers to contain its directories of unstructured data. In fact, these shared file and print servers duplicate filing cabinets. That is, we still maintained a paper paradigm despite being in a digital world. We stored our unstructured information just like we would have stored our paper memos and documents. When we consider duplication of electronic information, we must understand that documents were often sent to individuals using email. These individuals keep the email containing the document, open the document, and save the document on their personal drive. They may send a copy to other individuals. We often had twenty to fifty copies of electronic documents within our organization, including copies stored on personal drives, in email folders, and on other

drives. And if the document was shared among other organizations, we might have had hundreds of copies.

Typically, unstructured information is poorly managed. Unstructured information is kept on personal drives, in business silos, and is unsearchable. There have been many studies that looked at how much time people waste looking for information. In a typical office, people spend 25% of their time looking for information. The findability factor has become a critical factor in the ability to find and reuse information. It is not the ability to search that we need to consider but rather the ability to find. We talk a lot more about improving unstructured information find-ability in Chapter 16.

Information Delivery: How Information Flows in Your Organization

In every organization, information flows through the organization. It starts as data that enters the organization in some form. The data is turned into information as it is captured and entered into applications and stored in the infrastructure. When the information is manipulated and used, it turns into knowledge. At some point in time, the knowledge is no longer useful and converts back to information at the end of the information life cycle (Figure 10.3).

Finally, the information may be discarded or turned into data for research purposes. Personal information that is turned into data for research is often anonymized. For example, Corrections has a sophisticated case management system called CORNET. CORNET is used to track inmates from the time they enter the Corrections facilities until they leave the Corrections facilities, and even after

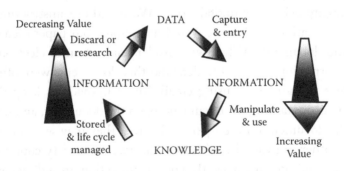

Figure 10.3 Information value circle.

that CORNET information is used by parole officers and others while the inmate is on parole. Once an inmate has left the system, the information is no longer needed and, assuming the inmate does not repeat and commit another crime, the information is end-of-life and can be discarded or used for research. CORNET tracks the events that happen within the Corrections facilities and presents a history of events for each individual inmate. It captures data and turns the data into information and knowledge about the inmates. That knowledge about inmates is extremely important as it helps guards and officials manage violent behaviors through the continuous efforts of entering these behaviors into the CORNET system, allowing the transfer of the knowledge of an event to other guards and officials.

Using another example of Customer Relationship Management (CRM), we can see the same cycle repeated. A new customer has data entered into the CRM system. As the data is entered, it becomes information about the customer. Salespeople and relationship managers use the information and, through analysis, determine customer needs, complaints, issues, and opportunities. This becomes knowledge about the customer. The more knowledge about a customer that is stored, the better the service. The better the service, the more sales. The more sales, the more value the customer is to the company. At some point in time, there may be a disconnect when the customer is no longer purchasing or maintaining products that the company sells. At this point, the knowledge is no longer needed and can be removed from active files. The information then could be discarded or turned into research data for additional analysis.

From a CIO perspective, the cycle of Data–Information–Knowledge–Information–Data must be managed. The information must be available to the business to use in maximizing the delivery of products. This means the CIO must ensure that information is delivered when needed and that it is protected and managed. The priority is information delivery; however, there may be times when information protection or information management takes priority. For example, if someone is trying to steal intellectual property, the priority is protecting that information to prevent someone from stealing it. If someone is trying to find information, then information management is the priority.

Organizing IT for Information Delivery, Management, and Protection

In my experience working for CIOs, I have often found that the organization of IT functions is critical in maximizing the value. If you split the functions along application development and operations, you often find that the development side is throwing new applications over the fence at operations. Operations is then left with the problem of picking up the pieces to maintain the application along with all the wrinkles. And you find that security is left as an afterthought, and retrofitting applications to make them secure is expensive.

In Table 10.1, I have restructured IT services into three areas that may help redefine organizations. If information is the most important product that a CIO delivers to the business, then reorganizing IT services will help facilitate delivering, managing, and protecting information. There is a trend toward considering the infrastructure as a cloud: that is, the infrastructure has very much become a utility. Much like electricity, the telephone, and even sewer, water, and streets, the maintenance and management of the infrastructure are contracted to a third party. There may be parts of the infrastructure that we consider integral in our organization and these may be kept separate. However, the vast majority of the infrastructure can be outsourced to specialists.

If you decide that information is the product you deliver, then you can reconsider how you allocate your budget and realign your resources. IT has been considered a technical operation and in most organizations as part of the plumbing, just like facilities. In some organizations, IT is moving into a more strategic role as executives recognize the value of the information. As discussed, information is the lifeblood of an organization, and as a CIO you must decide how to allocate your budget to best serve the organization and deliver information. In Table 10.1 there are three IT services that you should consider

Table 10.1   Organizing IT Service

IT SERVICE	ATTRIBUTES
Information delivery	Accessibility, availability, performance, infrastructure
Information management	Organization of information, source of truth, capture, life cycle, controlled vocabularies, applications
Information protection	Access controls, confidentiality, integrity security, audit

as foundations for delivering information to the business: information delivery, management, and protection. Each service requires different skills and expertise to manage. They should be tightly coupled and not siloed. It takes a team to deliver optimal services; the more highly integrated the team, the more effective the team. It is similar to professional sports, where the high-performing teams are always the teams that are highly integrated, everyone knows their part on the team, and everyone gives 100%.

We recognize that budgets are limited and that funds must be allocated to the most urgent business requirements. If you relegate security to a back-row function in your organization, then you should not be surprised when you have a serious breach that requires significant effort to remediate. Considering that information is the lifeblood of the organization, if the appropriate protection is not there, then information leakage, breaches, and downtime may be the alternative. In my opinion, you must allocate sufficient resources and budget to each of the three services to maximize the delivery of information to the business. It is not always the case that the split in budget is exact. So while the ideal model is that a third of your budget is allocated to each service, using information delivery, protection, and management as a means of organizing your organization, you may find that you need more budget this year to replace an application or replace servers. This is where the business is important—making decisions about the budget and how to allocate the appropriate resources. The balance that must be achieved is continuous improvement in all three areas of IT services.

Just like delivering any product, there are risks associated with delivering, managing, and maintaining information. Information delivery must consider processes and projects. Information management needs to look at how information is organized, including both structured and unstructured information. Finally, information protection must consider access controls, security, and audit, as discussed in Section III, Liabilities Management.

11

PROCESS MANAGEMENT

Processes can be looked at as something that gets hard-wired into organizations, similar to what happens inside our brains. Our brains are hard-wired to analyze information coming into our senses and, based on pattern recognition, will stimulate a response. An example is that touching a hot stove with your hand causes you to pull the hand away quickly. We know that a hot surface will cause us pain.

Similarly, we have specific processes such as manufacturing, sales, marketing, human resources, and application development that have been created, evolved over time, and now are hard-wired into our organizations. These processes should all support products or business outcomes eventually. We also have to remember that we have primary or core processes, secondary, sometimes tertiary processes or subprocesses that support primary (core) processes. For a small business there will be a smaller number of core processes. As the organization grows, there are more people and the complexity grows. There needs to be more processes. The following list represents some of the possible core processes in a medium-sized organization:

1. Marketing
2. Human Resources
3. Financial and Capital Management
4. Strategy and Vision
5. Sales
6. Product Development/Service Delivery
7. Accounting
8. Technology

As the organization grows, there are additional core processes added such as supplier management, legal and compliance, and security. There are many, sometimes hundreds, subprocesses. Business process management is the alignment of processes with business outcomes.

Processes are interdependent and linked activities, groups of tasks or procedures that use resources to convert inputs into some desirable output that eventually serves a purpose within an organization. Business process management is the management of these processes to create more efficiency and improve the effectiveness of the processes. Although we are not going to discuss business process management, it is important to note that every process should be aligned with a core process or core processes. The objective is to support business outcomes or products/services produced by the organization.

Processes are often overlooked as a means of improving your ROI in terms of time spent on managing the infrastructure and applications. It may also be very difficult to implement changes as many technical people feel they are doing a great job and are spending countless hours managing the infrastructure and applications. The heroics that go on in many organizations are commendable; however, many such heroics are self-induced. These heroics usually involve lots of unplanned work. In their book entitled *The Visible Ops Handbook*, Kevin Behr, Gene Kim, and George Spafford (2004–2005) described an approach to help organizations control their IT environment. The approach is outlined in four phases:

1. *Stabilize the patient:* This phase reduces the number of outages by freezing changes outside the scheduled maintenance windows.
2. *Catch and release; and find fragile artifacts:* This phase inventories assets, configurations, and services to identify those with the lowest change success rate, highest MTTR, and highest business downtime costs. Fragile systems are identified and special treatment applied.
3. *Establish repeatable build library:* The best return on investment is based on implementing effective release management processes. This phase creates repeatable build processes to make it cheaper to rebuild than to repair.
4. *Establish continuous improvement:* This phase implements metrics to enable continuous improvement to meet business objectives.

The objective is to reduce the MTTR and increase the MTBF for all your systems, especially critical systems.

Analysis of IT outages has demonstrated that up to 80% of the outages are caused by operator and application errors. (Donna Scott, 2004)

An event that occurred in the life-cycle management of an application within the Justice Sector emphasizes the fact that a lot of outages are caused by operator and application errors. During a routine upgrade, a critical application for managing inmates within Corrections facilities in British Columbia failed. During one of the maintenance windows, the objectives were to perform three separate operations: upgrade the database, upgrade the business process execution language, and upgrade the application. The database upgrade was successful. The business process execution language upgrade was not. The technical engineers felt that they could overcome this failure and proceeded to upgrade the application. This failed also, and there was no back-out or recovery capability once the engineers had proceeded this far. The application was unavailable for four days. The direct financial impact was $72,000 in staff overtime. However, there were intangible impacts of the outage on staff as the backlog of data entry for Corrections staff extended for several weeks after the event. The other concerns of such extended outages were public and personnel safety.

No events occurred that were related to the outage, but what we cannot predict is that there could be a correlation between this outage and some future event. If some detailed piece of information about the violent behavior of an inmate was not entered into the system because of workload, there is the potential that information could compromise the safety of personnel. This is analogous to the *butterfly effect*, which we will discuss in the chapter "Preparing for a 'Black Swan'" (Chapter 25).

MTTR and MTBF are the metrics that can be used to measure service delivery. One cannot be sure that all executives will understand MTTR and MTBF. What they do understand is the unavailability of their applications and the downtime impacts. Implementing the four practical and auditable steps as outlined in *The Visible Ops Handbook* (Behr, Kim, and Spafford, 2004–2005) makes sense. The objective is to move your team from a reactive position to a proactive position as much as possible. Being able to predict outages and durations is far better than reacting to an outage with no understanding of the time and no real understanding of what really caused the outage.

In my days as a Field Service Engineer for Digital Equipment in the 1980s, it was understood that there would be outages. Equipment failed. The routine maintenance that we performed sometimes induced failures. We stress-tested the equipment during these maintenance windows to help reduce intermittent failures. There is nothing more frustrating for customers than for the technical person to be called in for a failure, run all the diagnostics, stress-test the system, and still not identify the failing component. It was like we were chasing ghosts in the systems. Troubleshooting became a slow progression of component replacement and keeping detailed information in a logbook on-site so the next person could continue with the process. Operations in some of these places were 24/7, and the maintenance contract was the same with built-in escalation. Organizations paid thousands of dollars per month to make sure the equipment was operational and met their needs. Many of the systems were used in critical operations, such as the VAX 11/730 that controlled the huge dump truck routes in the mining operations at Quintette Coal to maximize fuel efficiency and safety. Another example involved the PDP11/05 computers that controlled the "pot" lines used for melting aluminum for the smelting plant at Kitimat, BC.

Today, computers are the heart of most operations, and the failure of email and other critical applications represents financial and productivity losses to organizations. Computers are an integral part of our lives and as the CIO you are responsible for making sure they are available and fully functional to deliver information services.

So why implement something like ITIL or the four steps in *The Visible Ops Handbook* (Behr, Kim, and Spafford, 2004–2005)? The objective is to minimize the impact that infrastructure and application outages have on achieving desired outcomes. This means reducing the MTTR and increasing the MTBF, making the systems more available and minimizing the impact from unscheduled downtime. A key point is to ensure that the work being done is auditable. That will help you in many of other requirements such as compliance with SOX, PCI, HIPAA, or whatever regulation, legislation, or industry standard requires your organization's compliance.

Auditability means that you measure. Dr. W.E. Deming developed "statistical process control," which measures processes to make sure the processes are performing as expected. When we look at systems, there are a number of different processes that we use to achieve expected outcomes; that is, the systems are performing as expected and producing the expected results. Watts Humphrey (1989), in his book entitled *Managing the Software Process*, described process maturity levels; these have been used as foundations to describe the maturity levels of many different standards such as COBIT. Maturity levels have the following general characteristics:

1. *Initial:* Until the process is under statistical control, orderly progress in process improvement is not possible. Where there are many degrees of statistical control, the first step is to achieve rudimentary predictability of schedules and costs.
2. *Repeatable:* The organization has achieved a stable process with a repeatable level of statistical control by initiating rigorous project management of commitments, costs, schedules, and changes.
3. *Defined:* The organization has defined the process as a basis for consistent implementation and better understanding. At this point, advanced technology can usefully be introduced.
4. *Managed:* The organization has initiated comprehensive process measurements and analysis. This is when the most significant quality improvements begin.
5. *Optimized:* The organization now has a foundation for continuing improvement and optimization of the process.

It is not the maturity level that you are interested in but rather the measurement. Measurement is a key to process improvement. Whether you define the stage your organization is at as one of the five above or use COBIT or some other standard, the intent is the same. You want to define what improvements you need to increase the efficiency and effectiveness of your teams to maximize productivity and reduce costs. The effect of continuous measurement is process improvement. Remember to base your view of the information on facts, calculations, and estimations, considering some quantifiable metrics and your interpretation of how confident you are in the information (confidence interval).

In their guidebook entitled *Practical Software Measurement: Measuring for Process Management and Improvement*, William Forac, Robert Park, and Anita Carleton (1997) characterized process performance with the following points:

- Measures used to characterize process performance should
    - Relate closely to the issue under study. These are usually issues of quality, resource consumption, or elapsed time.
    - Have high information content. Pick measures of product or process qualities that are sensitive to as many facets of process results as possible.
    - Pass a reality test. Does the measure really reflect the degree to which the process achieves results that are important?
    - Permit easy and economical collection of data.
    - Permit consistently collected, well-defined data.
    - Show measurable variation. A number that does not change does not provide any information about the process.
    - As a set, have diagnostic value. They should be able to help you identify not only that something unusual has happened but also what might be causing it.

In essence, what you want to discover are

- What activities are being done within your processes?
- Are these processes effective?
- Do these activities contribute to improving products?

Figure 11.1 depicts your budget. Within your budget, you usually have projects, operations, and part of the operations budget is consumed reacting to situations. In *Visible Ops* (Behr, Kim, and Spafford, 2004–2005), work is referred to as either planned or unplanned. In a budget cycle, you estimate one year in advance how much money you will need to operate. This usually is broken down into resources (personal and contract), projects, systems, salary, benefits, training, applications, network, maintenance, and miscellaneous. What you cannot

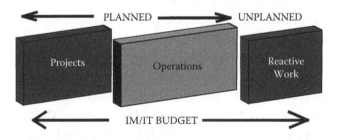

Figure 11.1   Planned versus unplanned work.

tell from your operations budget is how much money you will spend on unplanned work. In firefighting mode, your staff and contractors will consume significant portions of your budget. This is reflected in overtime, adding shifts, and adding contractors to make sure systems are operational—in other words, uptime. You want to reduce the unplanned or reactive portion of your budget. Your objective should be to decrease the unplanned or reactive work to less than 25%. A key metric for determining if your staff is spending significant time is to measure the uptime (and downtime). The more downtime, the more you are spending on unplanned work.

The first step is to complete some form of activity-based costing (or activity-based management) analysis on your organization's operations. This will give you information on where your staff is allocating their time and on what activities. There are a lot of activities that are above the ground, that is, staff can tell you exactly how much time they are spending on an activity. There are a lot of activities that are below the ground; that are not identified because they may only take ten or fifteen minutes and are cyclic. Those are the activities that often haunt us after we have done all the work in transforming the organization based on what information is being presented. In IT, they are often referred to as off-the-side-of-the-desk activities. Even so, the objective is to get an idea of the major activities that are consuming most of the time. Activity-based management will not by itself reduce cost, but it will help you understand your costs.

The next step is to benchmark your existing processes. You should focus on one thing to benchmark: your change control process. The entire change control process should be in scope. This includes updates to servers, workstations, applications, and databases. This is where we start to measure and, if possible, compare to industry standards. In their book *Visible Ops*, Kim, Behr, and Spafford (2004–2005) do not benchmark existing processes; however, it would be good to know your starting point. The benchmark can be internal, or you can hire someone to benchmark your processes against industry standards. Both have positive and negative points; the intent is to benchmark and make sure you understand that in a benchmark, you are dealing with people's opinions, estimates, and calculations—and typically very few facts.

The third step is to define where you want to be and in what time period. If you have discovered that your staff is spending much of its time in firefighting mode, more time than you would like, now is the time to declare where you want to be and when. This is the gap: you have benchmarked where you are and where you want to be in terms of productivity, processes, and budget. There is a gap and you need to plan with all your staff how you will move from where you are to where you want to be.

Most importantly, you must measure everyone on this. In government we did Employee Personal Development Programs (or EPDPs). The CIO should put the metrics within the EPDP of his direct reports to set targets for this change. Each direct report then sets targets within each of their staff's EPDP to contribute to their overall target. And the most important piece is tracking—*If you do not track and report on a periodic base, no one will take it seriously.* The most important is measuring the improvements and letting people know that you are tracking and reporting them. I suggest at least quarterly. There may be some shorter-term changes that need reporting. I also suggest that the metrics and baseline to demonstrate improvements be reported to the entire organization.

The fourth step is to make changes in your change management system based on ITIL, Visible Ops, or COBIT. Pick a standard that you are currently using or can adopt. I like Visible Ops because it is practical and appears to be the easiest to implement. The point is that you have to manage this across multiple disciplines and multiple workgroups. Everyone must be on the same page. It will take training, discipline, and demonstrated commitment.

One of the obstacles you have to overcome is inertia. Your organization has developed great applications and processes and a really good system development life cycle. This may work against making changes. Fitts' law (Figure 11.2) describes the relationship between experience in doing a process and the improvements in the time it takes to do the process. There is a log-linear relationship: the time to complete a process decreases in a linear fashion as experience in performing the process increases logarithmically. That is, doing a process many times makes you more proficient. For example, if you do a process ten times, you get a certain increase in performance. To get the next increase in performance, you need to do the process a hundred times. It highlights the law of diminishing returns. At some point in time, the improvement is marginal as compared to the changes that

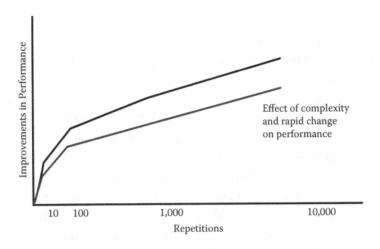

Figure 11.2 Fitts' law as it applies to IT.

were made during the first few repeats. Pro golfers shoot buckets of balls per day to practice. The difference between a good putt and a great putt is measured in inches. The difference could be the result of the 10,000 practice putts made.

Fitts' law is more in tune with repetitions that would apply to physical training. However, if we apply this law to IT, we see that there are similar results. However, there is a difference. The top line in Figure 11.2 represents repetition improvements in something like baseball or hockey. The bottom line represents the effect of complexity and change such as occurs within IT. In IT we have two characteristics that change the way Fitts' law works. Repetition is very important but there are two other considerations that impact the ability of an individual with reasonable skills to improve quickly: complexity and change. We recognize that the IT environment is very complex and that this complexity will reduce improvements in performance. The other is change, which is constant in our IT environment. The assumption is that the person is reasonably competent in technology. I know that once in a while I have to reconfigure my PC for some reason. I struggle with the settings and how to view the network. It may seem very simple to a network engineer; however, I do not repeat this daily or even weekly. It occurs once every two years. So the same results apply whether you are training people for incident response, business continuity, or playing golf; repetition is key as long as you consider competency, complexity, and change as factors that will impact performance improvements.

In early childhood, the human brain is making and breaking synaptic connections in response to sensory inputs. Repetition makes these connections permanent. Somewhere between three and six years of age, our synapses have finished "hard wiring" and we have developed a system for performing pattern recognition. After this, we develop patterns based on soft connections (our software) to manipulate our hard-wired templates in a virtual fashion (logic filters or gateways). We store these patterns as virtual connections between our primary hard-wired system. We can also relate this to organizations. We establish primary hard-wired patterns in our organizations, such as finance, IT, operations, and have soft or virtual patterns that allow us to transfer information between our primary hard-wired patterns (committees, teams, communities of practice).

Once people are trained and proficient in performing a task, there is significant resistance to change. Inertia may show up as passive resistance to change. Larger bureaucracies are more susceptible; that is, the larger the organization, the more the resistance. The more specialization there is, the more resistance to change. In his book entitled *Complex Organizations*, Charles Perrow (1986) talked about two kinds of authorities: specialization and official. *Specialization authority* is an authority based on technical competence; *official authority* is based on the incumbency of a legally defined office. In IT, we see a lot of specialization authority. When you have achieved technical competence in a specific technical field, there is a very high reluctance to abandon the technology that has taken years to learn. The reticence of people to learn new technology or even recommend new technology becomes apparent. It becomes a liability to corporations.

IT is constantly evolving. There are few technologies that have stayed or will stay constant. Some time ago I attended a presentation given by IBM. The presentation was on infrastructure commodities. When we think about telephones, electric power, water, roads, rails, and air, these are all infrastructure commodities. Computers and networks are now part of our infrastructure commodities. There is a definite move to outsource the network, storage, and processing capabilities. We call it "cloud computing" today. It really is not much different than having hosting services such as customers being serviced by a mainframe. The difference is in the contracts, performance, and capacities. We recognize that the skills needed are different. There is a definite requirement for more skills dealing with applications, business problems, contracts, negotiations, security, privacy, and information management. These must be considered in hiring as well as in retraining staff. As the complexity increases, there will be more need for specialists. Whether these specialists are on staff or are contracted depends on the needs of the business. The timing of getting these resources to solve business problems is critical. Often these specialists are in short supply and therefore in high demand. More contractual arrangements will be made with outsourcing and consulting firms to leverage these resources.

One of the critical aspects of processes is pulling together groups of people to solve business problems. Often, a business problem arises that requires a number of different skills to help solve the problem. The question is: Do you call these committees or teams?

In government we often pulled together committees to look at some problem. Committees were very often formed based on hierarchical decisions, not on skills. That is, people with formal official authority would delegate and task individuals who they wanted on the committee. This did not always resolve the problem in the most effective manner; sometimes the person who was designated the chair of the committee by the formal official authority had other agendas. Keeping in mind that organizations need to change from a hierarchical structure to a more developmental organization, we should consider changing the way we select groups to solve critical business problems. I am proposing that we should start using the word *team* instead of the term *committee* or *working group*. To me, the term *team* represents something that has a single purpose; I equate this to football.

I coached football for three years and learned a lot about specialty teams, teamwork, and repetition. In football we had specialists: the quarterback who could throw the ball with speed and accuracy, run the plays, do the handoffs, and had to be a good athlete for those times when the play broke down and he had to run. We had one kicker who could kick field goals and punt. We had linebackers, running backs, tackles, guards, the center, and receivers—most of you know football and the number of players. The point is that there were specialists but if you wanted to win games, these specialists had to perform as a team to win. I want to step through why we should start calling our groups *teams* and not *committees*.

In looking at both committees and teams, there are some unique differences that we can focus on; Table 11.1 outlines the differences.

Teams have a single focus on winning. In Table 11.1, teams are led by a leader, whereas a committee is led by a chair. A leader has some or all of the following characteristics:

- Knows what they want to do
- Tells people what to do but not how to do it
- Does his or her homework
- Leads by example
- Demands excellence
- Takes care of their people
- Is humble
- Has character (honest, truthful, and dependable)

Would you rather have a leader or a chair appointed by someone to run a project or solve a problem? Most people would prefer a leader. The problem to be solved needs the right person to lead the effort. Appointing a chair just because the person is liked or is on the executive list of possible candidates is not going to help solve problems. As a matter of fact, this may create more problems as smart technical and business people are forced to develop a solution based on some political requirement rather than solving the problem. I have seen a few instances of things going very wrong and having to fix problems created because the committee was comprised of political appointees and not skilled technical and business people. In my case, security was added as an afterthought long after

Table 11.1   Governance Committee or Team?

CRITERIA	COMMITTEE	TEAM
Governance	Formal	Informal
Focus	Hierarchical	Equal participation
Reporting	Chair	Leader
Selection	Management picks team	Selection based on skills needed
Participation	Management (chair) dictates level of participation	Everyone has voice, everyone must be heard
Purpose	Different agendas, different priorities	Single purpose
Resolution	Already determined; normally the sponsor will dictate how this should be resolved	Open; all ideas should be considered

the solution had been created, was presented, and work started. Then the issues surrounding privacy and security come to the front and the new application does not have security built in.

We need to change our hierarchical organizations to become more flexible. Innovation is what drives new companies, and they often compete in niche markets that already have a big company solidly entrenched. The problem is that the big company no longer listens to its customers and does not change fast enough. A good example of that occurred when I was working on a knowledge management strategy and the Manager for Information Management came to me with a proposal to implement TRIM™ (a records management solution from HP). He was new to information management and had been told that the recommended government solution for records management was TRIM. I was looking at the problem that the ministry was facing and knew that TRIM would not solve the problem. The problem with TRIM was a thick client and based on twenty-year-old technology. There was no Web-based or browser interface. Searches were done by keywords and there was a lot of up-front work that had to be done by each person in saving each file or document. I knew that the people would not do this work and that the system would fail. HP, which had bought TRIM in their 2008 acquisition of TOWER®, admitted that this was a legacy application and would not solve our business problems. (There is further discussion on developing information management solutions in Chapter 16.)

We have been driven by hierarchical structures for the past 10,000 years. Hierarchical organizations like the military and the church are based on blind obedience. There are places for this behavior but not in organizations that must be flexible and agile in order to keep up with changes in the market and technology. Teams are much more driven by a single goal. In sports, it's about winning. In corporations, it's about winning. When you have good participation, you get new ideas. When you are open to suggestions, you renew the innovative spirit that has been the driving force behind good companies. In so many studies such as those done by Aberdeen, they always talk about leaders and laggards. Leaders always seem to be on the leading edge of technology, always implementing the newest technologies. The important question is: Can you change from a hierarchical structure to a developmental structure?

Perhaps another way of looking at this is to classify organization structures. Dr. Frid, in his book entitled *The Frid Factor: A Pragmatic Guide to Building a Knowledge Management Program*, described three classifications of organizational structure:

1. *The Team:* two to six members bound by a loose association that targets a specific task or function. Within a team, the leader role will pass between team members, depending on the skill sets. Teams are a democracy and everyone has a voice.

2. *The Department:* consists of several teams. Studies have shown that it is best to keep teams in a department to six or less. Someone is designated the boss. Normally that is an official position designated by the organization. There are formal (official) and informal leaders within the department. Similar to teams, the leader role is passed among the members within the department, depending on the decision required.

3. *The Organization:* the formal political mechanism to manage multiple departments. There is an official position as the person with the formal line of authority to make decisions.

There are optimal sizes of organizational structures and the number seems to vary between five and nine, with an average of seven. There is something about the human mind and the capacity to retain five to nine objects or thoughts in short-term memory. Decision making with more than nine rapidly degrades as the size of a team increases. Hence, the committees with twenty members often cannot make decisions or get consensus. This is something to consider next time you need a team to look at some key operational issue that must be resolved quickly.

We have discussed operational risk and planned versus unplanned work. One final aspect of service delivery is projects. Projects are a defined set of tasks and activities with a set period of time and a specific objective. Projects within IT are usually about building and updating applications, installing and upgrading infrastructure, and installing and upgrading workstations. There are also some projects about building and improving processes within IT. Projects have risks associated with them. Usually, a project manager develops a risk registry and mitigation strategies. Some projects are risky; they have a lot of uncertainty and complexity. We discuss an approach to identify and manage risky projects in Chapter 12.

12

PROJECT MANAGEMENT

Organizations are complex, and in this global economy, change is constantly required to maintain efficiencies, a competitive edge, and to keep the organization secure and complex. No matter what triggers the changes—internal or external—the organization must manage those changes effectively. Otherwise, chaos ensues and the organization fails in its strategic objectives or ceases to exist.

Consider the organization as consisting of a standard hierarchy of many layers in a pyramid. A standard pyramid has a few executives at the top, more people in middle management between, and a lot more people doing the day-to-day operations of the company at the bottom.

- Executives focus on the longer-term vision and strategy of the organization—the business results and stakeholder value. These are the leaders of the organization.
- Middle management is hired and directed by those executives; they develop and maintain the organization structure. They are key enablers in organizational governance, in how to structure and change the organization, and how it operates. Middle management manages everything and must focus on the value to clients, the staff, and the processes. They create and measure how the business processes are performing and through something like a balanced scorecard, how it all fits together—the client value, the costs, the change, and the operational processes.
- Reporting to middle management are the people who execute business processes, using the IT tools and systems to deliver the services to the customers and the organization. They have to make sure the capacity of the operations delivers, measured by some indicators of success.

The increasing rate of change is a major challenge for all organizations. Managing changes in an efficient and controlled manner is a critical need for all organizations. Unmanaged change can result in the wrong changes being implemented, with the right changes being unrecognized and therefore unfunded. This leads to inefficient operations, unsecured information, and out-of-date processes.

Project management is all about change; it is changing the operational services and/or business processes, the IT systems, and tools to improve the value to clients, improve the process performance, or implement new visions and strategies (Figure 12.1). As the very term *project management* indicates, it is about management—the management of change.

The project management discipline has been instrumental in identifying the need for not only managing projects well but also in selecting and funding the right changes at the right time.

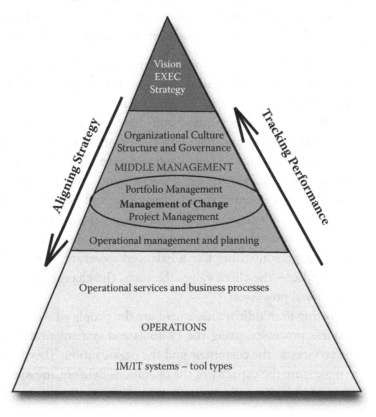

Figure 12.1 Project and portfolio management.

Portfolio management is the discipline and set of processes for the management of investments proposed or in process for changes to the business (Figure 12.1). From the CIO's perspective, portfolio management is about managing IT investments. Portfolio management is about leveraging the resources (time, money, infrastructure, and people) in the most effective way to achieve the best results or, in essence, getting the best value from your IT investments. Defined as a set of strategic-level processes and decisions that enable the most effective balance of organizational changes and business operations, portfolio management ensures that

- Strategic business decisions are made based on a clear understanding of the costs, risks, benefits, and impacts to business operations.
- All changes to business operations are made and monitored at the appropriate management layer and support business strategic objectives.
- Funding and resources are assigned to those changes aligned with the strategic objectives and prioritized changes.

Portfolio management is also responsible for managing the organization's structures and processes: from the organization-wide process architectures and value chains to the way information is managed and secured. From a total organizational view to the departmental, program, and finally project view, portfolio management must be well understood and consciously structured for success.

Usually structured in some kind of office structure, the organization-wide portfolio management office is staffed with a leader and analysts working directly for the organizational executives and may have subordinate portfolio offices working directly for departments or branches.

Regardless of the structure, the leader charged with managing the portfolio must recognize the complicated dynamics in the organization at the executive, political, social, and cultural levels. In addition, the leader must ensure that his or her portfolio follows the following principles:

- *Remain aligned with corporate strategy:* Understand and support the vision and strategy of the executives and how changes (projects) are selected, funded, and aligned.

- *Lead change:* Move the organization through the phases of the change acceptance curve—contact–awareness–understanding–acceptance–adoption—within the constraints set by the governance bodies (scope, time, cost) through common and standardized project management practices.
- *Envision and communicate a better future:* Prioritize change (project) investments to maximize the return on investment, while minimizing risk.
- *Focus on benefits and the threats to those benefits:* Identify and measure the realization of the benefits (results/outcomes) expected.
- *Design and deliver a coherent capability* through learning from experience and mature the organization to deliver the organization's products and services more effectively and efficiently.

All of this is required to support the executives in both managing the operations day to day but also in strategically managing the changes within the organization and ensuring that the strategic visions are implemented.

Projects

Projects are the means of getting new technology operational. Whether the technology is a new application, upgrading an existing application, or adding new hardware or functionality, we start with a project. By definition, a project has a start and a finish. Projects exist for a finite time. I have been involved with pilot projects that existed for years. There was no start or end time. When I put the question to business as to who should pay for the production model, the answer was "not me." Projects are great if they accomplish something that helps the business meet its goals. And one needs a sponsor to pay for the project. I have also seen where the project is paid for but not the ongoing costs of maintaining the application or software and hardware maintenance. As one of the directors in the Ministry of Attorney General said, he wants to see the total cost of ownership over five years to make sure that when the project goes into production, it is fully funded.

Projects typically start with a business case. There is a business problem or a need that is not being met. The problem or need may represent an opportunity for an increase in profitability or the avoidance of a cost or a risk. A project is the means to realize the opportunity or avoid the cost or risk. A business case should be completed prior to the project.

The business case should provide sufficient detail to allow a decision to be made. The decision should be go or no-go. In the worst case, the sponsor may need further information in order to make a decision.

One of the critical functions of IT is managing projects. Ideally, projects should be completed on time and within budget. The reality is that many IT projects fail outright, are over budget, or are not delivered on time. To help us understand why projects fail, we need tools that measure and report on projects. There are many reasons why projects fail such as lack of management commitment, scope creep, inadequate or vague requirements. Rolling up all these reasons, we have determined that there is an inability to predict the complexity or uncertainty of each project. Project risk profiling estimates the complexity and uncertainty of projects.

The Ministry of Attorney General and the Ministry of Public Safety and Solicitor General is referred to as the Justice Sector within the government of British Columbia. In 2007, the Auditor General audited the Corrections Network offender management system, also known as CORNET. The Auditor General released the audit of the CORNET System in March 2008. A recommendation from the key findings was to continue the development of a risk model and increase the security group's involvement with key security-related decisions made in the different Information Technology Services Division (ITSD) areas. As the director responsible for information security within the Justice Sector, I had to develop a methodology to help us manage risks within IT and reposition information security within the Systems Development Life Cycle (SDLC).

Our existing approach required a TRA and a Privacy Impact Assessment (PIA) for new projects or major upgrades. The PIA was mandated by legislation under the Freedom of Information and Protection of Privacy Act (FOIPPA). The TRA focused on the technical risks and did not provide an overall measure of project risks. Our SDLC followed a standard waterfall methodology, and project managers were expected to manage risks within their projects following standard project management practices as within the Project Management Body of Knowledge (PMBOK).

In my assessment I realized that TRAs were not adding sufficient value to our clients and, primarily, a TRA was completed as one of the gates they had to complete prior to the project going into production. We needed a better way to determine what controls we needed to streamline the process and add value. The article *Adaptive Agility— Managing Complexity and Uncertainty* by Todd Little et al. (2004) and the government's project management "Level of Project Management" scoring provided me with some ideas on how we can look at project risks. What I wanted was the answer to two basic questions:

1. Was the project risky?
2. What level of controls should we apply?

The first question was important because we outsourced our application development. If the project was risky to start with—scope, cost, technology, impact, timelines were not clearly defined—this may mean that the contractor might have to cut corners to save costs and meet unrealistic timelines. This may introduce risks in terms of availability, confidentiality, and integrity. In other words, poor programming has a greater chance of inducing failures in the applications and increases the likelihood of having more changes to the application to fix problems introduced by poor programming. Answering the first question would let us determine an answer to the second question. I developed a simple Excel™ spreadsheet that was to be completed by the business sponsor, the business manager, or the project manager. The risk profile of the project was given a ranking from Very Low to Very High, as described in Table 12.1.

The results were reviewed by a security analyst and any disagreements on the ranking were discussed. If the discussion could not produce an agreed-upon result, the decision was presented to me as the director and I determined the final ranking. Although some of these

Table 12.1 Project Risk Scale

RISK SCORE	PROJECT RISK PROFILE, LEVEL OF RISK
0–20	Very Low
21–40	Low
41–60	Moderate
61–80	High
81–100	Very High

were estimations, there were a number of facts that we could verify, such as cost, scope, stakeholders, and resourcing. Some areas were less certain, such as objective, visibility, and dependencies. I have included a sample of the project risk profile Excel spreadsheet in Appendix B.

Project risk profiles were determined based on a possible maximum score of 100. Risks were measured out of 5, and the scores were weighted out of 10. Table 12.1 provides how risk was scored. The Project Risk Profiling Process is described in Figure 12.2. Key decision points were the risk ranking of a project and vulnerability scanning.

Risk Ranking

We took a simple approach to ranking projects. Once the project risk was scored, we determined how much attention we could spend on what project. It was easier to determine which projects required more attention once we ranked the project risks: High and Very High risk projects demanded more attention, whereas Moderate and Low risk projects demanded less attention.

- *High and Very High risk projects:* More monitoring was required for High and Very High risk projects. At a minimum, a project plan, work breakdown structure, risk registry, and risk mitigation strategy were required. Periodic meetings were scheduled to verify that the project was tracking and that the risk profile had not changed.
- *Moderate and Low risk projects:* We still had to maintain some monitoring over Moderate and Low risk projects. We still required a project plan, a work breakdown structure, and a risk registry. Most of the Moderate or Low risk projects had shorter timelines so periodic reviews were not practical, given the constraints on resources and the risk profile. We requested that the project managers provide some updates that could be reviewed by a security analyst.

Vulnerability Scanning

Each project required a vulnerability scan prior to production. This was a system scan or an application scan. A system scan determined

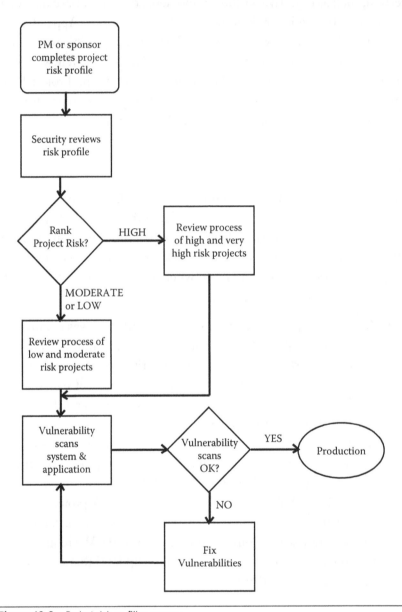

Figure 12.2 Project risk profiling process.

if there were vulnerabilities such as open ports or missed patches, whereas an application scan was used to determine if the application was properly coded. We used the Open Web Application Security Project (OWASP) list of top-ten vulnerabilities, which you can find at http://www.owasp.org/index.php/Category:OWASP_Top_Ten_ Project, to determine if the application was suitably coded to protect against the majority of hacker attacks. Either way, our objective was to reduce the possibility of the wrong information getting to the wrong person at the wrong time, and in this case we were trying to keep the hackers out.

Just to give you an example of how important vulnerability scanning is prior to systems going into production, we had an incident that emphasized this point. The system was rushed into a "production" state without undergoing testing for vulnerabilities. The system was compromised by a hacker from China running an automated script. The script simply entered the userid "admin" and default passwords in every system that had a specific identified vulnerability. Our administrators were so rushed that they set up the system with some default passwords. The script found and exploited that vulnerability. Luckily, an administrator found that the server was compromised before any damage could be done. If a vulnerability scan had been done prior to the system going into production, this simple error would have been detected.

Reporting

As a CIO, you need to report on the status of projects to the executive, especially to those executives who are sponsoring projects. The reporting depends on the size of the organization. We can safely assume that small organizations generally have fewer projects. For large organizations, there may be hundreds of projects.

For small organizations, there are few projects and the reporting should be quite simple. The CIO should report project status to the executive. A vulnerability scan of the application and the platform(s) should be required at the completion of all projects prior to production. The CIO would brief the executive on any vulnerabilities found and determine the criticality of the application in terms of business requirements versus the severity of the vulnerabilities. The executive might decide to take the risk and put the application into production with application vulnerabilities if there were sufficient business pressures to warrant the risks.

For medium- to large-sized organizations, the reporting becomes more complex. There are more competing priorities and dependencies. There are more projects and the competition for resources becomes more acute. For example, in the Justice Sector we often had forty projects at any given time and people were often over-committed to five or more projects. If you added up their time, you would often find they were allocated 150% or more to projects, and there were other operational and administrative tasks on their plate. The Justice Sector had multiple business areas and competing priorities, so resources for projects were juggled based on the political or business urgency of the day. Most medium- and large-sized organizations have similar competing priorities, and the only way to effectively manage all these is to implement portfolio management. Portfolio management allows you to develop appropriate governance mechanisms and assign business priorities. The governance allows the business to drive priorities. The CIO should not be the decision maker on the business priorities, perhaps better described as the focal point for IT-related projects.

In most situations, IT Projects are a component of a larger business project. The CIO should make sure that the IT components are well represented and that reporting on the status of the IT deliverables is the responsibility of the project managers. The aggregation of the reports is the responsibility of the CIO. The use of portfolio management would improve the reporting. It still requires everyone to input the data. That is where setting up a governance structure adds value, enforcing the reporting of data.

Whether you have a portfolio management application or manage by spreadsheets, you must report the status of projects periodically. The status should be kept simple but have the capability of drilling down into the details. Identified risks should have mitigation plans and these should be carefully monitored. Identified risks should be compared across projects to make sure it is not the same risk for multiple projects. At a high level, many project managers will identify resourcing as a key risk. Multiple projects will identify resourcing as a risk. It is up to the CIO to determine if there are sufficient IT resources that can be allocated for projects. If there are not sufficient

IT resources, then the CIO will identify that as a risk to the business and the business will determine project priorities. If the governance structure is set up, any issues that cannot be resolved at the management layer should be decided at the strategic or executive level. That is what periodic reporting does; it brings issues to the table and opens a dialogue. The more you can talk about issues and resolving these issues, the more the executive pays attention—especially if you are coming to the table with solutions and recommendations. Meaningful reporting is welcome. Identifying issues is good. Providing cost-effective solutions and demonstrating good governance is excellence.

13

IT Service Management

The focus is on service delivery, making sure the right information is available to the right person at the right time to positively affect outcomes. IT predominantly operates in silos even within the IT organization. The programmers focus on delivering code. The server technicians focus on maintaining the servers. The database experts focus on making sure the database is operational. Who is coordinating these efforts?

The ITIL is a framework for IT service management. As with any best practices, the intent is not to implement ITIL as fully described but rather to develop processes using ITIL as the model. Visible Ops is about implementing ITIL in practical and auditable steps. Visible Ops does not advocate all of ITIL. Whatever model your organization subscribes to, the result must be better IT service management.

IT service management must:

- Have a clearly defined set of products and services
- Not operate in silos
- Define the culture of the organization
- Enable IM/IT to be a service-based organization
- Have standard, well-documented, and followed processes
- Have customer relationship management
- Have automation for processes and workflows to manage the complex environment

As a CIO, you manage a budget. In some cases, the IM/IT budget is substantial. If your IM/IT budget is $40 million, you manage activities and assets that are valued at $20,000 per hour. So you must ask yourself: "What activities can I do to maximize my value to my organization?" Having good IT service management is about managing your budget effectively. If a big chunk of your budget is being spent on unplanned work, it means you are not delivering your services effectively. Executives are always looking to make the organization more cost effective, and one of the big threats facing CIOs and their staff is outsourcing. Using IT service management, you should be able to baseline

- Problems and problem resolution solutions
- Change management processes
- Time to market of new products and services

Make your staff proactive and not reactive. Executives are not interested in your problems, processes, and excuses; they are interested in the impact to the business. It is up to you to make the impact of IT positive or negative. As the following quote from Lewis Carroll says,

> Now, here, you see, it takes all the running you can do, to keep in the same place. If you want to get somewhere else, you must run at least twice as fast as that!

—"Through the Looking Glass"

Staff members are already running as fast as they can, and they are staying in the same place. You cannot ask them to run faster. You need to step out of your existing paradigm and spend time addressing the gaps. This means taking some of your very smart people out of production for a while and getting a really good facilitator to understand the problems and develop real fixes. "I can't!" You scream as the fires rage all around you. So who started the fires, and how did they get started? If you can stop the fires from starting, you may find that you have more time for delivering information more effectively, which is what you are paid to do.

IT service management does not solve all your problems. As described in Visible Ops, you have to take steps to manage your delivery of services to be more effective. ITIL provides a framework. IT service delivery develops the framework into processes and practices that improve service delivery.

Opportunity Capacity

IT service management is not enough! A CIO is fired from his job for not being innovative and missing opportunities to invest in new

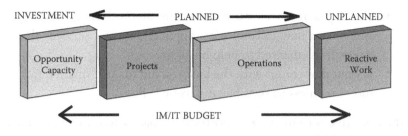

Figure 13.1   Opportunity capacity.

technologies to help drive the business further and faster. He was managing vendors, his service model was very good, downtime was minimal, his people were on top of projects, and he managed operations within budget. His organization was one of the top in their sector and they wanted to stay as a leader in their business. Where he failed was to understand and respond to unarticulated demands.

In most IM/IT organizations, budgets are being divided between unplanned and planned work. Planned work is further divided into projects and operations. There is nothing left for innovation or investment.

What does the business want from IM/IT? Not the status quo! Your competitors are not standing still, nor are your customers. What the business is demanding is IM/IT *opportunity capacity* (Figure 13.1) to exploit IM/IT to its maximum.

> Opportunity capacity is the power, aptitude, and ability to learn and create situations or conditions favorable for the attainment of goals.

In this case, it is the utilization of IM/IT to maximize investments. An example is using IM/IT to extend markets to new areas or countries that were not obtainable prior to making this investment.

Steps that must be taken are very much as above:

- Reduce unplanned work; reactive work means rework, which means that time, people, and resources are lost.
- Reduce or stop projects that do not add value.
- Streamline operations; get rid of or replace services that no longer have value.
- Get closer to the business; relationship management is important in understanding their needs and demands.

- Develop a team to work internally and externally to help understand new technologies, applications, and services that can be implemented to help business.
- Try out new things with the business but make it small, quick, and as painless as possible; everyone is busy.

The objective is to increase opportunity capacity to maximize investments in IM/IT.

14

REPORTING ON
SERVICE DELIVERY

In our discussion of metrics, we need to have ways of describing how we are doing in terms of outcomes. We often measure things like MTTR and MTBF. What we are really measuring is the downtime and uptime of the IT infrastructure. These are outputs and to affect outcomes we need to take this one step further and measure the impact on service delivery (Figure 14.1). That is a true measurement that executives can understand.

How much did IT downtime affect my business? That is a good question and one that you should be able to answer. Metrics must reflect what is important to business and outcomes. If you have significant downtime, you should have actions and plans in place to show how you can improve that metric.

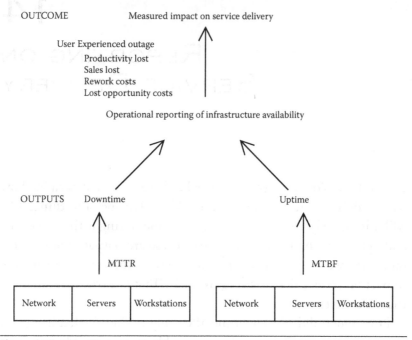

Figure 14.1 Reporting on service delivery.

15

SERVICE DELIVERY

Section Summary

IM/IT is important for service delivery. The objective of IM/IT is to ensure that the right information is available to the right person at the right time to get the job done in the most efficient and cost effective manner.

Service delivery is about outcomes. Outcomes are often confused with operational information. The uptime of a system does not indicate that the business is fully operational with IM/IT. The uptime of a system is an output measurement. An IM/IT infrastructure is very complex. For the front-line workers, they only see their input device. That device could be a laptop, desktop, hand-held, or terminal. If they cannot get the right information at the right time, they cannot do their job. The failure of one component in the infrastructure means the right information is not available to the right person at the right time to complete the task. That is the measurement we must measure. Until the service is back in full operation and they have fully recovered from an outage, we are not measuring the right outcome, and measurements like server uptime are meaningless unless presented as an input to service delivery outcomes.

Service delivery can be described as product management; that is, the processes and projects that achieve an organizational outcome. There are direct and indirect processes and projects that support service delivery. IM/IT has both direct and indirect processes and projects. Some of these processes and projects focus directly on ensuring that the right information is available at the right time to the right person. Others focus on improving the infrastructure and supporting the organization. Not every process or project directly focuses on service delivery. The rule should be that priority must be given to servicing business outcomes.

IM/IT can create its own problems. In every organization there is planned and unplanned work: people and process issues cause 80% of outages and IM/IT has a cowboy-and-hero mentality that "Joe Technician" is the only one who can fix the problem. To fix this means a fundamental change in culture and processes from "we fix on-the-fly" to a well-documented and strictly enforced process. Change management processes may be well documented, but if they are not strictly enforced and followed the process will fail.

Projects are an integral part of IM/IT. Projects should focus on service delivery. Some projects are high risk. We need to know if the project is high risk so that we can contain the risks. Every project should have a risk registry and mitigation strategy.

We can never predict with certainty every event that happens within our organization that may affect service delivery. A black swan is a highly improbable event that causes an impact on an entity. That entity could be a person or an entire country. A black swan may have impact on your organization and the delivery of IM/IT services. For example, a technical person may have a financial problem and steal customer files to pay back a debt. This leads to a security breach that gets published in the media. The story has a downward effect on stock prices. A bit of forward-looking risk management and planning may help.

ITIL sets a framework for good practices. IT service management implements these practices into your processes for service delivery by defining a set of products and services, building customer relationships, and automating these processes as much as is practical and possible.

PART III

LIABILITIES
MANAGEMENT

Corporations consider liabilities in terms of direct or indirect losses. A direct financial loss is a realized loss of money such as money being stolen or a payout of some claim. An indirect financial loss is a potential loss of money such as reputation loss, which may impact the stock price of a publicly traded company. The loss is not realized until the stock is sold.

Governments also consider liabilities in terms of direct or indirect losses with the added risks associated with state, citizens, and properties. Governments have broader consideration for liabilities, depending on what level of government it is. The H1N1 pandemic in 2008–2009 is a good example of liabilities that government must consider. Although corporations had to look at the risks of people not being able to get to work or staff reductions, government had to look at a much broader impact, including inoculations, panic, business impact, citizen impact, and country impact. When H1N1 first started in Mexico, there was a direct impact on tourism. Flights, bookings, and hotels were all affected. Mexico lost hundreds of millions of dollars. The government had to react to control the outbreak as well as manage media and international reactions.

A CIO is concerned with making sure the right information gets to the right person at the right time, as well as preventing the wrong person from getting the wrong information at the wrong time. This means making sure that networks, systems, security, policies, and procedures are properly maintained and managed.

In terms of information, there are three concerns that every CIO has to worry about:

1. *Personal information:* loss, theft, or disclosure of personal information such as credit card, medical records, credit history, and confidential information about people.
2. *Intellectual property:* loss, theft, or disclosure of intellectual property such as defense information, trademark secrets, industrial secrets, and case information.
3. *Decision information:* key decisions made using the wrong information to cause business failures, loss of life, loss of reputation, financial losses, safety.

Personal information and intellectual property are information that must be protected from inappropriate disclosure. That means the information should not be disclosed except to authorized personnel. This involves having the right protection mechanisms and deals more with the information security aspects of organization. Decision information is making sure that the right information is there to allow the best decision to be made and deals more with information management or knowledge management and appropriate disclosure.

In this section we discuss information security, information management, and e-discovery. There are many linkages between these three and all involve the life-cycle management of information. Information also may evolve through a sensitivity life cycle where the information may be very sensitive when it is created and devolve toward less sensitivity as time passes. We all know that some military information becomes declassified after a period of time. The same applies to a lot of other information.

From our previous discussions, we note that there may be a primary life cycle for information as well as secondary and tertiary uses as depicted in Figure III.1. This creates additional complexity in managing the protection and the life cycle of information. We need to consider this when looking at information security and management as well as e-discovery. If you consider primary information usage, a credit card transaction is a good example. The client information is collected and stored in a database. Specific protection mechanisms are enabled to protect the data. If you consider PCI compliance requirements, the focus is on the primary information life cycle. Now

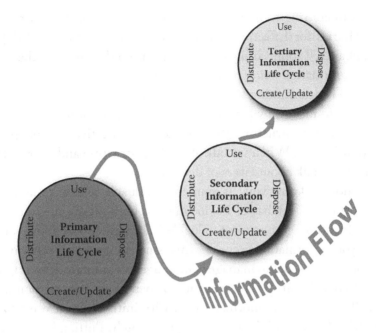

Figure III.1 Information flow primary to other uses.

consider if business intelligence software is used to extract customer information for marketing; this is secondary usage of information. What protection mechanisms are used to protect this information when it is stored on a separate server, perhaps on a workstation or, even worse, on a laptop? What if the information is extracted further and used by an affiliate or your advertising company to send out surveys, or telemarketing, or emails? What protection mechanisms are they using? Are they meeting your standards? If they have a breach, how will it affect you?

Some questions we need to answer to determine our risk management approach include the following:

1. What information are we trying to protect?
2. Where is the information being kept?
3. If this information is disclosed, unavailable, or changed, what are the consequences?
4. What are our current technologies, processes, and policies used to protect this information?
5. Are these technologies, processes, and policies sufficient?

It is interesting to note that in "The 20 Most Important Controls and Metrics for Effective Cyber Defense and Continuous FISMA Compliance,"* John Gilligan did not focus on determining the value of the information being protected. To me, the first and most important step is determining what it is that you are protecting. As a CIO, you need to focus on your most valuable assets, information, and not just on the infrastructure. That is the most effective way of spending your budget. When we talk about infrastructure and information security, we talk about layers of defense.

So, do you know what is your most valuable information? Is the information in databases, in documents, both, many different formats? Identifying your most valuable information will allow you to focus your information security. This is not to ignore all other information or assets, but to manage your budget accordingly. If your Chief Information Security Officer wants to spend hundreds of thousands of dollars on a new information security initiative, you want to be sure that the money is being spent appropriately. Putting in expensive protection mechanisms is useless unless you allocate the appropriate resources and time to manage and maintain. This means allocating some of your staff's time to review logs and respond to incidents. The total cost of ownership should be considered, not just the purchase and installation costs.

When looking at liability, we need to focus on controls to prevent or limit damage. There are a number of controls that we deploy in any organization, depending on the size of the organization, outcomes, budgets, people, and risks. Basically we can divide them into physical and logical controls. A lot of attention focuses on physical controls. We know about them. They have been around for thousands of years. Little has changed in physical controls. We always had watchmen. Watchmen are people who patrol the perimeter and watch to see if bad guys are coming. They had a tower that they could go back to for a changing of the watchman and to get out of the elements. To get a job as a watchman, you had to be known. Someone had to verify your credentials (someone spoke for you, either an elder, a mayor, or

---

* John Gilligan; The 20 Most Important Controls and Metrics for Effective Cyber Defense and Continuous FISMA Compliance; draft 1.0, February 23, 2009; www.gilligangroupinc.com/headlines/2009/feb-23-related/20090223-cag-draft-1.0.html.

someone who had position. For people coming in and leaving town, the watchmen would ask their business. Now we have cameras, a control center, and security guards. They still are watchmen. We also have doors, bars on windows, and alarm systems. We will look further into physical security and pay closer attention to identity, behaviors, and personality types.

Information security is not new. We have managed small quantities of sensitive information for centuries. Passwords were closely guarded secrets. Military plans were carefully guarded. However, as we adopted computers into our businesses and technology development began to accelerate, we began having more secrets. At first, these were stored on paper and in vaults and filing cabinets. Now these secrets are stored as electronic information. As a matter of fact, most of our information is now created and stored electronically. And we are not doing a good job of managing our information. The next chapters deal with information management. Then we take a look at information security.

16

INFORMATION MANAGEMENT

Most CIOs are well aware of the information contained in their applications and databases. Many CIOs are not aware of the information contained in spreadsheets, reports, documents, forms, Websites, and other records. An Aberdeen Group report in June 2009 estimated that 40% of sensitive corporate data is in unstructured formats. This includes file formats such as Adobe Acrobat™ (PDF), PowerPoint™, Word™, Excel™, email, audio, video, instant messaging, and Web pages (HTML). This means that CIOs do not know where 40% of their sensitive data is stored and how well it is managed. In some cases where the organization is focused more on information as opposed to transactions, the volume of sensitive data in an unstructured format is higher.

So what do we mean by *unstructured information*? When looking at a Microsoft Word document, we think we see structure. There are paragraphs, titles, tables, diagrams, sentences, subscripts, and superscripts. This is presentation structure; that is, the formatting of the information into a representation of the information. HypeText Markup Language (HTML) is one of the best examples of presentation languages and the most easily understood. While Word uses a proprietary presentation language, HTML is a World Wide Web (W3C) presentation standard. Almost every Web page that presents information uses HTML.

Basically, information can be structured or unstructured. There is a third kind of information called *metadata*. Metadata is important because it provides context to the content.

- *Structured information* is information that has associated metadata. Typically, structured information consists of databases, although more and more we are seeing XML documents that are structured information.
- *Unstructured information* has little or no metadata. A Microsoft Word document contains little metadata about the content.

Instead, it has information about how the document is presented, such as bolding, font, paragraph, page, which is presentation markup. HTML is a markup language used on the Internet to present the content of Web pages.

- *Metadata* is data about other data. Metadata adds context to content. An item of metadata may be described as an individual datum. Schemas define the structure of a database system and, in the case of XML, describe the datum. Metadata can also be used to format or present the information such as HTML or Word documents.

Managing information as a corporate asset is critical to every organization. Before buying into any technology, we need to determine what is important to the business. Is there IP that should be protected? How about personal information and the requirements from PCI? Do you have HR and medical information? Is your organization responsible for information under HIPAA or some other act or regulation? How well is your important information managed? If your organization is being sued, could you easily gather all the relevant information? What does it mean to your organization if the information is lost, stolen, or compromised?

The Value of Information

There are three basic reasons why information has value:

1. Reduces uncertainty
2. Influences behavior
3. Has market value

Any information that has positive value may also have negative value. Putting complete trust in the information we receive may be a bad thing. We need to filter the information based on verification of facts, calculations, estimations, or guesses. The more trust we put into the information we receive without verification, the greater the potential for bad decisions.

1. *Reduces uncertainty:* The right information at the right time to the right person makes for good decisions. The exact opposite is also true: the wrong information to the wrong person at

the wrong time makes for a bad decision. We make decisions that affect the organization, our budget, or some other economic pressure and must have information to bring about a desired outcome. The more information is based on facts and calculations, the better the decision. Transactional information provides certainty in terms of cash flow for retail and financial organizations. The accuracy of that information is very important.

2. *Influences behavior:* Information that influences behavior may have negative or positive economic consequences. Winning the lottery may have very positive economic consequences for a group of workers; however, there may be a negative economic consequence to the employer having to hire and train new workers. Receiving information about a negative financial situation at home may induce a worker to steal. This will have a negative, economic impact on the employer. Information about an individual may trigger emotional behavior that may be negative such as a distraught spouse getting revenge on their estranged partner. The same can be said about good or bad performance reviews. These may have a positive or negative effect on the employee. This does link to thinking about risk culture and risk tolerance. When information changes behavior, we have to reconsider how this behavior change may change the risk management profile of an individual and perhaps the risk culture of the organization.

3. *Has market value:* Information has value that is determined by how much someone is willing to pay to obtain that information. Personal information has value in terms of identity theft and fraud. IP has value in terms of competitive knowledge, intelligence, espionage, research, time-to-market for competing products, and even national interests.

Even small pieces of information can provide important pieces of a bigger picture, as we have seen in espionage and criminal investigations. It is detective work that uncovers the minute details that lead to the arrest and conviction of a felon. Forensics is about the details, whether it is looking through gigabytes of data to find and piece together a compromised event or sifting through hours of surveillance to determine who was in the computer room at the time of the event. Not all data is valuable. However, we sometimes do not put the right value on our information.

Information + Knowledge = Value

Information by itself has little value. Even the most valuable intellectual property has little value unless you know what it is and what to do with it. If a hacker broke into a computer system at Sandia National Laboratories and copied information from a system, that information may not mean much. If there is no market for the information that he can determine or find, then the information is of little value. It could be a formula for a new form of hydrocarbon that could replace gas and burn clean in our combustion engines with very little pollution. If the hacker knew that it was the formula for a new form of hydrocarbon, the next thing he needs to do is to find a market. It is a rather specialized marketplace and oil companies may not want this information disclosed. The important message is that information without context *and* knowledge may not have much value. However, the fact that there is applied knowledge to some information means it has value. The more applied knowledge, the more the value.

In his book entitled *Spies among Us*, author Ira Winkler (2005) discussed espionage. He divides it into two major categories: economic and military. The military speaks for itself and if your organization is in the business of building, supplying, manufacturing, or researching military weapons, then your organization is at risk for major espionage. Most organizations fall into the economic category and there are many people seeking your information. And you may not even be their primary target. The point is that the more knowledge that is captured as information, the more value that information has. It may present danger to your employees as your competitors and foreign governments may want that information.

Or look at it differently in a graph (Figure 16.1). There is a correlation between increasing knowledge that is stored as information and the increasing value of the information. Information is not a physical asset. It exists as bits and bytes in a computer and network. It is important to note that it is difficult to detect when your information is stolen. You may only find out after your competitor has upgraded its product that incorporates some of your new features. Unlike a physical

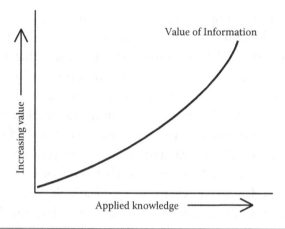

Figure 16.1   Value of information.

theft, there are few signs that information is stolen—especially if the theft is done by an authorized person who copies the files and sends them home.

In 1997, writers Leif Edvinsson and Michael Malone wrote a book on *Intellectual Capital*. In their book they noted that there is more than just tangible assets, that there are also intangible assets. Microsoft and Apple are prime examples of companies that have significant intellectual capital tied up in intangible assets. These intangible assets were called *human capital*:

Human capital + Structural capital = Intellectual capital

- *Human capital:* The combined knowledge, skills, innovation, and ability of employees to meet the tasks at hand. It also includes company values, culture, and philosophy. Human capital cannot be owned by the organization.
- *Structural capital:* Hardware, software, buildings, databases, patents, trademarks, and everything else left when employees go home. Structural capital also includes customer capital and relationships with key customers and can be owned, traded, or sold.

This also links us to that new employee, the knowledge worker. In essence, many of the intangible assets are tied up in your knowledge workers. When we consider the value of information, we need to understand knowledge. A simple example is giving a credit card to a sixteen-year-old from the jungles of the Amazon. That person has never seen a department store and knows nothing about credit, let alone credit cards and how to use them. Compare that to giving a credit card to your own sixteen-year-old daughter and watch as she flies out the door to meet her friends and go on a spending spree.

It takes years of education and learning to develop knowledge workers. That knowledge is your intangible asset and, if used carefully, will increase the wealth and prosperity of your company. It is knowing what to do with information that makes it valuable.

We need to determine what the organization's crown jewels are, what the important information assets are, what the important records are, and how to manage and protect them. So how do you do that?

There are four questions you should ask to help you understand the value of your information:

1. *Does this information reduce uncertainty?* Information can be used to help reduce uncertainty in making decisions. This is a very broad category and can include almost any information that helps people make informed decisions. There is a very large range in the value of this information, from information about a proposed merger/acquisition to information about the type of furniture being purchased for the office.

2. *Does this information influence behavior?* Information about an individual's behavior is very sensitive. In some cases, in the hands of a criminal, it can be used for blackmail and cause considerable damage to an organization as well as the individual. You need to think about personnel files, customer files, medical files, and any other information about people that your organization may have in its custody.

3. *Does this information have market value?* Intellectual property is the first information asset that should be considered. This could include research, copyright, nondisclosure, product, process, and any other information that may have market value. There is also information that has intelligence value. Simple information like market literature, email lists, company directories, product information, marketing plans, sales

plans, customer lists, personal files, or anything with credit card information that could be used to assume a person's identity so a criminal can commit fraud.

4. *If someone outside your organization knows about or gets this information, can it harm the organization, individual, or a group of people?* This relates to spies, criminals, terrorists, and fringe groups who may use this information to cause harm in some manner. You also have to think about the media and, if they got this information, could it harm the organization? There are many stories in the newspapers, Twitter, or any of the myriad newsletters, Rich Site Summary (RSS) feeds, and blogs that could damage reputation or cause significant efforts to manage damage control. This also goes to employees and getting information on another employee that could cause the employee harm. A simple example is inappropriate jokes that have racial overtones. These may offend employees to the point of taking legal action against the organization.

Some factors to consider about your information are provided in Table 16.1.

Table 16.1 Factors about Your Information That Should Be Considered

FACTOR	DEFINITION	CONSIDERATION
Freshness	Most current information	Most current date of information; reporting or other documents; stale or old information
Relevance	Information may be sufficient, insufficient, filtered, or diffused	Related to freshness, may also be a component of other information (i.e., report or spreadsheet)
Volume	Quantity of information	Some filings such as pharmaceutical testing are voluminous; case files, e-discovery
Location	Single location or multiple locations	Electronic information proliferates and may have wide distribution
Source	Origin of information	Single, original source of information (i.e., oldest date)
Creator/author	Individual(s) who created document	Authoritative, subjective, bias
Versions	Modified version of information usually document format	Drafts and partial copies
Duplications	Multiple copies of information	May be in different formats

Who determines the value of information? At an organizational level or at a business level, it is the individual responsible for the information who must answer that question. At the individual level, it is up to the user to determine if the information has value. The CIO cannot determine the value of the information except for information within the CIO's control (system configurations, policies, procedures, applications, etc.). Once information has a value, it is a combined effort to determine the necessary level of protection. The CIO, CISO, and the IT department can support the business in determining what protection mechanisms will work in the infrastructure.

Information can also have a negative value. If information is kept too long or not properly destroyed according to a life-cycle schedule, then there may be liability associated with that information. It is important to have appropriate life-cycle management of information.

The next sections deal with steps you need to take to help your organization improve your information management. As described in the Federal Information Security Management Act (FISMA), there are distinct steps that you need to manage your valuable information. The first and most important is to classify your information; that is, where your information is stored and what is valuable.

Classify Your Information: Value and Categories

Classification of information is divided into two parts:

1. Value/sensitivity of information
2. Categories of information

The first part deals with determining the value and/or sensitivity of the information. What information is of value, and what information is sensitive? Information may have value and may be sensitive, or it could just be sensitive in protecting an individual or decision.

The second part deals with the categories of information: how would you put different information into groups to allow you to determine the life cycle of the information? That is, to purge old or little value information from your systems when appropriate. Life cycle deals with information that has decreased in value to a point where it can no longer be considered useful. On the flip side, sometimes information can also increase in negative value if it is kept too long.

Value/Sensitivity of Information

Information comes in many formats and today is stored in many places. From databases to memory sticks and paper, we have so many ways of presenting and storing information. And with the Internet, there are more opportunities for your information to go outside your organization. So questions that should be answered about your information include the following:

- What information is of high value to the organization? That is, if the information is lost or stolen and disclosed to persons other than authorized personnel, what is the impact to the organization?
- Where is this information stored? In many instances, the information has been replicated and resides in many places and many formats. The application with that sensitive personal and customer data has been moved to a PowerPoint presentation and shared via email with twenty other people who need to know. It was also copied to a spreadsheet so the data could be manipulated. And do not forget the executive reports; the information was presented to the CFO as part of the monthly review of customer forecasts.
- So, do you know what is sensitive and where it is?

We often identify sensitive information with transactional information such as credit card data. As pointed out in many cases, the primary information cycle is very well protected. That is the aim of Payment Card Industry Data Security Compliance—to protect credit card data. In many cases, it is the secondary or tertiary usage that is compromised. The difficult part is to identify those secondary and tertiary usages of your information. Some of your sensitive information is moved into different storage media and the same rules you use for the primary information cycle no longer apply. So how do you manage this?

The first step is to classify your information. What information is personal, customer, IP, or unique process? The idea is to determine that if the information is lost, stolen, inappropriately modified, or disclosed, there will be some impact and some consequence. We know that if personal information is stolen by hackers, there is an impact and a consequence. We can predict with reasonable certainty that if IP is stolen, there will be an impact and a consequence. The impact may be that your competitor leapfrogs you with a more competitive product and the consequence is loss of market share and loss of revenue.

So how do you classify your information? There are a number of steps that you need to take to classify your information, as outlined below:

1. *Determine an information security classification schema that you will use to classify your assets.* Information should be put into categories according to the impact and consequences a compromise will have in terms of confidentiality, availability, or integrity. FIPS 199 (pp. 2–3; Federal Information Processing Standards) and the Canadian government use a simple classification schema of High, Moderate, and Low. The Canadian classification schema is included in Appendix D.

2. *Develop labeling for your information.* This may seem trivial but your information should have labels. Better yet, if you can embed this labeling into the documents and information using something like XML, you will be better able to electronically control your information. It is like the military where they stamp "TOP SECRET" on paper files and put everything in folders or envelopes so prying eyes cannot see the information.

3. *Develop information handling policies and procedures.* This should be very true for any information identified with a high impact. In the BC government, "Cabinet" documents, those handled by the ministers and top executives, had special procedures such as double-bagging sensitive material to avoid any embarrassment of inadvertently opening and reading this material.

4. *Document the policies and procedures.* Once you have written policies and procedures, you need to document them in a way that will allow people to access the policies and procedures quickly and easily. This was a problem in the BC government, where it was difficult to find the relevant policies and procedures for just about anything.

5. *Awareness and training.* You need to promote awareness among and provide training to people to realize that the

information they are handling is sensitive and must be treated accordingly.

6. *Identify your information assets.* This includes primary, secondary, and tertiary usage of sensitive information. You need to understand the business requirements for your sensitive information.

7. *Review your existing controls and procedures.* In the BC government, we used directories within Microsoft's servers to store our documents (called Shared File and Print). All documents were stored in the same server with no regard for the sensitivity of the information. The only protection was New Technology File System (NTFS). This does not preclude administrators from viewing, modifying, or deleting files. Make sure your controls are commensurate with the value of your information.

8. *Develop an implementation plan.* Make sure you have sufficient time for consultation. This will help you when you deploy the classification schema.

If you follow FIPS 199 as described in the section "FISMA, NIST, and FIPS" (see Chapter 17), you will look at your information and determine the impact of a compromise in confidentiality, availability, or integrity. FIPS 199 uses broad impact categories of Low, Moderate, or High. If you want to get more granular in your measurement of impact, you can use the table in Appendix C (Risk Impact Scale), which will allow you to measure financial impact and define the potential impact and consequence in more detail.

Categories of Information

We know that organizations have sensitive information. In a broad sense, sensitive information falls into categories such as

- IP (industrial property—research, product, service, inventions, industrial design; copyright—artistic or literary works, designs, images)
- Personal (identifiable information about a person including employee files, credit records, medical records, dispute

information, customer files, any unique personally identifiable information about a person)
- Contractual (agreements, memorandums of understanding, nondisclosure)
- Processes (methodologies, procedures such as incident response, business continuity)
- Financial (not publicly reported)
- Transactional (case files, credit card, customer, shipping)
- Military and government secrets

That helps us understand how our valuable information is categorized. However, there is a lot more information used by organizations. That information runs the organization. It helps people understand what is important and who to talk to when there is a problem with their computer. This is the broader aspect of classifying information into categories. Records managers are more concerned with this aspect of classification. These categories are used to help determine the life cycle of information. In any organization there are similar categories and there are specialized categories relating to the industry segment or some aspect of the organization. We can easily categorize some information, whereas some other information is more difficult to classify. Here are some example classifications of information:

- *Intellectual property:* documents pertaining to trade secrets or proprietary information that has substantial value to the organization.
- *Personal information:* customer, employee, or other personal information such as medical records, health records, or insurance claims.
- *Operational procedures:* information relating to the operations of business units such as manufacturing, bill processing, decisions, business continuity, and disaster recovery.
- *Facility, engineering, network:* diagrams relating to the building, infrastructure, or network that provides valuable information about building or network layouts.
- *Administrative:* documents related to org charts and phone lists.
- *Financial:* documents related to financial information, such as spreadsheets, contracts, orders, and invoices.

- *Marketing and sales:* documents relating to sales and marketing programs.
- *Regulatory or legal:* documents related to statutory requirements or documents on hold due to e-discovery or court proceedings.
- *Research:* documents relating to research.
- *Miscellaneous:* the all-important category where everything else is dumped.

Classifying information takes a lot of work. While I was managing the records unit, the records analysts were being asked to help with classifying records for various business units. The research often took six months to carefully understand the business requirements and map the information into categories. The important point is to understand the business requirements. It allows the analysts to grasp what information is important and what information is less important. Once it is understood what is important, you can create appropriate controlled vocabularies to improve retention and search capabilities.

Controlled Vocabulary, Taxonomies, Keywords, and Search

How do you find information on the Internet? You "Google it." The company that currently owns searching on the Internet is now a verb. Google is the established search engine on the Internet and there are few challengers. How many remember AltaVista? AltaVista was launched in 1995 as a full-text searchable database of a large part of the World Wide Web. The search engine was powered by twenty multiprocessor machines with 130 GB of memory and 500 GB of disk storage in 1998. Traffic increased from 300,000 search requests on the first day to more than 80 million search requests a day by 1997. Compare this to Google today and we can see a very large difference. Google has over one million servers in data centers around the world and processes over one billion search requests each day. Google has the dominant market share in the U.S. market, with 65.6% of all searches going to Google. Google indexes billions of Web pages. Users search for information using keywords and operators (using special symbols to allow you to specify search parameters). This begs the question: How do you find information at your organization?

As a CIO, you are responsible for your information at your organization. Given that 40% of your information is unstructured, where is it stored? How do your users get access to it? Assuming you have controls over your sensitive information, how do users who may have a need and the right to see get access? How do you make sure that that information is not going somewhere else or is being viewed, moved, changed, or destroyed by users?

Ideally, you structure all your information so you can put context to your content; that is, using metadata you can control and find your information. This is the major reason you need taxonomies. So what is the difference between taxonomies and keywords?

- *Keywords* arc thc words used to search for information in search engines such as Google. Keywords usually refer to a specific topic. Using keywords to search using a search engine means that the search engine has indexed the information in a database or, in simpler terms, created a detailed list of words arranged alphabetically. The search engine searches for all information in the database containing the specific word or words and displays the results in a list. Normally the word or words are highlighted in some manner, and a reference such as a URL links the search results to the Web page or item.
- *Taxonomy* is the practice and science of classification according to natural relationships. Taxonomy is derived from the science of classifying organisms. Taxonomy has been expanded to include aspects of information management and not just used as a scientific method of classification. Taxonomy has its foundation in its Greek roots *taxis* (arrangement) and *nomos* (law). Taxonomy separates elements of a group or division (taxon) into subgroups or parts (taxa). Under Drupal (open source content management platform), taxonomy is created from vocabularies that contain related terms.

Whether using keywords or taxonomies, we are talking about controlled vocabularies. The next section discusses controlled vocabularies, defining what it is, why it is needed, and what standards are available to help your organization better manage your information.

Controlled Vocabularies

In any organization there is vocabulary that is used to describe the business. There is vocabulary that is used to describe IP, personal information, sensitive information, and processes, events that all correlate to the business and the sector. This vocabulary may be translated into multiple languages, adding a level of complexity to managing information. So why do we need a controlled vocabulary? According to the National Information Standards Organization Z39.19-2005 standard "Guidelines for the Construction, Format, and Management of Monolingual Controlled Vocabularies,"

> Vocabulary control is used to improve the effectiveness of information storage and retrieval systems, Web navigation systems, and other environments that seek to both identify and locate desired content via some sort of description using language. The primary purpose of vocabulary control is to achieve consistency in the description of content objects and to facilitate retrieval.

There is a need for vocabulary control because of two basic features of natural language:

1. Two or more words or terms can be used to represent a single concept.
2. Two or more words can have the same spelling but represent different concepts.

And this is only about a single language. When we add multiple languages, we can get multiple spellings, concepts, and meanings. For now we focus on a single language—English. English has expanded from about 5,000 words in Shakespeare's day to over 600,000 words today according to the *Oxford English Dictionary* (2nd edition). Estimates are that we add approximately 25,000 new words every year.

We all know that the English language has many words that have many meanings. For example, "fiber" can mean fiber as in plant or animal tissues, having character such as a morale fiber, or fiber in terms of optical fiber used for communications. We also know that we can represent the same concept with different words, such as *confidential, private, secret, protected, restricted,* or *privy.* We also have compound terms that represent a single concept, such as *duct tape* or *optical fiber*; if these words are separated, the meaning is lost.

So according to the "Guidelines for Monolingual Controlled Vocabularies," a controlled vocabulary is defined as follows: A list of terms that have been enumerated explicitly. This list is controlled by and is available from a controlled vocabulary registration authority. All terms in a controlled vocabulary *must* have an unambiguous, nonredundant definition.

Note: This is a design goal that may not be true in practice; it depends on how strict the controlled vocabulary registration authority is regarding registration of terms into a controlled vocabulary.

At a minimum, the following two rules *must* be enforced:

1. If the same term is commonly used to mean different concepts, then its name is explicitly qualified to resolve this ambiguity. *Note: This rule does not apply to synonym rings.*
2. If multiple terms are used to mean the same thing, one of the terms is identified as the preferred term in the controlled vocabulary and the other terms are listed as synonyms or aliases.

Controlled vocabularies are used for organizing information and providing a mechanism to detect the usage and movement of sensitive information such as in data loss prevention. There are five objectives of controlled vocabularies:

1. *Translation:* provides a means of converting the natural language of authors, indexers, and users into a vocabulary that can be used for indexing and retrieval.
2. *Consistency:* promotes uniformity in term format and the assignment of terms.
3. *Indication of relationships:* indicates semantic relationships among terms.
4. *Label and browse:* provides consistent and clear hierarchies in a navigation system to help users locate desired content objects.
5. *Retrieval:* serves as a searching aid in locating content objects.

Controlled vocabularies are used to describe content by assigning terms to represent metadata associated with content objects or organizing content as shown in Figure 16.2.

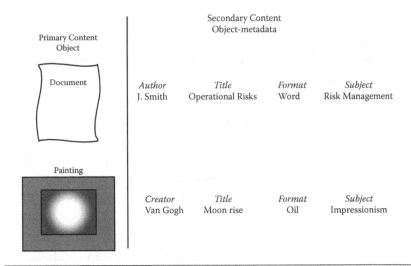

Figure 16.2   Primary and secondary content object example.

- *Terms:* one or more words used to represent a concept. Terms are selected from natural language. If multiple terms can be used to describe the same thing, then one of the terms should be the preferred term.
- *Content objects:* any item that is to be described for inclusion in an information retrieval system, website, or other source of information. Content objects may be electronic such as documents, PDF files, or spreadsheets or may exist as other entities such as paintings, sculptures, computers, books, or paper records. There are two classes of content objects:
  - Primary is the item itself, whether it is in physical form (print, movie, tape, DVD) or electronic form
  - Secondary is the metadata that describes the primary content object

There are four important principles to help guide the design and development of controlled vocabularies:

1. *Eliminating ambiguity.* Ambiguity occurs in natural language when a word or phrase has more than one meaning. The term *mercury* represents four different concepts: automobile, planet, metal, and mythology. A controlled vocabulary must compensate for ambiguity by assigning one meaning to each term.

2. *Controlling synonyms.* Synonymy is where a concept can be represented by multiple terms having the same or similar meaning. The term *computer* can also be described as a laptop, desktop, PC, workstation, and even a Mac. A controlled vocabulary must compensate for synonymy through a single preferred term. The other terms should be listed as nonpreferred terms.

3. *Establishing relationships among terms.* Concept objects may have different semantic relationships such as hierarchical or associative. A controlled vocabulary may use semantic relationships to describe groups of terms.

4. *Selection, testing, and validation of terms.* The process of selecting terms that should be included in a controlled vocabulary involves consulting with various sources of words and phrases and the following criteria: natural language used to describe the content objects, language of the users, and the needs and priorities of the organization. The controlled vocabulary needs to be tested and validated by users.

Maintaining a controlled vocabulary will have a positive impact on information retrieval. The effectiveness of information retrieval is measured by two parameters:

1. *Recall:* a measure of a search system's ability to retrieve all relevant content objects. Recall is expressed as a percentage, calculated by dividing the number of retrieved relevant content objects by the number of all relevant content objects in the collection.

2. *Precision:* a measure of a search system's ability to retrieve only relevant content objects. Precision is expressed as a percentage, calculated by dividing the number of retrieved relevant content objects by the total number of content objects retrieved.

Recall and precision tend to be inverse ratios. When your recall goes up, precision goes down. Both recall and precision are directly affected by the type of controlled vocabulary. There are four types of controlled vocabularies. They are determined by the increasing complexity of the structure and the level of control. Figure 16.3 reflects these controlled vocabulary types (list, synonym ring, taxonomy, and thesaurus). As

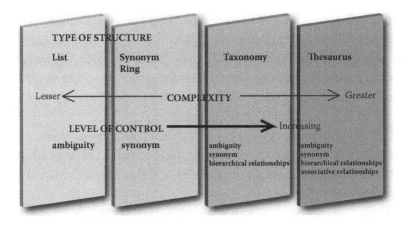

Figure 16.3 Controlled vocabularies structure versus control.

the complexity of the structure increases, so does the level of control. The better the control, the better the recall and precision. Table 16.2 provides the definition and level of control for each structure.

The intent of a controlled vocabulary is to make it easier to search and find relevant information—with the emphasis on find. We use the two metrics from above—recall and precision—about finding relevant information. A controlled vocabulary defines the terms from word, user, and organizational perspectives to improve the searchability and

Table 16.2 Types of Structure

STRUCTURE	DEFINITION	LEVEL OF CONTROL PROVIDED
List	Sometimes called *pick list* or *keywords* Limited set of terms arranged as simple alphabetical list or in some logical manner	Reduces ambiguity by providing a meaning for each term on the list
Synonym ring	Set of terms considered equivalent for the purposes of information retrieval	Use of multiple terms that have similar meanings or concept Used for retrieval to allow users to find the concept with different words or phrases
Taxonomy	Controlled vocabulary consisting of preferred terms connected in a hierarchy or polyhierarchy	Adds hierarchical relationships between terms through a classification schema
Thesaurus	Controlled vocabulary arranged in a known order and structured so various relationships among terms are identified	Adds association relationships between terms by grouping words into similar meanings (semantics)

finding of information. With each type of controlled vocabulary listed above, the first step is to define the terms. This will standardize search terminology. If I call it a widget and you call it a gadget, yet we both mean the same thing, unless we use synonyms we will never find each other's terms. I will discuss each type of controlled vocabulary: lists, synonym rings, taxonomy, and thesaurus.

List. A list of terms is useful. The problem is that we associate a list of words with searching for documents or records. A list of words has little value unless the words are defined in terms. Terms are used for searching and indexing.

We should not confuse terms with words or keywords. In records management, we often use keywords. Keywords are created by the user to add some metadata to their record, making the record more searchable for the user. Unfortunately, each user creates his own keywords. These keywords are never standardized; in other words, the terms are not defined. Without a standardized and controlled vocabulary, we do not get the maximum value out of our information. And it may be important information that can be used to make better decisions. Sometimes information is all we have and if it is bad information, we will make bad decisions. The better you manage your information, the better the decisions made.

When I was creating a strategic plan for knowledge management for a ministry within the BC government, I was adamant about creating a taxonomy or a set of taxonomies. However, the manager for information systems could not see the value in creating taxonomies. He preferred to create keywords. It was a matter of scope. A taxonomy would serve the ministry better in the longer term. A list would enable him to get something accomplished this year in enabling the storing of records. In the end, it was not my decision and my recommendation was to create a standardized list of keywords that could serve the ministry. At least we would define the terms in the list so everyone called the same object by the same term.

Synonym Ring. While the guidelines for controlled vocabulary consider a synonym ring as a type of controlled vocabulary, it is different from a list, taxonomy, or thesaurus. If you are using a search engine and indexing your information, a synonym ring cannot be used during the indexing process. A synonym ring is useful for retrieval. Because synonymy is the same concept described by multiple terms, a synonym ring is useful if the research is trying to locate something like medical terms that describe a number of concept objects using different terms yet would have the same concept or context. An example is speech disorders, which also may be described as speech defects, defective speech, speech deficiency, and flaws in speech.

Synonym rings is a set of terms considered equivalent for retrieval purposes. Rings usually are lists that allow a searcher access to all content objects or database entries containing any one of the terms on the lists. It is still better if you establish a preferred term, and all others terms that describe the concept will be listed as nonpreferred terms with reference to the preferred term. Synonym rings are generally used for retrieval systems and provide access to content represented in a natural language.

Taxonomy. A taxonomy is a controlled vocabulary arranged in a hierarchical manner using preferred terms. In my strategic plan for the ministry, I identified several levels of taxonomies that could be used. I defined four levels of taxonomies: government; ministry; communities of practice, and folksonomies.

1. *Government:* The first was corporate- or government-wide. This was to establish a controlled vocabulary of government terms to facilitate and improve information management and sharing of information across ministries.
2. *Ministry:* The second level was ministry-specific taxonomies. Each ministry had specific goals and mandated outcomes. As an example, the Justice Sector, which was comprised of the Ministry of Attorney General and the Ministry of Public Safety Solicitor General, had the common goal of justice for the people of British Columbia.
3. *Communities of Practice:* Each ministry was further divided into Police Services, Court Services, Criminal Justice Branch, and Corrections, which were directly involved with the delivery of justice. Each of these branches had its own mandate and priorities. These branches represented the third level, Communities of Practice, which may have other areas of other ministries involved in creating, managing, operating, or contributing to specific outcomes. Some examples of Communities of Practice are Policy Analysts (each ministry had one or more policy analysts involved in legislation or high-

level policies), Strategic Human Resources, and Ministry Information Security Officers.

4. *Folksonomies:* A final level was something that I interpreted from a SharePoint document called "Folksonomies," which are user-based terms that could be used to search content. If you look at records management or SharePoint or any content management software, these user-based terms could also be described as keywords. Keywords are words or terms that a user describes as metadata to search for a specific document.

From an organization perspective, a taxonomy may be useful as a subject map to an organization's content. The taxonomy should reflect the organization's purpose, industry, functions, responsibilities, products, services, research, technologies, business, and other elements of the organization. The following is a list of taxonomy elements that has been compiled by a number of researchers. The list offers eight perspectives or groups of taxonomies that apply to an organization. It should be noted that more perspectives might not increase the effectiveness of the organization.

Organizational perspectives of taxonomic elements (Sharma et al., 2010) include

1. *Industry Segments:* Marketing/positioning/competitive intelligence perspective; industry segments may overlap with products and services.
2. *Organizational Functions:* The organization breakdown of a business or organization by function or responsibility.
3. *Business Relationships:* The intensities and types of other companies or organizations a business deals with, including customers, vendors, regulators, associations, partners, etc.
4. *Business Issues and Events:* Economic, legal, Mergers and Acquisitions (M&A), regulatory, environmental, labor, safety, other government interfaces, etc.
5. *Products and Services:* Products sold; Maintenance, Repairs and Operations (MRO) materials; indirect services; direct materials; and services purchased.
6. *Technologies:* Applicable to the industry or industries in which the firm participates. Basic or applied sciences are also included as appropriate.

Table 16.3   Associative Relationships

RELATIONSHIP TYPE	EXAMPLE
Cause/effect	Accident/injury
Process/agent	Velocity measurement/speedometer
Process/counter-agent	Fire/flame retardant
Action/product	Writing/publication
Raw material/product	Peanuts/peanut butter
Concept or object/property	Steel alloy/corrosion resistance

7. *Geography:* Referring to location, particularly region or jurisdiction.

8. *Document or Record Types:* This perspective provides valuable reduction of results based on the document's purpose and its connection to the information need.

A corporate taxonomy may be viewed as a conceptual map, an information access tool, and a communications and training device all at the same time, providing history, expertise, and corporate information that can assist business activities.

In the realm of digital resources, Noy and McGiness (2001) suggest that taxonomies are particularly useful to (1) share common understanding of the structure of information among people or software agents; (2) enable reuse of domain knowledge; (3) make domain assumptions explicit; (4) separate domain knowledge from the operational knowledge; and (5) analyze domain knowledge.

Thesaurus. Most of us associate a thesaurus with groups of words with similar (synonyms) and opposite (antonyms) meanings. In this context, a thesaurus adds more than hierarchical groups. A thesaurus uses other types of relationships, equivalence, hierarchical, and associative. Synonymy is an equivalence relationship; taxonomy is a hierarchical relationship. The only one we have not explored is associative relationships. There are a number of associative relationships that could be used in a thesaurus. Some examples are included in Table 16.3.

Summary

Most of us can immediately see the benefits of using a controlled vocabulary as a necessary element of information management. The first benefit is improving the ability to find information. The second benefit is to help us determine when our most valuable information is accessed, modified, or removed. To do this we need data loss prevention or digital rights management. The purchase of any product will require a controlled vocabulary anyway to make the product effective. Otherwise, what are you looking for or trying to prevent from leaving the organization? A controlled vocabulary is essential once you classify your information assets.

Identify Information Assets

Do you know where your valuable information is stored? Are there lots of duplicate copies? Once you have classified your information and defined a controlled vocabulary, you need to look at where you store your information.

There are two ways to manage information:

1. *Structured information* is information that is typically transactional, such as customer, credit card, shipping, case,* employee (time sheets, expenses, training), and managed through an application and a database. In some cases this is now managed outside the organization; however, the information is still proprietary to the organization.
2. *Unstructured information* is typically working documents, which includes spreadsheets, Word documents, presentations, HTML, graphs, charts, pictures, images, movies, etc.). In some cases, the information is managed outside the organization using a third-party service provider.

The volume of structured and unstructured information varies by organization. This is based on the type of organization and the type of work. In the case where knowledge workers comprise a high percentage of the workforce, there tends to be a higher percentage of unstructured information than structured information. For example, consulting firms tend to have a higher percentage of knowledge workers and more intellectual property than trucking firms.

---

* Case work can be associated with processing claims, legal, social, financial, and customer.

To determine where your information is stored, you need to consider the types of information your organization processes. In any case, you will have both structured and unstructured information. You will need to consider what information is extracted from your structured information and stored in an unstructured format. This is a secondary or tertiary usage of information, the primary usage being transactional. In other cases, the primary usage is stored in an unstructured format such as research papers. The data for the research paper may come from a database.

Your analysis of your information assets needs to determine the following:

- What information does your organization have?
- What type of information (structured or unstructured) does your organization have?
- What storage does your organization have? Does your organization have shared drives, personal systems (policy allows personal employee computers to be used), memory sticks, DVDs, CDs, tapes, other backup media, home drives, collaborative or social networks, instant messaging, email?
- Do your policies allow outside collaboration? The sharing of information using Microsoft's collaboration suite (Groove™, SharePoint™), GoToMeetings™, Google apps, content management collaboration such as Alfresco™, Open Text™.
- Do your policies cover email retention? Email is now considered one of the most likely sources of information during e-discovery. E-discovery is the process of discovering all relevant information for litigation. There is a chapter dealing with e-discovery later in this book (see Chapter 18).
- Do you know what files are stored on your systems? Are you familiar with all the different extensions used to describe all file formats? Do you allow .MOV and .MP3 files to be stored on your network? Are you sure you are not breaking copyright laws through a lack of policies? In the BC government, we restricted the transfer of certain file types such as .EXE through filters at the Internet gateway. The way around that was to rename the file extension to something

benign and send the file through the gateway. Once we had received the file, we simply renamed the file extension back to its original format.

Some considerations when you are looking at your unstructured information include

- *Information stores:* Includes disk drives, tapes, other media (what system is your information stored in?).
- *Storage space:* How much storage space is being used. Should include information like file count, size of files, percentage of disk space.
- *File extensions:* What types of files are stored on your systems.
- *File owners:* Group files by owners.
- *Duplicate files:* Identify duplicates (multiple copies of same file). Note that there also may be multiple versions of a file as a file goes through iterations during edits, especially when there is collaboration on a file.
- *Storage charges:* Represents the amount of money being allocated, such as in a chargeback setting where there is a cost associated with storage. This could be real (outsourced storage) or calculated to represent a cost to the business unit (in some instances, IT is bundled into a single expense item and the cost of storage is buried in that cost).

Some additional information that may be useful and will be discussed in the information life cycle includes *last access* and *last modification* dates. These may be useful in determining when to move these files to less expensive storage or to delete or archive the information.

Determining where your information is stored is critical in developing an overall information management strategy for your organization. You may look at restricting where you store your sensitive data to improve your controls. This can be done by policies, practices, technology, and procedures.

Information Has a Life Cycle

How long do you keep information? That is a very important question that you need to answer. Google wants to keep everything forever.

Google has petabytes* of information. The current estimates from researchers indicate that the amount of digital information on the Internet will exceed a zetabyte some time in 2010. Your organization will not store that much information. Even as disk prices go down and the cost to store huge volumes of information reaches into pennies per gigabyte, you do not want to store all your information forever. Information has a value. In some cases, that value could be negative. If the information is wrong (we know that sometimes we are given erroneous information) and it is used to make a decision, wrong decisions could be made, costing the organization money. It could even cost you your job.

We have to recognize that most of us are poor records managers. We do not have great filing systems. Even worse, some of us keep everything. For individuals, it is an inconvenience and annoyance to collect information and manage information. For organizations, it is critical. So do you have information retention schedules as part of your information management strategy? This includes your databases; too often we do not consider that our databases continue to grow and a lot of data is no longer valid. So how do you manage the life cycle of your databases?

If you are following the steps, you would have classified your information, and determined its value and where it is located. The next step is to determine how long you keep your information. It depends on regulatory, legal, operational, compliance, and business requirements. For example, corporations are required by the Canadian Revenue Agency (CRA) to retain their financial records for two years after the dissolution of the corporation. The CRA further requires merged or amalgamated corporations to retain all financial records of each amalgamated business on the basis that the new corporation is a continuation of the amalgamated corporation.

To determine the life cycle of information, you consider how long you *need* to keep information based on how long you *must* keep information. The information life cycle should be based on regulatory, statutory, legal, operational, and organizational requirements. As an example, provincial governments divide documents into administrative and operational and treat all documents as records. There are two

---

* Petabyte is one million gigabytes; a zetabyte is one million million gigabytes.

classifications of records: the Administrative Records Classification System (ARCS) and the Operational Records Classification System (ORCS). ARCS, or administrative records, are documents that provide administrative or housekeeping support to the government. ORCS, or operational records, are related to the mandate or program delivery of an entity (branch, department, agency, or business unit) within government. A detailed analysis of records is done prior to developing ARCS and ORCS for a department or agency. Then a schedule is determined to help decide the life cycle of records. The life cycle is simple: create, use, and dispose. Disposal could mean destruction of the document or archival. Archival is determined by regulatory, statutory, legal, or the requirement to retain organizational history regarding decisions.

Organizational decisions are important history of organizations. In some cases these decisions should be captured to help understand how and why decisions were made, such as in the case of the Aboriginal Treaty process. The treaty process takes upward of twenty years to negotiate one treaty. What was said ten, fifteen, or twenty years ago about a specific point of negotiation will be forgotten unless there is a record of the decision and the background information that supports the process of arriving at the decision. This also may be true in legal cases where it may take five to ten years to complete a trial.

There are a lot of different categories and a lot of different documents. Keep in mind that a document could be a picture, video, map, movie, graph, report, and in many different formats. It could also be on many different media types, so storage and retrieval are important considerations especially if you need to keep something for a long time. This may require different technology. We have witnessed the evolution of technology and for some of us we have seen different media evolve as technical innovations have pushed the boundaries of storage media. Just as an example, I remember 5.25-inch floppy disk drives that stored an amazing 320 KB of information. Compare that with memory sticks that now store 32 GB. The obsolescence factor is an important consideration when thinking long-term storage of information.

Information can be transitory, meaning there is little value, or they can be official records that have value to the organization. Typically when a decision is made, there should be a record kept. The problem is that for some decisions there is a lot of discussion that may lead up to that decision. The history of that discussion may be very useful in understanding how the decision was made, the criteria considered, who was involved, and who made the final decision and when. Sometimes that information has negative value, such as the time we received a Freedom of Information (FOI) request for all drafts of an important report prepared for one of the executives. The problem with the drafts was that there were a lot of blue-sky options proposed that contradicted the final outcome. We negotiated with the requestor and managed to boil it down to a single request for the first draft. We had to redact the first draft significantly to avoid confusion with the final copy. There was a lesson learned about keeping drafts. I encountered a similar situation at another ministry, and our approach was to destroy all drafts once the document was finalized. This may hold true for a lot of organizations.

Whether your organization has records managers, librarians, or clerks, just remember that they do not determine the value of information; they determine the life cycle of information based on a schedule. Schedules must be developed for all information. Each category should have a retention and disposition schedule. How long the organization keeps each document or record is what is important. Retention of administrative records is generally three years. It really depends on the type of information and the value, regulatory or legal requirements. For example, the State of Alaska keeps complaints from citizens, employees, and consumers for one year after resolution.

When a record has reached its end of useful life, there is the choice of archiving the record or destroying the record. The life cycle should determine what is done with each record. We discuss destroying information in the Data Loss Prevention section (see Chapter 17). When we discuss destroying information, we need to consider what media the information is stored on. The most obvious is paper. There are a number of other media types, including microfiche, film, CDs, DVDs, tape, cartridge, memory stick, disk drive, and even floppies.

Working for the Justice Sector was invaluable as the elevated sense of protection permeated all our work. This included disk drives. While the rest of government was running laptops without encryption, we were carefully implementing encryption using Pointsec™ on our critical laptops, especially for Criminal Justice Branch staff, who were the most strategic in deploying protection technologies to protect their sensitive information. We also implemented a policy of drilling any hard drive prior to disposal to make sure it was difficult to recover information. After an embarrassing incident involving the sale of magnetic media with sensitive information, the BC government instituted a disposal program to shred all magnetic media using very large shredders. There still was the issue of transportation of the disk drives to the shredder location. Although these may have come by courier, there have been a number of incidents where the tape or disk has fallen off the back of a truck or mysteriously vanished. You need to consider using either shredding disk drives, proper wipe-out technology, or full encryption.

For paper you can shred on-site, have mobile shredding, or shred at a contracted location. There are costs associated with all of these, and policies and procedures should be developed, adopted, or added and—the most important step followed—audited and monitored. Policy should be strictly enforced and people will get the message that there is zero tolerance. Your information is valuable and it must be protected. The end of the life cycle is sometimes where your information is most vulnerable. That is where information can be in some filing cabinet, on a personal disk drive, or on some backup media that is scheduled to be destroyed. How often have you heard about some box of records or some important papers being lost and found, much to the embarrassment and possibly to the detriment of an organization or an individual? The fact that the information is to be destroyed does not lessen its value, especially if the information could have a negative value to the person or organization. That is when care must be taken to ensure that the information is destroyed properly.

Database Information Life Cycle

Believe it or not, your databases grow at exponential rates. The question you need to ask: Is there data that is no longer relevant in my databases? In some cases, such as with the Corrections Branch and its CORNET application that manages inmates, the information is kept as long as the person is alive. For CRM systems, do you keep the data on a customer when they are no longer a customer? There is a lot of data in databases that is no longer relevant to the business and yet is kept in the database. This can slow performance and increase storage costs as well as backup and recovery costs and time. Do you know how much your data has grown since the application came on-line? Do you know the growth pattern? Do you know the data usage pattern? When we implemented an application to digitally record court proceedings, we did not understand how much data was being recorded across all the courtrooms. However, we soon found out that our initial estimates of volumes were significantly lower than actual. We had to increase the size of storage by terabytes.

You need to consider an information life cycle for your databases. Whether you choose to archive or simply dispose of data that is no longer relevant should depend on your business requirements. Here are some simple steps to help determine your database information life cycle:

1. Define business requirements for data (based on how the business wants to use the data will help determine what method you should use (archive, dispose, hybrid). You may want to consider a hybrid model, depending on the business requirements and any regulatory or legal requirements. In many instances, such as CRM, customers leave and return.
2. Plot your data growth over time (annualized growth of your database).
3. Develop data retention policies.
4. Evaluate automation for implementing policies (develop an in-house retention program or archive or purchase a package). The alternative is manual intervention, which is typically more expensive, error prone, and time consuming.
5. Implement policies (keep it simple, implement one rule at a time, and verify results).
6. For archiving, develop restoration procedures and test.
7. Verify that policies and programs work.

Information Flows

Information flows through an organization much like blood flows through your veins. Cut off information to a part of the organization and it slowly withers and dies. Cut off information to the heart of the organization and it dies. Cut off information to the brains

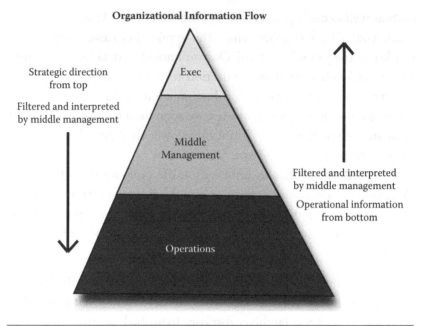

Figure 16.4   Standard view of organizational information flow.

of the organization and it stagnates. Information is the lifeblood of the organization.

In a typical organization, information flows up and down (Figure 16.4). Strategic directions come from the executives through middle management, who filters and interprets this information to operations. Information flows up from operations and is filtered and interpreted by middle management to the executives.

In reality, information flows not only up and down but also in all directions and can be either controlled or uncontrolled (Figure 16.5).

- *Uncontrolled information:* Information naturally flows into an organization through many channels and through all layers. It is uncontrolled information that enters the organization and is collected by individuals, and it may be kept by the individual or disseminated to the rest of the organization through various media.
- *Controlled information:* Information must flow out from an organization. Whether through customer relationship management, marketing, mergers, sales, or other distribution channels, information is what is needed to create sales and

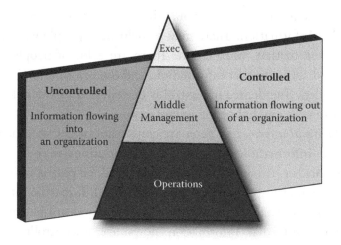

Figure 16.5 Organizational information flow.

profits; or in the case of not-for-profit or government institutions, the information that is necessary for operations, products, and services provided to their customers or clients.

In most organizations there is a need to manage the information flowing out of an organization. This is to protect the reputation; make sure the right message is being sent to customers, partners, and suppliers; protect intellectual capital and personal information; and prevent any litigation. There will always be tension between controlled and uncontrolled information flowing out of an organization. We can refer to the uncontrolled release of information as data or information leakage. We deal with data or information leakage in Chapter 17.

Information Flow Analysis

To determine how information flows in an organization, you need to investigate how information is used in the organization. There are formal information flows and informal information flows:

- *Formal information flows* are related to business processes. CRM is a good example of formal information flow. Customer information is used to manage the relationship between the organization and a customer. Various people need access to manage the account. The salesperson needs access to that information. The manager needs access to that information. There may be help-desk people who need access to that information. There are a lot of people who need access to that information, and the information is controlled. The degree of control is determined by the risk culture and appetite of the organization.

- *Informal information flows* are conversations between people and information leakage. The conversations may be electronic, in person, over lunch, overheard, or passed on (as in a secondary conversation after a meeting). It may be internal or go external. There may be a degree of control but mostly these informal information flows are uncontrolled. The degree of control depends on the organization and more so on the individual who has access to that information. As discussed earlier, people have ethics. And for most people, that ethical behavior is determined by the situation. Give a person a few drinks in a social setting and we could have loose lips sinking ships.

To find where your information flows, you can determine the formal information flow by looking at your business processes. In simple terms, you look at your applications that you use to support your business processes and determine who has access and why. Keep in mind that there may be secondary and tertiary uses for the information to create reports, spreadsheets, and marketing information. Figure 16.6 depicts a transaction such as a banking transaction. The source is the customer. They create a transaction by going to an ATM. They get money or perform some other banking transaction. And they use the money. Information is processed by an application and the information has a primary life cycle within the application. The customer information about the transaction is stored within a database. At some point in time, that information could be accessed by some business intelligence application to perform some analysis. This would be a secondary usage. The information could then be used to write a report for the CFO, which is a tertiary use of the information. The information could also be extracted to a specific request to have a customer service representative call the customer, representing more tertiary usage of the same information that was protected very well in

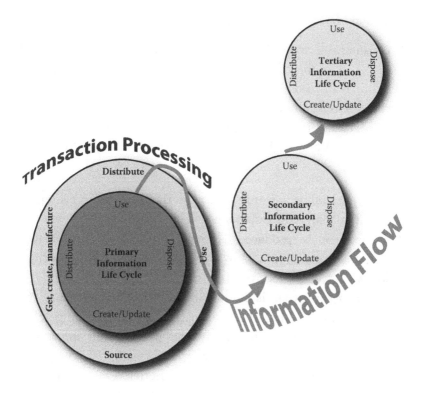

Figure 16.6   Transaction information flow.

the primary life cycle within the application. We know that information protection gets diluted the further downstream that information moves from the source. In other words, this is where your information is more at risk.

A good example of not knowing where your sensitive information is flowing was a story related to me by a vendor of data loss prevention. The vendor did a risk assessment analysis of a financial institution for its CISO. The analysis revealed that one of the analysts at the financial institution was taking work home electronically. The initiative of the analyst should be applauded; however, there was a serious risk to the financial institution based on the information being extracted and taken home. It turned out that the work involved analysis of credit card information and if this information was lost or stolen, it could cause a breach in the financial institution's PCI Data Security Compliance, possibly leading to fines and expensive remediation costs.

Information Management Strategy

CIOs manage electronic information. Whether the CIO is directly responsible or is the custodian is not important. The CIO is most likely to be held accountable if the information is compromised. The question is: Do you have a strategy to manage information?

To understand information, we must describe what we mean by information. What is the difference between data, information, and knowledge?

- *Data* are numbers, words, or images that have yet to be organized or analyzed to answer a specific question.
- *Information* is produced through processing, manipulating, and organizing data to answer questions, adding to the knowledge of the receiver.
- *Knowledge* is what is known by a person or persons. It involves interpreting the information received, adding relevance and context to clarify the insights the information contains. (*Source:* Improving Information to Support Decision Making: Standards for Better Quality Data, Audit Commission, November 2007. www.audit-commission.gov.uk/Products/NATIONAL-REPORT/AE298947-73F0-4dcb-AF77-D2520EECBCFB/ImprovingInformationToSupportDecisionMaking.pdf.)

Data does not have any association with other information to allow it to be useful. An example of data is latitude 10 South, longitude 80 West, which is a point on a map.

Information is data with context and is associated with other data. That is, information has meaning and may have associated metadata. An example of information is there are large schools of bluefin tuna at latitude 10 South, longitude 80 West. We should define information further and in more detail.

Information is raw data that

1. Has been verified to be accurate and timely;
2. Is specific and organized for a purpose;
3. Is presented within a context that gives it meaning and relevance; and

4. Leads to an increase in understanding and a decrease in uncertainty, change in behavior, and/or has some market value.

Information can be in many formats:

- *Document:* organized collection of content that is formatted, authoritative, and plays a transactional role within business processes.
- *Record:* applies to authoritative documents that provide evidence of decisions or events occurring in the execution of a business process.
- *Form:* a special type of document with the content being provided by one or more persons and retained as a record of contribution and authority.

Knowledge is the interpretation of information, and value is added to the information. A fishing captain on a fishing boat knows there are large schools of bluefin tuna at latitude 10 South, longitude 80 West, off the coast of Peru and has the means to get them. It is also very close to the Milne Edwards Trench, which has a depth of 6,369 meters, or roughly 19,750 feet. The captain also knows the weather, the market for bluefin tuna, and whether it is profitable and safe to go out to that point in the ocean. His knowledge will make the difference between safely returning with a catch of tuna that has good market value and will pay him and his crew and not going out or, worse, drowning out there.

There is also some confusion in the marketplace about records, document, content, and knowledge management. They all deal with information and the management of that information.

- *Records management:* Records management evolved from the procedures and technologies originally designed to manage paper records. If we consider the paper paradigm, we used to manage information in filing cabinets and in/outboxes. Documents and records were sent via mail or courier. Sensitive information was stamped with a designation that indicated the document was or should only be viewed by authorized individuals. To some extent, records management is still involved with physical documents. We still manage paper invoices, contracts, letters of acceptance, forms, and any other document that requires a signature for authentication purposes.

- *Document management:* Document management evolved from records management. It controlled documents during their "working life." Document management included features that helped people find, share, revise, and finalize electronic documents. Document management helped organizations manage both workflow and documents. Document management is undergoing changes and evolving toward content management as the Internet continues to evolve.

- *Content management:* Content is the persistent expression of meaning that can be exchanged in a variety of formats. Content management is the management and associated processes for efficiently executing and continuously improving strategic business processes. It is dependent on the business processes being supported and content types. A good example of content management is Microsoft SharePoint™. SharePoint has workflow, version control, collaboration, and presentation components. There are other content management vendors, such as Open Text, Alfresco, Documentum, and some more specialized companies for Web content management such as SDL Tridion, Sitecore, and Percussion. Web content management focuses on maintaining a high-quality Web presence and may be either software or software as a service (SaaS).

- *Knowledge management:* Knowledge management comprises a range of strategies and practices used in an organization to identify, create, represent, distribute, and enable adoption of insights and experiences. These insights and experiences comprise knowledge either embodied in individuals or embedded in organizational processes and practices.

Any one or all of these is about managing your information. Unfortunately, most organizations manage information in silos. There is no overall strategy. Sharing information is limited to communities of practice or within business units. This typically means multiple solutions, requiring different expertise, adding costs, and preventing the more effective use of information, not to mention the risks associated with finding information when liability knocks at the door. In other words, how you manage your information is about managing risks. We cannot forget that lots of important information is in

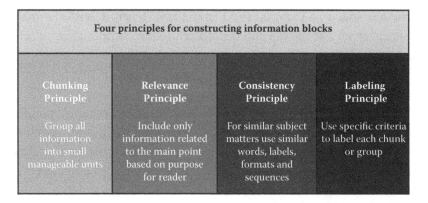

Figure 16.7 Principles for constructing information blocks.

databases. That information is often extracted to reports, presentations, spreadsheets, and documents. It still must be managed.

The Internet is playing a greater role in moving information into different formats and often has "chunks" of information. If you perform a search on Google, you get a brief description of the topic. Notice that the word or words that you used for search are **boldface**). For example, if I search for "content," I get back the following:

> Content - Wikipedia, the free encyclopedia
>
> **Content** or contents may refer to: **Content** (algebra), the highest common factor of a polynomial's coefficients; **Content** (measure theory), an additive real ... en.wikipedia.org/wiki/**Content** - Cached - Similar

That brief description could be described as a relevance block of information containing the search criteria. Robert Horn (1989), in his book entitled *Mapping Hypertext: ...*, described information blocks as the basic subdivision of a subject matter replacing the paragraph as the fundamental unit of analysis and presentation in functional and task-oriented text. He further said that information blocks are composed of one or more sentences and/or graphic structures constructed according to four principles: chunking, relevance, consistency, and labeling (Figure 16.7).

Barbara Minto (2007), in her book entitled *The Minto Pyramid Principle: ...*, discussed logic in writing, thinking, and problem solving. The Minto Pyramid Principle is a methodology for presenting information in a pyramid manner. We could view this as similar to taxonomies in the sense that a taxonomy is a hierarchical classification schema. That is, a pyramid is a hierarchical structure with the main concept or idea at the top and the structure links similar ideas or concepts together.

Minto's limiting factor is groups of seven. It appears that most of us can only hold seven items in our short-term memory. George A. Miller (1957), in his article entitled "The Magical Number Seven ...," pointed out that the mind cannot hold more than seven items, plus or minus two. Because we cannot remember more than seven things at a given time, the presentation of information should be grouped into objects or blocks of information containing a maximum of seven points.

The Cluetrain Manifesto, written by Rick Levine et al. (2000), is about the art of conversation on the Internet. When we want people to remember things, we tell a story. We have a conversation. How many times have you attended a presentation and remembered very little? How many times have you heard a story and remembered that story? Information management is about telling stories. The Internet and intranet are about conversations and telling stories. If you want people to remember, you tell a story so they can relate to it. How you organize your stories is important. It presents a message to people. If we do not use building blocks or pyramids, how can we expect people to remember? The building blocks for information management must have some form to present the information.

The paper age is evolving into the digital age. Although we still print as our standard way of presenting information, more and more information is now electronic in databases, documents, and in many other media formats. We are progressing toward that paperless office that was envisioned in the 1990s. Just don't throw out the printers and paper; paper is still a good presentation medium for information.

Just to sidetrack, if you are envisioning getting rid of printers and going electronic, you need to consider the desktop as the view into corporate information. In his presentation at TEDTalks at the 2007 EG Conference, Kevin Kelly (2007), who was the editor for *Wired Magazine*, talked about the next 5,000 days on the Internet. He referred to the Internet as the machine and all devices such as desktops, hand-helds, and laptops have a view into the machine. If you are moving to mostly electronic viewing of information, you should make sure your organization has the maximum viewing capability on the desktops; that is, invest in the biggest and best monitors.

I have encountered this situation twice in my career. The first time was at the Department of National Defence when we were building the intranet in 1996. We had to argue to increase the size of the monitors from fourteen inches to seventeen inches. The Department had a standard size of fourteen inches for any server monitor. We argued that these would be used more as an editing station for HTML to develop the content for the intranet. We won that battle.

The second time was with the BC government in 2009. The BC government was hit with a budget crunch and at the same time deploying new workstations with twenty-inch monitors. The technical folks saw an opportunity to save some money by not deploying twenty-inch monitors. We saved $500,000. The problem they did not see was the operational problem. If you cannot view your information electronically, what do you do? You print the document. I was one of the lucky ones who got a twenty-inch monitor. The advantage was one of being able to open multiple windows at the same time and view them at the same time. This was a productivity gain. The technical folks did not see that either. So we lost on our ability to reduce printing costs and improve productivity. Measuring this across 10,000 workers, I can say with certainty that it cost us more in terms of productivity and printed paper than we saved.

We still might print documents but the approach should be to minimize the number of printers in an organization. If you consider the cost of paper, toner, and printers, you may determine that there is an ROI in reducing the number of printers by improving the viewing capabilities.

Designing Information Management across Large Organizations

In a typical organization there are many business units. In a simple example, you may have human resources, finance, information technology, records management, administration, and operations. In a complex example such as the Ministry of Attorney General, there are a number of business units (e.g., Criminal Justice Branch, Court Services Branch, Family Maintenance and Enforcement, Criminal Justice Reform), each with a separate mandate and different priorities. The Justice Sector had four main participants: Police, Criminal Justice Branch, Courts, and Corrections. Each of these had different mandates and priorities. You could leave it up to the individual branches to solve their information management problems or you could develop a strategy that would work for all the business units. Further on, I describe an approach that we proposed for the Justice Sector that could be used as a model for all the business units in the Justice Sector as well as the other ministries.

Information is unique to the organization. There are some common areas, such as

- Personal information
- Customer information
- Intellectual property
- Business intelligence
- Organizational
- Financial
- Administrative
- Facilities, buildings, equipment
- Human resources
- Procedures, policies, guidelines

Returning to our discussion on where to find your information, in larger organizations it is spread across multiple platforms. For example, in the BC government we had Microsoft file servers that we named Shared File and Print (SFP). These were logically divided into ministries, and some of the larger ministries had more than one SFP server. These logical units managed all unstructured information in one big bucket. The security was limited to NTFS. There was no ability to find information in other ministries unless you knew someone who told you about a document that was pertinent to your research. In essence, these were great big electronic filing cabinets. Management of information was performed by users. We had "home" drives that we could use personally; these were not shared. We had taken the paper paradigm of filing cabinets and converted it to an electronic format. We still had in- and outboxes, thanks to email. We had many copies of documents across many branches and ministries.

There were some glimmers of information sharing using Wikis and SharePoint. Typically these were communities of practice or IT groups. There was not a common strategy for information management across the government. Information was not classified. There were no controlled vocabularies. Nobody knew where information was kept. Does this sound like your organization? As a CIO, your job is to manage information. If you are not managing information, are you the enabler to creating business chaos?

There are three types of information: structured, unstructured, and metadata. In most organizations, the unstructured information is not being managed well. The structured information is typically in databases, and metadata is used to describe the information. These are typically managed well. The problem occurs when that information contained in the databases is used elsewhere and ends up in the unstructured pile.

Databases are used for applications to manage transactions. What is being transacted is your business. In the Justice Sector, applications are used to manage inmates. The database of these applications contains some very sensitive and personal information about inmates, guards, and facilities. Business intelligence software is used to analyze the information. Additional reports are developed for judges, courts, police, and researchers.

The important message is that your most sensitive information may be used in other ways by other businesses within and external to your organization. To illustrate that point, we should look at some generic models and step through an example from the Justice Sector to see how information is processed.

In any transaction, something is processed. Material is sourced, something is created, distributed, and used. Information is created and used for the transaction to be completed. This is the primary usage of the information and what the database and application were created for. An example is processing an order where a credit card is used to purchase some goods. Information about the credit card is processed as well as information about the goods to help manage inventory. Customer information may also be kept for awards programs and marketing. Amazon is a good example of companies that use customer information. They send you tracking information about your purchase, letting you know that the item has been picked and shipped. Amazon is very good at sending information about new books that may be of interest to people who have purchased books via email. It is not just any books but books that are related to subject areas based on books purchased. They also match your purchase books with other books of similar characteristics, adding financial incentives to get you to buy more.

Now think about where your information goes from your primary business. There may be secondary and tertiary uses, as described in

Figure 16.6. Your partners may have access to your information. How well protected is that information? In the CardSystems Solutions breach in 2005, the credit card information was moved from the primary system to another system for further analysis. The hackers breached a secondary system that did not have the same level of protection as their primary system. It would have been good if there had been a controlled vocabulary that alerted someone that the credit card information had been moved to another system. If you are using third parties to conduct business, you need to consider what agreements are in place and what level of protection is being placed on your valuable information.

As an example, within the Justice Sector in BC, we proposed an approach to managing information that is different than the way it is being managed today. We recognized that the same information was being processed by different entities within the Criminal Justice process. Figure 16.8 reflects the process and how we were going to change the way information was being managed using policy enforcement points as a means of allowing the appropriate level of access to the information.

The process used in Canadian criminal justice is different than in the United States. Once the police solve the crime, they present the case to the Crown or the Prosecutors. The Crown determines if the evidence is sufficient to proceed with the case. The case is prepared by the Crown, including evidence gathering and statement preparation. The information is also made available to the person being charged, which is known as e-disclosure. In cases where the person charged is in custody, the information must be provided within the corrections facility where the accused is being housed. The Crown presents this information to the courts where the judge—and, if present, the jury—get access to the information. Once the person is convicted and sentenced, the information is turned over to Corrections. As seen in previous examples, Corrections manages the information through its own applications. At some point in time, the person is placed on probation or is released with some conditions. Other services such as social, health, and housing assistance may require access to the information.

What we proposed was to have a single repository of information that will have appropriate control points to allow authorized access to the information. That way, we are not duplicating information and can have the right level of protection assigned to the most sensitive information.

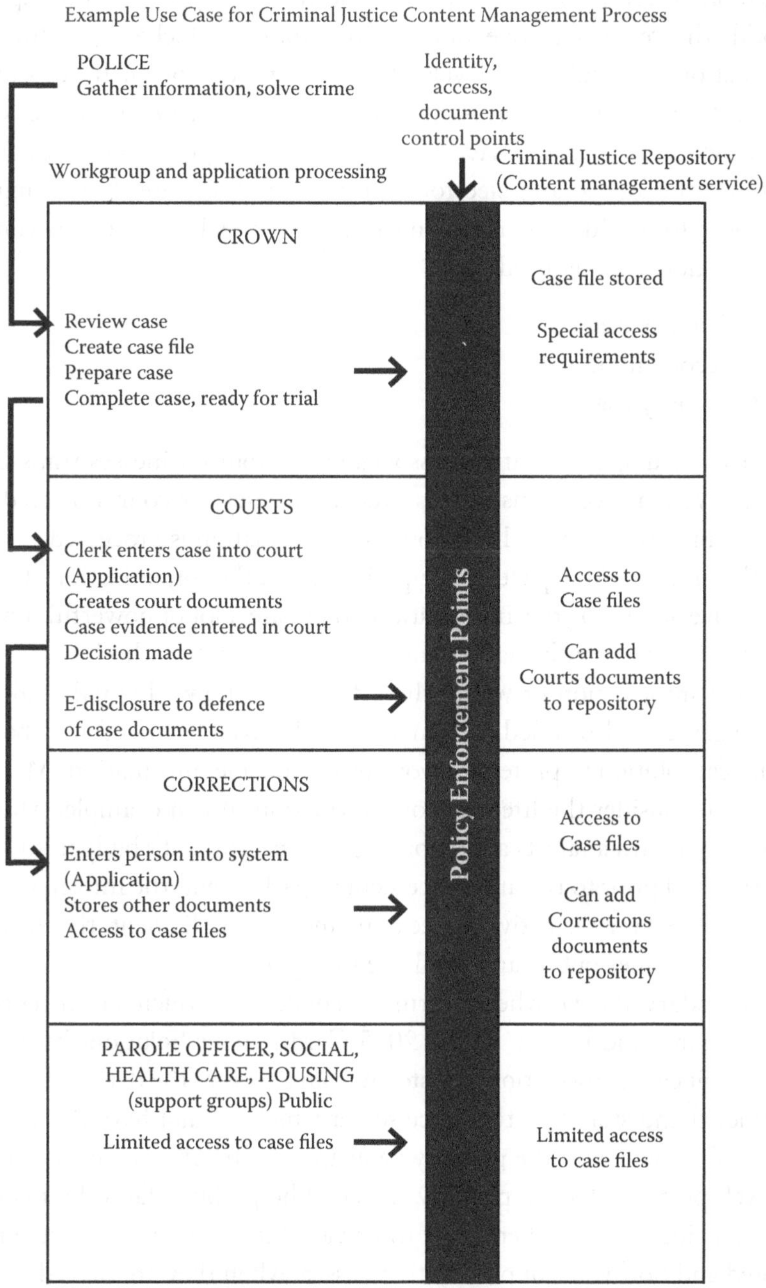

Example Use Case for Criminal Justice Content Management Process

POLICE
Gather information, solve crime

Identity,
access,
document
control points

Workgroup and application processing

Criminal Justice Repository
(Content management service)

CROWN

Case file stored

Review case
Create case file
Prepare case
Complete case, ready for trial

Special access
requirements

→

COURTS

Clerk enters case into court
(Application)
Creates court documents
Case evidence entered in court
Decision made

E-disclosure to defence
of case documents

Access to
Case files

Can add
Courts documents
to repository

→

CORRECTIONS

Access to
Case files

Enters person into system
(Application)
Stores other documents
Access to case files

Can add
Corrections
documents
to repository

→

Policy Enforcement Points

PAROLE OFFICER, SOCIAL,
HEALTH CARE, HOUSING
(support groups) Public

Limited access to case files →

Limited access
to case files

Figure 16.8 Justice content management process.

This example shows that information is reused many times and the appropriate levels of protection that need to be applied. In a paper world, the really sensitive information would be locked in a filing cabinet or in a vault with levels of physical protection such as locks, burglar alarms, fire-suppressant systems, doors, etc. Within the electronic world we not only have to contend with the physical protection, but also the logical and electronic protection. There are three things you need to consider when looking at who, what, where, and how your information is being used:

1. Primary usage
2. Secondary usage
3. Tertiary usage

Primary usage is what you associate with your businesses transactions. Whether your business is preparing cases for courts or credit card transactions for on-line shopping, information is processed.

This must include partners, suppliers, and other organizations that may have access to your information. There are a lot of powerful tools for manipulating information and you may not know who has access to what information or where the information flows. Digital Rights Management (also called Information Rights Management) may be a practical solution to protecting your most valuable information. Make sure you consider the life cycle of information. As an example, when Treasury Board analysts are preparing the government's budget information and prior to the announcement in parliament, the information is considered very sensitive. Once announced in parliament, the information becomes public and available to anyone.

Secondary usage is when information or data is extracted from a primary source and reused. In the 2005 CardSystems Solutions breach, the credit card information was stolen from a server. The data had been extracted and stored on the office server which did not have the same level of protection as the primary database servers. This server was not as well protected as the primary servers. The problem faced by many CIOs is identifying where your most valuable information assets are stored and how you can protect these assets when they are moved.

Tertiary usage often occurs when the information is reused by partners or other parts of the organization. Consider that Business intelligence may extract specific records from a database and use them in reports. These reports may also be further reused in presentations, or certain information may be extracted again. Once again, the problem facing CIOs is the level of protection being used to protect this information.

> Information management should be a priority for every CIO in every organization.

Within government there is a lot of focus on records management. Records management is based on paper and filing cabinets although a lot of records managers will tell you otherwise. I had the records management division reporting to me for a few years and the Ministry Records Officer (or MRO) always insisted that records included electronic information of all types. The problem was that the Document Disposal Act, which is what all information life cycle was based on, was written in the 1950s and updated in the 1980s. The act was written by archivists who wanted to keep records of decision for the government, and their entire process derived from a paper paradigm.

In the 1950s, a memo was printed on paper, duplicated a few times, and the original was kept in a filing cabinet by the Office of Primary Interest (OPI). When filing cabinets became full, the records were sent off site in boxes. A retention period was set for each piece of paper and special instructions were given to the off-site storage site. The Government Records Officer had to authorize the destruction of each piece of paper as per the Document Disposal Act. This was a cumbersome and inefficient process. When government started relying more on computers and the amount of electronic information exploded, the Document Disposal Act became a problem. Because it deals with paper and not electronic information, it is not an appropriate way to manage electronic information. As technology continues to evolve, storage space is rapidly becoming unlimited in terms of floor space as compared to filing cabinets. This is a two-edged sword; and although the paper problem is eliminated using electronic information (note that we now produce more paper than ever and will continue to do so until the technology for viewing the information becomes as easy to view as paper), we now have multiple copies of information stored in multiple places. When we use hierarchical folders and our own naming conventions and have a separate home drive for each user, we often have multiple copies of documents.

So we have multiple problems: proliferation of information, multiple copies of the same information, and potentially multiple copies of the information with multiple revisions in different formats. I encountered a problem with having multiple revisions of a document under the FOI Act. We had a request under the provisions of the FOI Act from a reporter for all revisions of a report showing all changes to the document. An access request under the FOI Act requires the government to produce the information requested within 30 days of receiving the request. The executive responsible for the division did not want to release all the revisions because some of the key decisions from the report had multiple outcomes and each revision showed different outcomes, potentially harming government. We negotiated with the reporter and refined the request to only the first revision. We satisfied the request and at the same time learned a valuable lesson that we can apply to records management and also to e-discovery requirements. We need to be careful about keeping copies of all revisions of documents when the final document is produced. Only final documents should be kept as a record.

Information management of unstructured information is becoming a huge problem, especially when it involves litigation. In her article entitled "E-Discovery and Electronic Document Retention in Canada using Symantec Enterprise Vault and Symantec Technologies," Constantine Karbaliotis provided a few examples of how day-to-day document retention policies can affect the outcome of litigation. In the case of *Coleman v. Morgan Stanley*, the storage folks found an additional 1,600 backup tapes in a closet that were not disclosed to the judge. The judge instructed the jury to assume that the bank acted with malice or evil intent, and the jury awarded Coleman $1.6 billion. The cost of not managing unstructured information is going through the roof, especially if litigation is involved. Criminal cases now involve hundreds or thousands of documents, video, audio, and pictures, all produced as evidence. Evidence management is becoming a time-consuming process without the appropriate tools. We discuss e-discovery and the issues surrounding e-disclosure in Chapter 18.

Within the Justice Sector of the BC government, we proposed a content management strategy to help manage the mountains of electronic information that were continuing to grow at an ever-accelerating pace. Key elements of our strategy were

1. *Governance:* Three levels should be incorporated into governance: executive sponsor, a steering committee of the business stakeholders, and a coordination team to provide continuity across all tactical investments.

2. *Business orientation:* All investments should be geared toward realizing both short- and long-term business benefits. Any investment in content management technology should be balanced by an equivalent investment in business process improvements. There should be some amount of emphasis placed on training and education.

3. *Standards:* Establish standards for content management, including an information model governing the interchangeable content metadata and information assets at various points in their life cycle.

4. *Architecture:* A technical architecture must be established to implement the concepts underlying the standards and support a more complete content management solution through a series of incremental investments.

5. *Workgroup repositories:* The BC government has made a substantial investment in workgroup tools, including Microsoft's collaboration suite.

6. *Sector repositories:* Next level up is by sector. For example, Criminal Justice is a sector. A sector typically shares information between workgroups. These repositories are considered active.

7. *Archival repositories:* To manage the overall life cycle of content assets created or received by the Justice Sector and, in accordance with retention schedules, content is migrated from active storage to secondary storage when file retrieval falls below a specific level (i.e., file has not been opened or viewed in twelve months). The content will remain accessible through search.

8. *Search services:* Capacity to perform searches across all repositories, depending on content security classification. This capability will include both metadata and full text search.

9. *Security:* The importance of making sure that the content is secured commensurate with the value of the information cannot be understated. Sensitive information must be appropriately

protected to prevent unauthorized viewing. Identity management will play a critical role in determining access controls. A defense-in-depth strategy must be utilized.

Within any organization, especially those organizations that are information centric (such as pharmaceutical, research, consulting, and justice), there is an increasing need to manage unstructured information. As a matter of fact, there is a need to move unstructured information to a more structured format using eXtensible Markup Language (XML). Microsoft has made a huge investment in integrating XML into Microsoft's Office products. If there are standard reports, the next step is to embed XML into the report to add context to the content.

Steps to Better Information Management

I have already provided this information and thus this is a summation of the chapter to help you with some basic steps. There is a lot to each of these steps.

1. *Governance:* It may be too soon to set up a governance structure but you need to identify one person responsible for setting up an information management program. The program should be targeted and specific to meeting a business need. An executive should sponsor the information management program.
2. *Identify information assets:* Information has value. What information is most valuable to the organization? The business needs to identify what information is most valuable. Where is this information located? Take into consideration operational requirements, as well including incident response and business continuity documentation and how systems and firewalls are configured, as well as what patches have been applied.
3. *Classify your information:* If you do not have one, develop a classification schema. Then develop retention and disposition schedules for your different information categories. Finally, put your information into their respective categories.
4. *Develop controlled vocabularies:* There are terms that you want to standardize across the organization so that everyone is

talking the same language. It makes it easier for search and find, as well as protecting information.

5. *Determine levels of protection:* Identity and access management is one of the first levels of protection. Consider data loss prevention to protect your most valuable information assets. Determine what databases have sensitive information that needs the most levels of protection. Consider physical, logical, and procedural methods.

6. *Look at technology solutions:* There may be easy ways to automate your information management. It is not one-size-fits-all. However, you may want to look at content management or records management solutions to manage your most valuable information.

7. *Develop policies, procedures, and technologies:* Information management is about managing information. Specific policies are critical to supporting information management. Procedures should be developed to manage the distribution of information, including primary, secondary, and tertiary uses. Create appropriate life-cycle management policies based on the value of the information. IP may be kept in perpetuity. Technologies are essential in providing the infrastructure to support information management. Make sure the policies, procedures, and technologies are practical, implementable, and auditable.

8. *Implement policies, procedures, and technologies:* Initiate programs to prioritize and implement new or revised policies, procedures, and technologies.

9. *Monitor policies, procedures, and technologies:* Audit the policies and procedures to determine if they are being followed. Make sure the technologies are working according to what is needed. Adjust where practical.

10. *Develop metrics for measuring the success or failure of your policies, procedures, and technologies* in protecting and managing the information.

Setting up an information management program is not simple. In the Justice Sector we initiated Enterprise Content Management using the Oracle Collaboration Suite. What we tried to do was meet all expectations from all the businesses within the Justice Sector and regulatory organizations that comprised the Attorney General and Public Safety Ministries. This failed because we could not meet all expectations. The person responsible for information management must focus on one primary requirement and meet that requirement. Part of the consideration needs to be the architecture and standards that will be implemented within the organization. A lot of people will be disappointed in just setting up standards, policies, and procedures. When we discussed setting up content management with the business, there was a sense of dissatisfaction with the progress when we worked on setting up standards, policies, and procedures. The expectations were much higher to define and meet business needs. Information management must be taken slowly. There are a lot of changes that must be made in order to meet all the requirements. The reality is that there must be an ROI, whether it is measured corporately or by a business unit. That is why a business requirement should be a focus point for information management.

Security is one of the aspects of information management that is often overlooked. When you identify your most valuable assets, you need to consider what controls you should have to protect your assets. Do you need some form of digital rights management or information rights management?

Should you encrypt some of your information? All your information? The Criminal Justice Branch took the approach that its information was of high value and thus encrypted all their information. When we moved to the Vista platform, they were caught in a quandary. The encryption software was not functioning 100% the same as within the XP environment. A lot of work went into fixing the problems associated with Vista and the new environment. One of the suggested approaches was to decrypt all the existing information. The problem was that the sensitivity of the information did not permit the decryption as this might have exposed information such as police informants, witnesses, and case files to all the administrators who managed the servers, thereby putting the administrators at risk. We also had to consider that the information had to be available for e-discovery and e-disclosure before and during the trial. This means they had to decrypt case information at a point in time, keeping the most sensitive information encrypted. What this means in terms of information life-cycle management is that you have to consider moving information from high value to low value and what mechanisms, policies, and procedures apply to making that happen.

One of the other quandaries is the whole aspect of long-term storage of electronic information. If you encrypt your information, can you decrypt it in the future? If you use technology to protect your information, can you continue to use the same technologies in the future, or do you have to make the investment in changing the technology, including the conversion from one format to another? In his book entitled *Blindsided*, Jim Harris (2002) pointed out that the average life expectancy of giant multinational companies is forty to fifty years. One third of the 1970s Fortune 500 companies ceased to exist by 1983. In the case of the encryption software we were using to encrypt the Criminal Justice Branch's sensitive information, we originally bought from a small company in Australia that was bought by SafeNet. We also went through a technology change on the desktop, which further complicated things. We had originally purchased laptop disk encryption Pointsec™. In moving to Vista, we could now deploy Microsoft's BitLocker™ as our standard for disk encryption and no longer needed Pointsec. As encryption and other technologies converge toward the desktop, we need to consider obsolescence in our purchase strategies because the software we use today may be different tomorrow.

In terms of information, using international standards will probably safeguard your information over a long period of time. I recommend that you look at slowly converting all your unstructured information into XML. There are ways to convert documents using standard products like Microsoft Word, Excel, and PowerPoint. These all use XML embedded in their structure. The major advantage is that if you are duplicating a lot of information in various forms or templates, you can reuse the information by creating "smart documents." This may also be a way to index and manage your documents automatically.

17

INFORMATION PROTECTION

Electronic information security is really a new phenomenon. In the days of filing cabinets and paper, information was secured physically. There was a standing joke about how the Turkish Army managed their sensitive information. The sensitive information was stored in a box. The box was put in a room with one door and no windows. A guard with a gun was put in the room and sat on the box. If you came into the room and you were not authorized to be there, the guard shot you. Effective security, but not something we can do today in our electronic world. In the 1980 and 1990s, we were not really concerned with securing the Internet. The Internet was new. I was heavily involved with electronic data interchange (EDI) and electronic commerce, and we were not considering using the Internet at that point in time. EDI was point-to-point communications. As a matter of fact, when I was working for Bank One, we were conducting penetration testing on the mainframe application to determine if there were any holes in our use of Frame Relay technologies to access the mainframe in Georgia.

Although Robert Morris was the first person convicted under the Computer Fraud and Abuse Act of 1986 when he released his "worm" onto the Internet in November 1988, it was not until MafiaBoy unleashed his denial-of-service attack on Amazon, Dell, Yahoo, and eBay in February 2000 that we really sat up and took notice of information security on the Internet. Since 2000, information security has been steadily increasing in importance.

What we are now seeing is the emergence of a new and very sophisticated criminal element. We only hear about the ones who got caught. In her book entitled *Data Mining and Predictive Analysis*, Colleen McCue stated

What we are left with, then is a sample of information. In other words, almost everything that we know about crime and criminals is based on a relatively small amount of information gathered from only a fraction of all criminals—generally the unsuccessful ones. (2007)

This means our information security is based on what we know about unsuccessful cyber crime. That is, what we know about convicted criminals who used computers to commit a crime. This means we know very little about the successful criminals. As a matter of fact, even our information about the unsuccessful criminals is limited. These are people who may not be reliable and forthcoming with information to help the police. The information can also be filtered by the very police who have made the arrests. The time required to prepare and report a crime is often insufficient because the police's job is protection and arrest, not prosecution of the criminals.

We have always divided hackers into three groups: *script kiddies* (someone who has very little training and sophistication who downloads and runs a script to perform some malicious act), *hackers* (someone who has training and a level of sophistication who can actually write code and understands what is being done when a script is executed), and *professionals* (someone who can hire hackers or is very sophisticated and can cover their tracks so you do not know that they have been in and out of your network). Your information security should at minimum keep out the first two groups. Remember that they only need one mistake to gain access. That is why audit and review are very important components of information security.

If you read any book on information security, you will find a common theme. Information security is about layers of defense. You can think about it in physical terms, like a castle where you have walls, a moat, gates, defenders, procedures, and rules. We define information security in much the same way; there are layers of defense starting with access controls, firewalls, intrusion prevention, anti-virus, server hardening, policies, and procedures. In terms of today's environment, the outer walls are seemingly porous as we allow users access to information in mobile environments through multiple methods. Remember Kevin Kelly (2007) in his presentation at TED talking about the one machine. We are now facing the same dilemma in our organizations. The business requires access to its information in many ways to accommodate its users. We are also faced with issues surrounding access to social networks such as Facebook, MySpace, and Twitter, where information is shared among friends and kept by the social networks. Is our sensitive information being posted and stored in Twitter or Facebook? What are your policies about accessing social networks from work? As new generations enter into the workplace, they have certain expectations. If your organization does not meet these expectations, can you get the brightest and best?

Information security is moving from the technical space to the boardroom. It is now one of the most important issues for the U.S. government. The release of the National Institute of Standards and Technology (NIST) standard 800-53 and the requirement to comply with the Federal Information Security Management Act of 2002 will have a ripple effect. As government agencies tighten their controls, attacks will become more sophisticated. The war in cyberspace is just beginning. Science fiction is becoming science fact. William Gibson introduced us to cyberspace with *Neuromancer* in 1984. Now we are faced with cyberwar and our economy depends on this vital resource. On May 29, 2009, President Obama announced a new cybersecurity push by the U.S. government. Part of that was the release of NIST standard 800-53.

> ... Through the process of risk management, leaders must consider risk to US interests from adversaries using cyberspace to their advantage and from our own efforts to employ the global nature of cyberspace to achieve objectives in military, intelligence, and business operations. ... For operational plans development, the combination of threats, vulnerabilities, and impacts must be evaluated in order to identify important trends and decide where effort should be applied to eliminate or reduce threat capabilities; eliminate or reduce vulnerabilities; and assess, coordinate, and deconflict all cyberspace operations. ... Leaders at all levels are accountable for ensuring readiness and security to the same degree as in any other domain. ...

> **—The National Strategy for Cyberspace Operations, Office of the Chairman, Joint Chiefs of Staff, U.S. Department of Defense**

In their publication "The Financial Management of Cyber Risk," the experts from ISA and ANSI combined to create a framework for managing risks generated by information systems.

The bottom line is that the biggest risks are people. At the executive level there is misunderstanding. At all levels there are insiders and hackers. Insiders are your biggest threat next to misunderstanding. The focus of executive is on the business. The reality is that business runs on information systems. Compromise information systems and you compromise the business. There are so many examples to demonstrate that even the best organizations, such as the Department of Defense (DoD) and the Federal Bureau of Investigations (FBI), all have had insiders and hackers break into their systems and steal secrets.

A good example of a trusted insider was Brian Patrick Regan, who was employed by TRW as a SIGINT specialist with broad access to multiple sensitive information systems. He entered the U.S. Air Force in 1980 and retired in 2000. In 2002 he was charged with attempted espionage. He had been working from July 1995 to August 2000 at the headquarters of the National Reconnaissance Office (NRO) as a Signals Intelligence Specialist. Although he swore an Oath of Office and Security Acknowledgments, signed a Classified Information Nondisclosure Agreement, held Top-Secret clearance, and had served in the U.S. military, he spied for foreign governments. He felt that for his twenty years of service that he deserved more than the small pension he would receive. He was a trusted insider with high credentials who printed secret and top-secret material that was to be delivered to foreign governments. Fortunately, he was caught prior to his leaving the country after falsely telling his supervisor that he was vacationing in Florida with his family when he was really traveling to Switzerland to contact agents in embassies. Consider that he was a trusted person with Top-Secret clearance. He had passed background checks by the U.S. military and TRW. His motive was simple: money. He had access to secret information. That information had value. All he had to do was print the information and deliver it to foreign governments. Nobody questioned why he was printing this information. In all probability, nobody even knew he was printing this information. Nobody looked at the logs, assuming there were logs. Does your security include looking at logs? And what are they looking for?

We capture millions of events every day and do not have the means to look at all events. As human beings we have learned to skim. That is, we can look at large volumes of information and determine relevant information. Normally we use keywords that we look for in skimming the material to determine if this information is relevant—something similar to what most search engines do when you submit a word or phrase to search for information. The unfortunate problem is the volume of information we have to process. We also have to interpret the results. If someone has three to five log-on failures, does that mean there is a problem with fingers or is someone hacking his account? Is there a relationship between his normal work and the information he is accessing after that log-on failure? How do you know?

Only by continuous monitoring and comparing against regular activities can you detect abnormal actions. This is where a risk assessment should be performed. This is where classifying your information assets is extremely important. Knowing where to focus your efforts and managing your resources effectively will reduce your risks and identify where you should allocate your limited budget.

Security Controls

Information security can be broken down into controls. It is good practice to have layers of defense, including ingress (or incoming) and egress (or outgoing) controls. Ingress is what we are most familiar with in terms of firewalls, anti-virus, and access controls. Egress is now a necessary set of controls to know what information went where and why and by whom. Egress tools include data loss prevention or information rights management. We break down each layer of protection to provide an overview of what each layer does, why it is important, and when and where each layer should be applied.

Two types of controls should be considered: preventative and reactive. Preventative controls are generally controls that stop something from happening. Reactive controls are generally controls that mitigate or reduce the impact after something has happened. Table 17.1 provides a list of the different types of controls that can provide a defense-in-depth strategy. The more these controls are embedded into the culture, environment, and organization, the better the management of risks. Note that some of the controls have both preventative and reactive components.

Ideally, all these controls would be fully implemented, practiced, and tightly managed. The reality is that with limited budgets, a practical approach must be taken to determine what can be implemented

Table 17.1   Preventive and Reactive Controls

PREVENTIVE	REACTIVE
Education and awareness	Audits and reviews
Training	Incident response
Anti-virus	Forensic tools
Policies	Log management
Firewalls	Intrusion detection
Intrusion prevention	Procedures
Data loss prevention	Compliance requirements
Digital/information rights management	
Encryption	
Procedures	Regulatory, legal, court, law requirements (e.g., e-discovery)
System hardening	Identity and access management
Patching	Post-incident reviews
Separation of duties	Public relations, management, legal advice
Classification of information assets	Business continuity management
Application secure coding	Human resources management
Identity and access management	
Background screening and checks	

and how much. Some controls are essential and must be done. For example, an education and awareness program should be instituted in every organization. The question is how much money should be spent on education and awareness? This is where a practical approach will allow maximum benefit for your budget. Start with a basic foundation of what is essential for good security; that is, provides the best value for the dollars spent.

Some basic questions:

- *What information is most valuable to your organization?* This is the most important question to answer. You need to know what information is most valuable to the organization to determine what controls are necessary to protect the information. Is your information
  - Personal (you process credit cards or handle people's information in some capacity, such as medical records);
  - IP (you have significant investments in research and development); and/or
  - Public safety or government or national security?

According to NIST 199, government agencies must classify their information assets. Most organizations do not classify their information assets. If you start looking at your information, you will find that there is very sensitive information in spreadsheets and word documents, on intranets, and on personal drives. Chances are that you do not know what your most sensitive data is, where your most sensitive data is kept, or how it is distributed. We further discuss a classification of information in Chapter 16.

• *Is your organization transaction or information centric?* This is an important question to answer to determine where you allocate your dollars. Transaction centric usually means that your organization processes some form of financial operation. You should focus your dollars on protecting your transactions. Information centric means your organization is more focused on processing knowledge or IP. This requires different controls than transaction-centric operations. In most cases, organizations have a combination of both.

Essential Controls

There are a lot of controls listed in Table 17.1 and most of them are important in managing information security. The U.S. government has spent considerable money on developing standards such as NIST 800-53 (Information Security). NIST 800-53 organizes security controls into seventeen control families and three general classes (technical, operational, and management). Each control defines a specific security capacity that protects a particular aspect of an information system. The combination of controls provides a defense-in-depth strategy.

As much as possible and practical, you should embed security into operations. Technologies such as anti-virus, firewalls, intrusion prevention, system hardening, and patching should be managed by the operations teams. You will also need to put some form of security metrics into their job descriptions to make sure they understand the importance. One of my former bosses said that security was everyone's business; however, she could not force the operations folks to take that seriously, especially when there was a problem with service delivery. They were measured on uptime and productivity, not security.

One of the most important aspects of security is metrics. Going back to our original requirements, we want to minimize the impact of a security breach on the organization. We have seen all kinds of metrics reported, such as the number of viruses stopped at the Internet Gateway, malware detected on intrusion detection systems (IDS), number of investigations performed, etc. The real metrics should reflect the impact to the organization and link directly into service delivery. Executives sometimes want a single value for showing how well IM/IT is being utilized and CIOs struggle to present this single metric. I have also seen charts or graphs showing green, yellow, or red, which is really meaningless. Colors are often used in projects to depict measurements. The bottom line is that metrics should be presented to show impact to the business. As we discussed in service delivery, the impact of a system outage has a much longer duration and higher impact than what IM/IT operations consider. The server may be back in operation but the front-line operations still have to catch up to get back to full production.

Controls can be divided into three broad categories: personnel, technology, and information. There are some essential controls that you need for each category to have a minimum level of security.

Personnel (Includes Management and Operations)

For personnel you need, at a minimum,

- *Background checks:* Do you know where your people worked before? Do they have a criminal record? Are there financial difficulties? The level of background check should be commensurate with the job. A database administrator has the keys to the kingdom and his or her background check should be fairly intense. Note that there are some new types of personal checking. One such check is called B-Scan, which assesses the degree to which a person responds to challenges of organizational responsibility and effectiveness expressed in their behaviors, attitudes, and judgments. B-Scan is still not available. Also consider periodic background checks for key personnel. Things change. Remember that they work only part of their day with the organization; what do they do the rest of the day?

- *Education and awareness:* A program must be in place to make people aware of information security and their responsibilities. This should include reporting potential breaches. The program must include information about social engineering, that is, how people manipulate other people to gain information.
- *Policies and procedures:* As boring as it sounds, policies are what can protect an organization from harm, especially when it comes to behavior. There are many cases where there have been no policies in place and when a person's behavior warrants discipline, there is no recourse except a legal one. Having the right policies will reduce the risk of lawsuits. One of your policies needs to deal with remote administration of devices.
- *Governance:* Often overlooked, a process of governance is important in managing information security and risk management. Executive buy-in is a must.
- *Identity and access management:* One of the most important aspects of managing access to critical assets is identity and asset management. This should include the audit of all access to assets, especially valuable assets. You need to have the capability of knowing who did what and when.
- *Incident response and management:* If there is a security incident, you need consistent procedures, including escalation to manage the incident. This must include forensic capabilities to manage and preserve information in case you need court evidence. Forensic capabilities can be a service. Incident response should be part of your IT team that manages service delivery.
- *Business continuity management:* Is it critical that your IT operations support the business 24/7? Do you have contingency plans that will enable this to happen?
- *Audit and review:* Making sure that you review logs is important, especially access logs. One of the most time-consuming aspects of security is the audit and review of logs. There are tools that can consolidate and automate logs. It is better that you, rather than the auditors, review the logs. Having said that, it is good practice to have auditors internal or external audit your systems and procedures.

- *Physical access controls:* Make sure that only authorized people have access to your systems and facilities. How many broom closets contain sensitive network routers and switches? How do you control access to these closets? In my days as a field engineer for digital equipment, I serviced equipment that was located in a dusty closet under the stairs. The door was left open to allow for air circulation. I wonder how many remote offices still have this level of trust and prop doors open during those hot summer days? And how many laptops and computers are stolen daily?

One of the most critical controls that you must consider is your hiring process. Is the person you are hiring suitable for the role and responsibilities that you are considering hiring that person for? Have you evaluated the responsibilities from a risk perspective? If the person is unreliable or irresponsible, should you hire that person for a position that is critical to operations? In his book entitled *Without Conscience*, Robert Hare (1993) discussed the screening process for a nuclear power plant. An industrial psychologist described the process as careful with the usual screening procedures—interviews, personality tests, and references. These procedures do not always succeed in detecting individuals with psychopathic behaviors. These individuals were notorious for being unreliable and irresponsible, not people who you would want managing or watching a nuclear power plant. The question you need to answer before you hire an individual: Is he or she suitable for this critical job? What is the impact if he or she is not?

Technology

For technology you need, at a minimum:

- *Asset management:* What assets are on your network? What legitimate hardware and software has your organization purchased and maintained? Asset management is often underutilized as a method of managing risks. If you know what hardware and software is appropriate, then everything else is inappropriate.

- *System hardening:* Removing unnecessary services and applications from servers is important. Reducing the attack surface means less places to attack and easier defense. Make sure all ports that are not required are closed.
- *Patching:* Need I say more? Keeping systems patched with the latest software updates from vendors means reduced vulnerabilities. Systems that are not patched are most vulnerable to internal and external attacks. A compromised system can allow attackers access to other systems.
- *Firewalls and other information protection services:* Firewalls are the most common devices used in protecting organizations. The problem is that the network is now like Swiss cheese, full of holes to allow users access to applications. Firewalls are still very useful in establishing zones such that access to your most valuable data is limited. Look at other devices such as intrusion prevention or unified threat management (UTM), wireless protection, or digital rights management to help manage the protection of valuable and sensitive information.
- *Identity and access management:* Still the most important control to help manage access to applications and information. Using something like two factor will help reduce your risks. In extreme cases, you may consider three factor. The audit portion is often overlooked or does not have rigor applied.
- *Application secure coding:* Cyber criminals have moved from operating system compromise to application compromise. That is not to say that you ignore hardening systems but you need to consider how you protect applications, especially public-facing or Web applications. Consider using OWASP secure coding standards as a means of setting minimum standards for your code. Institute secure code testing into your SDLC as a final test prior to applications going into production (see Chapter 12).
- *Resilience of infrastructure:* If there is a requirement to have 24/7 operations, do you have enough redundancy built in your infrastructure to maintain operations?

Information

For information you need, at a minimum:

- *Information security identification and classification:* Identification and classification of your information is one of the most important steps in managing risks. You need to know where you want to maximize your protection. Much like a castle, there are layers of defense and your most valuable assets (the crown jewels) should have the most protection.
- *Information management:* Linking information security classification with information management means that you manage your information according to its life cycle. As the value of the information declines, you can move information from the most secure and expensive to less secure and less expensive protection. It also means that you are less likely to incur significant costs when you are asked to produce information for litigation.
- *Access management:* Because you have to manage your access anyway, using a holistic approach to identity and access management (IAM) will permit you to maximize your investment in IAM and reuse technologies appropriately.
- *Data loss prevention:* This is still a new technology but is being adopted by leaders in preventing sensitive information from leaving the organization.

These are the minimum requirements. Anti-virus controls are also important but are becoming difficult to manage both from the vendor's and your perspective. Because most anti-virus software is signature based, you are still vulnerable to new viruses until the vendor creates and releases a signature to protect against that virus. And with the newer viruses mutating or changing, the signatures that worked yesterday will not protect against a newly mutated virus today.

Access controls and identity proofing is one of the most important aspects of information security. When we consider userid and passwords as our primary method of identifying a person accessing our applications and information, we have no assurance that the USERID and password have not been compromised or shared. A sniffer or keyboard logger can capture userids and passwords easily and unknown to a person. Often, userids and passwords are hard coded into an application to facilitate a data transfer. Userids and passwords are a risk to every organization, and the sooner we move to two-factor or better access controls, the better security.

One aspect of access management is identity proofing. We have to consider that even when an individual presents him- or herself in person with the appropriate identification papers, we can be fooled. Frank Abagnale Jr. was a well-known confidence trickster and check forger in the 1960s who impersonated an airline pilot, doctor, lawyer, and even a prison inspector. His story demonstrates that social engineering represents a huge risk to organizations and individuals. If we want to continue to deploy new systems and applications, we must make sure we have proper identity proofing to minimize identity spoofing.

Digital rights management and information rights management are now important. Vendors such as Tripwire, Oracle, and IBM are all selling some sort of product that detects changes to files or does not permit files to be viewed, changed, or content extracted. Like any protection mechanisms, there are ways to get around these. It could be through social engineering, bribing someone to obtain information, for example, or some other method such as when information is moved from the primary source to a secondary or tertiary source as part of some operational requirement.

Controls can be viewed as either incoming or outgoing; that is, ingress or egress.

Ingress

Ingress means controlling incoming electronic access and information to your network, servers, workstations, and information. Remember that there are billions of electronic events every day. When we look at a simple workstation and go through the logs, there are a number of different interactions recorded. How much information you want to capture and how long you need to keep it will dictate what type of logs you need. One of the key decisions we had to make in managing our electronic logs was the volume. While I was with the BC government, CIO were capturing three different logs and storing these logs on the mainframe. We captured Netflow, Websense, and Intrusion

Prevention logs. The volume was significant. We actually had to limit the time we kept these logs due to the volume and the cost associated with storing these on the mainframe.

Egress

Egress means controlling outgoing information or connections. Most importantly, what information should you be allowing to leave your organization? When looking at the multiple ways of communications today and in the future, you need to consider applications like Skype, Facebook, MySpace, Instant Messaging, and Microsoft's Collaboration Suite as they all allow files to be shared. So what information are your users sharing, and should you be concerned? Our three key areas of concern are personal information, intellectual property, and poor decision information. The first two—personal information and intellectual property—comprise the information we need to be most concerned about when talking about egress controls. To protect that information, we need to consider technologies such as encryption, digital rights management, and information rights management. Encryption will protect your information from unauthorized access but will not prevent authorized users from sending the information in an unencrypted format to external parties. When we implemented Microsoft's Collaboration Suite, the lawyers who represented government were very concerned about these tools and having government's information shared in this manner. They initiated specific guidelines for controlling their use. We worked with them to make sure the appropriate mechanisms, policies, and procedures were in place to reduce the risk of a court-ordered search of all electronic information, including the Collaboration Suite.

Do you know what sensitive information has left the organization? Do you know if it has been printed? Do you know if someone is storing it on a memory stick? An important consideration for egress controls is data loss prevention or information rights management. This involves developing metadata that allows more control over sensitive information. Keywords are identified as critical words that communicate sensitive issues. Documents containing these keywords are considered sensitive. There are software and hardware solutions that look for these keywords and flag the transmission, printing, or saving of these documents.

Database Security and Monitoring

Much of our sensitive information is transactional. We process a large amount of information using applications and databases. Within the Justice Sector for the Province of British Columbia, there were a number of large applications such as JUSTIN and CORNET. JUSTIN is the Justice Information System and provides an integrated case-tracking solution to support the core business processes of criminal case processing. CORNET is the Corrections Network System and tracks all offenders, both adult and youth, from admission through to discharge. Both of the applications were audited. I am more familiar with the CORNET audit, as I prepared the response. There were ninety-two recommendations in all. A recommendation is when they find something wrong. Of the ninety-two recommendations, most were minor. There were nine key recommendations, as follows:

1. A process should be implemented for promptly informing key staff when user access must be modified because an employee's status has changed.
2. Exception reporting and regular monitoring should be conducted to identify and remedy incorrect access.
3. The database access levels should be corrected and regular monitoring conducted to ensure that access remains properly set and that all entries made directly to the database are detected.
4. Strategies, including effective monitoring, should be adopted to address the risk of users having full access.
5. Remove the ability to overwrite the audit trail from all users accessing the database directly.
6. The Oracle userid should be locked and only authorized support staff allowed to access it through their own userids.
7. Firewall settings should be reviewed and any excessive access removed.
8. A patching strategy should be adopted and implemented to address security-related vulnerabilities.

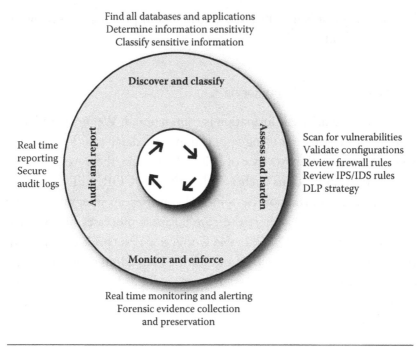

Find all databases and applications
Determine information sensitivity
Classify sensitive information

Figure 17.1   Database security.

9. A strategy should be developed to ensure adherence to security policies in the implementation of security settings and processes.

Although we addressed all the recommendations, I still found that we had not completed the work. I had recommended that we put in place real-time database security and monitoring (Figure 17.1). I wrote a request for funding and the request was rejected by the financial branch. Our response to the audit was to perform periodic reviews of user access. These were manual reviews and did not provide much information in terms of what users were doing daily. According to FISMA, PCI Data Security Standard (DSS), and most information security analysts, we should be performing continuous monitoring. If you are protecting sensitive data, I recommend that you adopt real-time database security and monitoring. I have taken liberal license from the *Guardium Quick Reference Guide* to represent in Figure 17.1 what I feel would be a good approach to database security and monitoring.

Two critical elements of database security and monitoring are

1. *Classifying your sensitive information:* Discussed further in Chapter 16. It is critical to determine, using a risk assessment, what your most valuable information is. The risk assessment should also include recommendations for protecting your information.
2. *Data Loss Prevention (DLP) strategy:* An important aspect is to know where your sensitive and valuable information is going. An important aspect of DLP is a controlled vocabulary. A controlled vocabulary enables you to audit and in some cases control what information is being moved, changed, or copied.

Defense in Depth

A *defense-in-depth strategy* should have both ingress and egress controls. A defense-in-depth strategy is analogous to a castle with its layers of defense. It includes both physical and logical controls. The objective is to make it more difficult for someone to penetrate your defenses. We also must consider insider attacks, which are much harder to defend against. If we take lessons from spies, hackers, and even simple stories like the Trojan horse and the city of Troy, we can mitigate many such threats. I do not advocate managing by threats. I would rather manage risks and vulnerabilities. There will always be a new threat that we never saw coming, perhaps a black swan that will cause significant disruption. Our strategy should be one of managing risks and mitigating impacts. That is why a defense-in-depth strategy works effectively. We already discussed the minimum set of controls that you should have in any organization. Most of the controls are ingress oriented; that is, we are looking at incoming packets to determine if they should be allowed to proceed. We need to move toward having more egress controls; that is, having the ability to know what information is moving out of the organization.

When you consider a defense-in-depth strategy, you must consider dependencies. In simple terms, the dependencies are complexity and uncertainty. We already know that the more complexity we have, the harder it is to defend. For example, if you are geographically distributed around the globe, then you have to deal with many locations in many countries with many cultures and many languages. As you know, that creates significant complexity in itself. We often transpose our own values and references on other locations and cultures, thinking that writing a single policy should be enough. However, the policy may not have the same meaning or is translated differently. A simple example is in Mexico where they do not work "9 to 5" as is expected in the United States and Canada. They work different hours, having the main meal at 3:00 p.m., which is family time. We have mistaken the siesta time as the time they go to sleep, whereas they are and will always use that time for family gatherings and their meal. They also go back to work and work until 8:00 p.m. We need to understand these different customs, cultures, and languages to develop the right policies and practices.

One final note on a defense-in depth-strategy: You need to have a monitoring capability and that means you need people. In many cases you can automate the processes but at the end of the day, there still needs to be someone who can interpret the results.

Audit and Compliance

How do you know if you have the right controls? Controls must be considered in terms of your requirements. What are the requirements that you must meet? Do you have a requirement for regulatory or industry compliance, such as PCI data security requirements? How about Sarbanes-Oxley? Are there local, state, or federal requirements? There are a lot of different compliance requirements that you must meet, and typically there are a lot of crossover requirements between each of these requirements. In terms of liabilities, what protection mechanisms will mitigate most of your liabilities, including the compliance requirements?

One of the most important aspects of information security is audit. Audit is the measurement of your controls; in other words, are you doing the right things at the right time with the right people? An audit should answer the following question: Do we have the right controls?

The first step is an audit of the existing controls. The audit can be internal or external. I prefer an external audit to make sure you are getting a third-party review of your controls. What you need to consider is the depth of the audit. How much you want to spend on the audit will determine the depth of the audit. At a minimum, the audit should cover the following:

- Access management
- Application security
- Operational processes
- Policies
- Compliance requirements (PCI, SOX, etc.)
- Incidents/breaches (the past may not reflect current but a history of incidents may indicate problem areas)
- Controls (what controls, ingress and egress, are deployed; technical, procedural)

Information security is one part technical controls, one part procedural controls, and one part monitoring (i.e., auditing to make sure controls are working).

Documentation

One of the first things I did when I took over responsibility for information security within the Justice Sector was to create a Justice Sector Information Security Framework. It describes how information security is managed within the Justice Sector and our relationships with our partners.

The document was arranged in sections as follows:

- *Governance:* describes how information security is managed within the ministry.
- *Business Requirements:* describes what the requirements are for security and how that integrates with the information resource management plan.
- *Architecture:* describes alignment with enterprise and other architectures.
- *Principles:* describes key security principles.
- *Policies:* describes ISO 17799 and government policies.
- *Defense-in-Depth Design:* describes the security deployed to protect the information and information systems.

- *Business Enablement Design:* describes the security deployed to enable users to access and manage information and information systems securely.
- *Strategic Planning:* describes future plans.

This framework was our guide and overarching document that was accepted in the Justice Sector as to how we manage information security. Further operational and more detailed procedures were created to link to the framework. Our framework did not contain any sensitive information and could be published across the government. As a matter of fact, many of the ministries used the Justice Sector Information Security Framework as a foundation for their own information security frameworks.

One final aspect of the framework was security architecture. We adopted SABSA as our architecture standard. SABSA links neatly to Zachman and provides a nice framework to deliver cohesive information security solutions to organizations. Like Zachman, you only implement the portions that apply to your organization.

Information Security Architecture

According to Wikipedia, enterprise information security architecture was formally introduced by Gartner, Inc., in their whitepaper entitled "Incorporating Security into the Enterprise Architecture Process." The white paper was published on January 24, 2006. As seen in Figure 17.2 from Wikipedia (http://en.wikipedia.org), information security architecture is now aligned with business, information, and technology architecture. This diagram represents a one-dimensional view of enterprise architecture. Enterprise architecture is now adopted as a formal method of describing the structure of an organization's complex enterprise systems. Probably the most recognized framework for enterprise architecture is the Zachman Framework. Twenty years ago it was recognized that organizations were spending more money building IT systems and it was difficult to keep these new IT systems aligned with the business. "Enterprise architecture" was created to address these two problems. Enterprise architecture initially started out dealing with business, information, and technology. Sometime in the early 2000s, it was recognized that

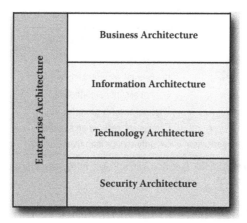

Figure 17.2   Aligning security architecture. (*Source:* From http://en.wikipedia.org.)

security was critical in the success of organizations, hence the need for information security architecture.

At a high-level concept, security was always a consideration of business, information, and technology to create enterprise architecture. Security architecture in Zachman's Enterprise Architecture was identified as something for the detailed representation and mostly dealt with people. Given the importance of information in organizations today, it made better sense to add security as an architecture to elevate its importance in enterprise architecture.

Information security architecture is a method of applying a methodology to describe the existing and future structure for an organization's security processes, systems, personnel, and units to align with business goals and strategies. Enterprise security architecture answers the problem of ad hoc building of security requirements based on a specific business, technical, or information need. Many security solutions were developed, designed, acquired, and installed on a tactical basis. Each solution operates independently and there is no opportunity to consider each of these solutions on a strategic level. These ad hoc solutions often cost more to maintain than if the organization had invested in an overall strategic solution that solved multiple business problems. Strategic solutions require a thorough understanding of the business requirements, such as cost reduction, modularity, scalability, operability, usability, and integration with enterprise IT architecture and its legacy systems.

Table 17.2 Security Architecture Views

VIEW	ARCHITECTURE
Business view	Contextual security architecture
Architect's view	Conceptual security architecture
Designer's view	Logical security architecture
Builder's view	Physical security architecture
Tradesman's view	Component security architecture
Service manager's view	Security service management

Source: From SABSA Executive White Paper; http://www.sabsa-institute. org.

Information system security (anti-virus, firewalls) is a small part of information security. Information security has been called information assurance or information risk management. Information security is a part of business risk management, which also includes business continuity and physical security. Any enterprise security architecture should consider all these different aspects.

SABSA appears to be the model and methodology used by many information security architects. SABSA actually started around 1995 with a model and methodology for developing enterprise information architecture. The primary characteristic of the SABSA model is that everything must be derived from an analysis of the business requirements for security and risk management. The SABSA model is similar in layout to the Zachman Enterprise Architecture model. The top categories are arranged a bit differently: Zachman uses What, How, Where, Who, When, and Why, whereas SABSA uses What, Why, How, Who, Where, and When.

SABSA has layered architecture views, as shown in Table 17.2:

- The *business view* is the description of the business context in which your secure system must be designed, built, and operated. The business view is called the *contextual security architecture.*
- The *architect's view* defines principles and fundamental concepts that guide the selection and organization of the logical and physical elements at the lower layer of abstraction. The architect's view is called the *conceptual security architecture.*
- The *designer's view* involves the identification and specification of the logical architectural elements of an overall system.

This view models the business as a system. It shows the major architectural security elements in terms of logical security services and describes the logical flow of control and the relationships between these logical elements. The designer's view is called the *logical security architecture*.

- The *builder's view* is the technology model that can be used to construct the system. The builder can take the logical and architectural elements of the system to create physical security mechanisms and servers. The builder's view is called the *physical security architecture*.

- The *tradesman's view* comprises the coders, installers, and integrators needed to construct the technology. These specialists are referred to as *tradesmen* and they work with hardware, software, and interface specifications and standards. The tradesman's view is called the *component security architecture*.

- The *service manager's view* concerns the operations, maintenance, and management of the systems. After the system has been designed and built, someone has to run it. The framework for operating, maintaining, managing, and monitoring the system is called the *security service management architecture*.

The SABSA framework places heavy emphasis on the duality of risk: the risk of negative outcomes and the opportunity of positive outcomes. Many definitions of operational risk focus on the negative aspects of risks and potential loss events. This is unfortunate; there are opportunities to develop operational excellence, and improved service and product delivery to customers. It can also contribute to meeting the performance goals of the organization.

I spoke with John Zimmermann, who was the Chief Information Security Architect for the Justice Sector in the BC government; he was using SABSA to develop an overall security architecture for the Justice Sector. He was working within fiscal restraints to adopt SABSA by leveraging the ICON project to help create some architectural standards for information security. Specifically, he was using the business drivers for ICON to help understand the key business attributes that must be protected by information security. He was looking to establish key performance indicators and key risk indicators to enable him to perform a gap analysis on the existing controls to confirm that the controls were sufficient or that there was a gap. In the end he hoped to pick a few areas that would produce some information security standards that he could take forward to the Justice Sector as a whole and to the government CIO to get these approved as government standards.

Whether you use SABSA or some other security architecture model and methodology, the important part is the business focus. Taking into consideration both positive opportunities and negative risks, you can achieve balance. Systems are very complex, and complexity with constant change will cause failures. A poorly designed architecture will be more expensive to build and operate.

Reporting on Information Security

One of the most difficult aspects of information security is reporting something meaningful that gets the attention of the executives. We reported viruses stopped at the gateway, investigations per year, and security incidents; these may have grabbed the attention of middle managers and directors but did not really get the attention of the executives. There are a lot of security metrics that have meaningful information but as it gets filtered to the top, it is severely reduced in significance. Executives have their sights on outcomes. What concerns them are the impacts to their outcomes. It takes more work but the focus must be on the impact to service delivery. When you consider that a virus infection means you have to clean the system and the system is unavailable, the impact can be measured in time. That is, the time the system is unavailable. If the system is compromised, there are many other factors but there is an impact to service delivery, especially servers containing mission-critical applications and sensitive data. There could be a very heavy impact to the business if a server is compromised and information is lost or stolen.

So what security events impact have an impact on business outcomes? We can definitely say that a security breach where credit card information is stolen is an event that has an impact on an organization. However, that is a crisis situation and the whole organization is affected by such a breach as there is damage to reputation, brand, and customer trust and loyalty. There will always be minor breaches and security events that need to get the attention of the executives.

Creating awareness at the executive level promotes information security—or as we have been discussing, information protection. In discussing DLP with Symantec, there may be exception reporting that specific sensitive information has been accessed by an unauthorized person. This could indicate a security breach where information may be stolen. The fact that an exception report was generated by a control mechanism will help demonstrate that controls are working and executives are getting good value from the expenditure. It shows that you spend your dollars well and the organization gets good value.

It should be noted that the Federal Information Security Management Act of 2002 was changed to move agencies and federal departments toward continuous monitoring of information security controls to give leaders a sense of the state of security for their information systems. NIST created a series of publications to guide federal agencies in the implementation, certification, and accreditation of federal information system security. In August 2009, NIST released a major revision of Special Publication 800-53.

So what do FISMA and NIST mean by continuous monitoring of information security controls, and how is this reported? It would not make sense to report every event. In a large network, there are millions of events. What is a significant event and what is routine? In the case of insider threat, most insider activities are routine events. Authorized access is still access that is authorized, and the activities associated with authorized access are routine. So what are the anomalies? What events should you be concerned about? In simple terms, anything that touches your most sensitive and valuable information.

In most organizations, our information management practices are abysmal. As an example, in the Provincial Government of British Columbia, I proposed that we classify our information through a series of projects that would develop a set of information security classification building blocks. One of the outcomes of this was the adoption of a government-wide information security classification schema. This schema was proposed by the Canadian federal government through the Public Sector CIO Council in 2004. It appears to be adopted by both the provincial and federal government. A sample of the schema is included in Appendix D.

For the most part, the remainder of the proposal was ignored and most information within the province is still not properly classified.

U.S. Federal Government Requirements for Information Security

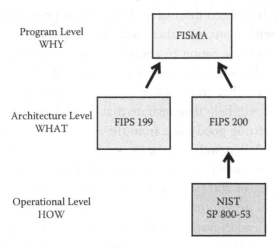

Figure 17.3 U.S. government information security requirements.

This means that the information is not properly identified and the proper protection mechanisms put in place. The one exception that I am certain about is the Criminal Justice Branch, which has determined that it easier to classify all their assets at a high level and they have encrypted all their information.

FISMA, NIST, and FIPS

The U.S. government has spent billions of dollars making sure they have the right security. FISMA outlines the requirements for information security. The purpose was to secure cyberspace and the economic and national security interests of the United States. The U.S. Congress and the president recognized the importance of electronic information, and FISMA is the overarching requirement for federal government agencies to develop, document, and implement an agency-wide information security program. Figure 17.3 describes how the U.S. government has prescribed a framework of *Why, What,* and *How* at the different levels to help agencies comply with the requirements for good information security. According to FISMA, an information security program should include the following:

- Periodic assessment of risks
- Policies and procedures

- Subordinate plans
- Security awareness training
- Periodic testing and evaluation
- Process for planning, implementing, evaluating, and documenting remedial actions
- Procedures for detecting, reporting, and responding to security incidents
- Plans and procedures to ensure continuous operations for information systems

Why

FISMA prescribes an oversight responsibility for all agencies in terms of information security and their information and information systems. FISMA describes that the head of each agency has overall responsibility for providing information security protection commensurate with the risk and magnitude of harm resulting from unauthorized use, disclosure, disruption, and modification or destruction of information and information systems. This may be delegated to the CIO, who may designate a senior agency information security officer to carry out the CIO's responsibilities under FISMA.

To support FISMA, a number of standards and guidelines were developed. Although there have been several standards developed, the three that are key to enabling information security are (1) Federal Information Processing Standard (FIPS) 199, (2) FIPS 200, and (3) NIST Special Publication (SP) 800-53.

What

FIPS 199 is the "Standards for Security Categorization of Federal Information and Information System" (http://csrc.nist.gov). The intent of FIPS 199 is to establish security categories for federal agency information and information systems. Security categories are based on impacts to information and information systems for the following three security objectives: confidentiality, integrity, and availability. Table 17.3 outlines the three security objectives and potential impacts. These impacts are classified as Low, Moderate, and High. I have included another way of looking at risk impacts in Appendix C; the Risk Impact Scales

Table 17.3   FIPS 199 Impact Scale

	POTENTIAL IMPACT		
SECURITY OBJECTIVE	LOW	MODERATE	HIGH
CONFIDENTIALITY			
Preserving authorized restrictions on information access and disclosure, including means for protecting personal privacy and proprietary information. [44 U.S.C., SEC. 3542]	The unauthorized disclosure of information could be expected to have a limited adverse effect on organizational operations, organizational assets, or individuals.	The unauthorized disclosure of information could be expected to have a serious adverse effect on organizational operations, organizational assets, or individuals.	The unauthorized disclosure of information could be expected to have a severe or catastrophic adverse effect on organizational operations, organizational assets, or individuals.
INTEGRITY			
Guarding against improper information modification or destruction, and includes ensuring information non-repudiation and authenticity. [44 U.S.C., SEC. 3542]	The unauthorized modification or destruction of information could be expected to have a limited adverse effect on organizational operations, organizational assets, or individuals.	The unauthorized modification or destruction of information could be expected to have a serious adverse effect on organizational operations, organizational assets, or individuals.	The unauthorized modification or destruction of information could be expected to have a severe or catastrophic adverse effect on organizational operations, organizational assets, or individuals.
AVAILABILITY			
Ensuring timely and reliable access to and use of information. [44 U.S.C., SEC. 3542]	The disruption of access to or use of information or an information system could be expected to have a limited adverse effect on organizational operations, organizational assets, or individuals.	The disruption of access to or use of information or an information system could be expected to have a serious adverse effect on organizational operations, organizational assets, or individuals.	The disruption of access to or use of information or an information system could be expected to have a severe or catastrophic adverse effect on organizational operations, organizational assets, or individuals.

Source: From FIPS 199; http://csrc.nist.gov/publications.

provide a financial impact and use a logarithmic scale based on some defined value to represent risk impacts to an organization.

FIPS Publication 200, "Minimum Security Requirements for Federal Information and Information Systems" (http://csrc.nist.gov), provides federal agencies with the minimum security standards for federal information and information systems. FIPS 200 defines seventeen security areas for federal information and information systems. FIPS 200 is not prescriptive; it dictates the minimum security requirements. It is up to each agency to determine how to implement these requirements. The following section provides a listing of the seventeen security areas as defined by FIPS 200.

Specifications for Minimum Security Requirements Access Control (AC): "Organizations must limit information system access to authorized users, processes acting on behalf of authorized users, or devices (including other information systems) and to the types of transactions and functions that authorized users are permitted to exercise."

Note: Access control usually equates to password control. For good security, access control must consider both physical access and logical access. I think that two-factor authentication should be the minimum for cyber access control.

Awareness and Training (AT): "Organizations must: (i) ensure that managers and users of organizational information systems are made aware of the security risks associated with their activities and of the applicable laws, Executive Orders, directives, policies, standards, instructions, regulations, or procedures related to the security of organizational information systems; and (ii) ensure that organizational personnel are adequately trained to carry out their assigned information security-related duties and responsibilities."

Note: Awareness and training are ongoing processes. There is no such thing as train once in cyber security. Threats are continuously evolving.

Audit and Accountability (AU): "Organizations must: (i) create, protect, and retain information system audit records to the extent needed to enable the monitoring, analysis, investigation, and reporting of unlawful, unauthorized, or inappropriate information system activity;

and (ii) ensure that the actions of individual information system users can be uniquely traced to those users so they can be held accountable for their actions."

Note: One of the most important aspects of audit is monitoring. If you do not look at the logs, there is no way of detecting anomalies.

Certification, Accreditation, and Security Assessments (CA): "Organizations must: (i) periodically assess the security controls in organizational information systems to determine if the controls are effective in their application; (ii) develop and implement plans of action designed to correct deficiencies and reduce or eliminate vulnerabilities in organizational information systems; (iii) authorize the operation of organizational information systems and any associated information system connections; and (iv) monitor information system security controls on an ongoing basis to ensure the continued effectiveness of the controls."

Note: Interesting thing about certification and accreditation: The system could be noncompliant the moment after it has been certified and accredited due to changes made by system administrators to fix a problem.

Configuration Management (CM): "Organizations must: (i) establish and maintain baseline configurations and inventories of organizational information systems (including hardware, software, firmware, and documentation) throughout the respective system development life cycles; and (ii) establish and enforce security configuration settings for information technology products employed in organizational information systems."

Note: Good idea. All systems should be baselined. Any failures in the system (especially when infected with a virus) should result in the system being reformatted to the baseline configuration.

Contingency Planning (CP): "Organizations must establish, maintain, and effectively implement plans for emergency response, backup operations, and post-disaster recovery for organizational information systems to ensure the availability of critical information resources and continuity of operations in emergency situations."

Note: Business continuity planning must be in place to ensure critical operations and information are available when needed. The one question that you need to answer is how long do you wait until you enact your business continuity plan?

Identification and Authentication (IA): "Organizations must identify information system users, processes acting on behalf of users, or devices and authenticate (or verify) the identities of those users, processes, or devices, as a prerequisite to allowing access to organizational information systems."

Note: There is a requirement for two-factor identification and authentication. In cyberspace, we have no identity unless it has been properly validated.

Incident Response (IR): "Organizations must: (i) establish an operational incident handling capability for organizational information systems that includes adequate preparation, detection, analysis, containment, recovery, and user response activities; and (ii) track, document, and report incidents to appropriate organizational officials and/or authorities."

Note: Incident response is important. Getting the system back into operations is critical. The next step is the Post Incident Review (PIR); this tells you what happened. It also gives you historical information to determine if this is something that is occurring frequently and, if it is, what steps you need to mitigate.

Maintenance (MA): "Organizations must: (i) perform periodic and timely maintenance on organizational information systems; and (ii) provide effective controls on the tools, techniques, mechanisms, and personnel used to conduct information system maintenance."

Note: This is critical. The most important part of maintenance are the updates. Software updates fix vulnerabilities. There will be pushback from the database folks, and these updates should be put into the context of operational requirements. A bad upgrade can definitely affect system uptime.

Media Protection (MP): "Organizations must: (i) protect information system media, both paper and digital; (ii) limit access to information on information system media to authorized users; and (iii) sanitize or destroy information system media before disposal or release for reuse."

Note: How do you know when an authorized user is taking information for inappropriate intentions? Do you search all users for media?

Physical and Environmental Protection (PE): "Organizations must: (i) limit physical access to information systems, equipment, and the respective operating environments to authorized individuals; (ii) protect the physical plant and support infrastructure for information systems; (iii) provide supporting utilities for information systems; (iv) protect information systems against environmental hazards; and (v) provide appropriate environmental controls in facilities containing information systems."

Note: Physical access to equipment means easy compromise.

Planning (PL): "Organizations must develop, document, periodically update, and implement security plans for organizational information systems that describe the security controls in place or planned for the information systems and the rules of behavior for individuals accessing the information systems."

Note: Plans are good. However, I have seen too many plans collect dust on shelves.

Personnel Security (PS): "Organizations must: (i) ensure that individuals occupying positions of responsibility within organizations (including third-party service providers) are trustworthy and meet established security criteria for those positions; (ii) ensure that organizational information and information systems are protected during and after personnel actions such as terminations and transfers; and (iii) employ formal sanctions for personnel failing to comply with organizational security policies and procedures."

Note: This is where monitoring and audit are so important. Detecting anomalies for authorized users is difficult.

Risk Assessment (RA): "Organizations must periodically assess the risk to organizational operations (including mission, functions, image, or reputation), organizational assets, and individuals, resulting from the operation of organizational information systems and the associated processing, storage, or transmission of organizational information."

Note: Risk assessments are good. Again, the system may be in compliance during the risk assessment and drop out of compliance the next moment.

System and Services Acquisition (SA): "Organizations must: (i) allocate sufficient resources to adequately protect organizational information systems; (ii) employ system development life cycle processes that incorporate information security considerations; (iii) employ software usage and installation restrictions; and (iv) ensure that third-party providers employ adequate security measures to protect information, applications, and/or services outsourced from the organization."

Note: Use an international standard such as OWASP to ensure that the coding is done securely.

System and Communications Protection (SC): "Organizations must: (i) monitor, control, and protect organizational communications (i.e., information transmitted or received by organizational information systems) at the external boundaries and key internal boundaries of the information systems; and (ii) employ architectural designs, software development techniques, and systems engineering principles that promote effective information security within organizational information systems."

Note: All communication should be encrypted.

System and Information Integrity (SI): "Organizations must: (i) identify, report, and correct information and information system flaws in a timely manner; (ii) provide protection from malicious code at appropriate locations within organizational information systems; and (iii) monitor information system security alerts and advisories and take appropriate actions in response."

Note: Standard defense-in-depth strategy should include anti-virus. Although anti-virus is not effective against zero-day threats, it is effective against most other threats.

FIPS 200 mandates the use of NIST Special Publication 800-53 (http://csrc.nist.gov).

How

National Institute of Standards and Technology (NIST) Special Publication (SP) 800-53, "Security Controls for Federal Information Systems," is a set of baseline security controls. SP800-53 provides guidance for agencies in applying these baseline security controls. The application of these security controls should demonstrate that the agency is in compliance with governmental, organizational, and institutional security requirements. The organization has the responsibility to properly select the appropriate controls and implement these controls effectively.

There are seventeen security control families. These align with FIPS 200. In NIST SP800-53 there is one additional control family (Program Management), which is designed to provide security controls at the organizational level rather than the information or information systems level. NIST SP800-53 further categorizes these into three general classes of security controls: management, operational, and technical.

NIST SP800-53 provides a concise statement of the specific security capabilities needed to protect an aspect of information and an information system. These are designed to provide the minimum level of security based on the categorization of the information and information system (FIPS 199 categorization based on Low, Medium, and High).

In Chapter 3, NIST SP800-53 provides a fairly good risk management strategy for the life cycle of information security. An outline of the six steps follows:

Step 1: Categorize information systems according to FIPS 199/ SP800-60.
Step 2: Select security controls based on FIPS 200/SP800-53.
Step 3: Implement security controls SP800 series.
Step 4: Access security controls SP800-53A.
Step 5: Authorize information systems SP800-37.
Step 6: Monitor security controls SP800-53A.

Of course, the devil is in the details. In the electronic world, information propagates and replicates quickly. When I worked on the certification and accreditation of the Defence Information System (DIN) for the Canadian Department of National Defence in 1997/1998, we found that the system was used for more than unclassified information as we had designed. The intent of the DIN was to allow members and staff to post information for sharing. When the users discovered that they could post and share information, some of them posted information at a higher classification than the systems were designed for. This occurred after we had completed the certification and accreditation of all the systems. So although we had completed the work and submitted the certification and accreditation for review, information was constantly changing on the DIN. The point of this is to emphasize that although you may classify the information system as having a low impact for confidentiality, integrity, and/or availability, you may be surprised at the information that propagates onto the system, especially for unstructured information systems. Chapter 16 contains more on how to categorize information sensitivity.

Payment Card Industry Data Security Standard

If your organization processes credit cards, then you need to be in compliance with the PCI Data Security Standard (PCI DSS; https://www.pcisecuritystandards.org). The PCI DSS is not a standard for protecting all your information assets; it is a mandatory protection of cardholder data, specifically,

- *Cardholder data:* Primary account number (PAN); cardholder name, service code, and expiry date (these three data elements must be protected only if stored in conjunction with PAN).
- *Sensitive authorization data:* Full magnetic stripe data; CAV2/CVC2/CVV2/CID; and PIN/PIN block. *Sensitive authorization data is not permitted to be stored.*

The PCI DSS was developed for the benefit of the card issuers. It is a risk management strategy adopted to reduce the theft of credit card information. For the organization that processes credit cards, there are some key considerations that must be determined. PCI DSS applies to all system components. System components include all networks, servers, or application(s) connected to the cardholder data environment. The cardholder data environment is that part of the network and systems that processes cardholder and/or sensitive authorization data. The PCI DSS defines this further by network, server, and application. Any network component that is connected to the cardholder data environment is within scope. Any server, including but not limited to the Web, application, database, proxy, email, network time protocol (NTP), and domain name server (DNS) is in scope. All applications, including purchased, custom, internal, and external, are in scope. The best an organization can do is to limit the scope of the assessment for compliance.

One of the most effective methods of limiting the scope is network segmentation. Restricting access to the cardholder data environment using firewalls, routers, and access control lists (ACLs) will reduce the scope of the assessment. This in turn will reduce the cost of PCI DSS scans, which must be done quarterly and the yearly audit for compliance. It will further reduce the cost of maintaining the specific controls needed to maintain the cardholder data environment. Finally, it will reduce the risk to the organization by containing the information in specific controlled areas.

A further way of reducing this risk is to ensure that you have documented all cardholder data flows. This includes primary, secondary, and tertiary data requirements for cardholder information. Knowing where your cardholder information is stored and used is critical to successfully defining the scope of your need for scanning and accessing the environment.

At a high level, the PCI DSS is divided into six areas and twelve requirements, as summarized in Table 17.4.

PCI DSS compliance is mandatory if you process credit cards. In an Internet.com Tech Brief, Alan Radding talks about PCI DSS compliance. He outlines five mistakes that organizations make when dealing with PCI DSS:

1. Treating PCI as a checklist
2. Focusing primarily on costs
3. Not practicing PCI all year long
4. Failing to look at the big picture
5. Not doing enough to detect harmful things in the card environment

Table 17.4 PCI Data Security Standard High-Level Overview

AREA 1: BUILD AND MAINTAIN A SECURE NETWORK

Requirement 1	Install and maintain a firewall configuration to protect cardholder data.	
Requirement 2	Do not use vendor-supplied defaults for system passwords and other security parameters.	In a crisis, the focus is often on availability and not on security. A process must be in place to check that the defaults have been properly changed for any incident or event that requires upgrades, rebuilds, or changes to systems, applications, or networks.

AREA 2: PROTECT CARDHOLDER DATA

Requirement 3	Protect stored cardholder data.	Limit access and encrypt all data.
Requirement 4	Encrypt transmission of cardholder data across open, public networks.	Make sure you understand where decryption occurs and why. Encrypted data cannot be interpreted by data loss prevention systems.

AREA 3: MAINTAIN A VULNERABILITY MANAGEMENT PROGRAM

Requirement 5	Use and regularly update anti-virus software.	Mitigates risk of end-point infection and unauthorized access. Consider who accesses the data and what devices are used.
Requirement 6	Develop and maintain secure systems and applications.	Conformance to OWASP is a good starting point for applications. Regularly install patches as required. Develop secure coding practices and security sign-offs for SDLC.

AREA 4: IMPLEMENT STRONG ACCESS CONTROL MEASURES

Requirement 7	Restrict access to cardholder data by business need-to-know.	Make sure you know where the data is being used and stored. Primary usage is usually protected. Secondary and tertiary usage and storage are often overlooked.
Requirement 8	Assign a unique ID to each person with computer access.	Consider using two factor and replace userid and password for all critical applications.
Requirement 9	Restrict physical access to cardholder data.	Do not overlook printed data. Sometimes reports are printed and thrown out. Dumpster diving is still a way of getting sensitive information, so shred all documents.

AREA 5: REGULARLY MONITOR AND TEST NETWORKS

Requirement 10	Track and monitor all access to network resources and cardholder data.	Continuous monitoring should be enabled for all access.

Continued

Table 17.4 (*Continued*)   PCI Data Security Standard High-Level Overview

Requirement 11	Regularly test security systems and processes.	Penetration testing does help. Periodic review of security controls improves security.
AREA 6: MAINTAIN AN INFORMATION SECURITY POLICY		
Requirement 12	Maintain a policy that addresses information security.	It is not enough to have policy. Policies must be realistic and enforced.

Although compliance for onsite assessments boils down to a check-list of a yes or a no for compliance status, the real value of the controls that must be put in place is lost. This includes the cost, monitoring, and detection. In other words, PCI DSS can be treated like a baseline for good information security.

Analysis of Good Information Security Practices

I have presented several information security standards as well as my own thoughts on good information security practices. ISO 17799 (or as it is now called, ISO 27001:2005) is a good starting point for information security practices. Table 17.5 provides an outline of ISO 27001. We used ISO 17799 as our framework for information security policies at the BC government. Unfortunately, the writers were a little too enthusiastic about ISO 17799 and wrote a policy on every single section of ISO 17799. The problem was enforceability. I worked on the policies as a subject matter expert and my comments about the size, scope, and enforceability were mostly ignored. Policy people tend to get carried away and love to write exquisite policies. If the policies are not practical, not enforceable, and not measurable, then it is merely a paper exercise.

Table 17.6 provides a comparison of ISO 27001, NIST SP800-53, and PCI Data Security Standard. One of the measures of a good organization is compliance with standards. I still think that ISO 27001 is one of the better standards against which to measure your information security practices. PCI DSS focuses on credit card information, and the comparison shows that if you use PCI as the baseline, you will have gaps in your information security. Credit card information is sensitive information. We all know that, based on Ponemon and other studies, there is a significant cost if this information is inappropriately

Table 17.5   Summary of ISO 17799

DOMAIN	RECOMMENDED PRACTICES
1. Security Policy	Establish a comprehensive information security policy.
2. Organizing Information Security	Establish an internal security organization. Control external party use of your information.
3. Asset Management	Establish responsibility for your organization's assets. Use an information classification system.
4. Human Resource Management	Emphasize security prior to employment. Emphasize security during employment. Emphasize security at termination of employment.
5. Physical and Environmental Security	Use secure areas to protect facilities. Protect your organization's equipment.
6. Communications and Operations Management	Establish procedures and responsibilities. Control third-party service delivery. Carry out future system planning activities. Protect against malicious and mobile code. Establish backup procedures. Protect computer networks. Control how media are handled. Protect exchange of information. Protect electronic commerce services. Monitor information processing facilities.
7. Access Control	Control access to information. Manage user access rights. Encourage good access practices. Control access to network services. Control access to operating systems. Control access to applications and systems. Protect mobile and teleworking facilities.
8. Information System Acquisition, Development, and Maintenance	Identify information system security requirements. Make sure applications process information correctly. Use cryptographic controls to protect your information. Protect and control your organization's system files. Control development and support processes.
9. Information Security Incident Management	Report information security events and weaknesses. Manage information security incidents and improvements.
10. Business Continuity Management	Use continuity management to protect your information.
11. Compliance	Comply with legal requirements. Perform security compliance reviews. Carry out controlled information system audits.

Table 17.6 Comparison of ISO 27001, NIST 800-53, and PCI DSS

ISO 27001	NIST 800-53	PCI DSS
1. Security Policy	Awareness and Training (AT)	12. Maintain a policy that addresses information security
2. Organizing Information Security	Planning (PL)	
3. Asset Management	Configuration Management (CM)	3. Protect stored cardholder data
4. Human Resource Management	Personnel Security (PS)	
5. Physical and Environmental Security	Physical and Environmental Protection (PE)	9. Restrict physical access to cardholder data
6. Communications and Operations Management	Media Protection (MP) System and Communications Protection (SC) System and Information Integrity (SI)	1. Install and maintain a firewall configuration to protect cardholder data 2. Do not use vendor-supplied defaults for system passwords and other security parameters 5. Use and regularly update anti-virus software
7. Access Control	Access Control (AC) Identification and Authentication (IA)	7. Restrict access to cardholder data by business need-to-know 8. Assign a unique ID to each person with computer access 10. Track and monitor all access to network resources and cardholder data
8. Information System Acquisition, Development, and Maintenance	Maintenance (MA) System and Services Acquisition (SA)	4. Encrypt transmission of cardholder data across open, public networks 6. Develop and maintain secure systems and applications
9. Information Security Incident Management	Incident Response (IR)	11. Regularly test security systems and processes
10. Business Continuity Management	Contingency Planning (CP)	
11. Compliance	Audit and Accountability (AU) Certification, Accreditation, and Security Assessments (CA) Risk Assessment (RA)	

disclosed, lost, or stolen. Compliance with PCI DSS is mandatory if you want to continue processing credit cards.

A comparison is useful because it allows you to look at what standards your organization must be in compliance with and how using these standards could improve your controls. If you are using compliance as the metric for your security program, you are not leveraging your investments fully.

Compliance is an output of specific controls. Good security is an outcome of a good security program.

There are a lot more requirements for information security that may cost your organization big money for noncompliance. It depends on your industry sector. We have not even discussed HIPAA or SOX, or privacy legislation such as California SB 1386. The question is: Do you react to each one separately, or do you have a coordinated risk management strategy that encompasses your compliance and security requirements?

Whether you are dealing with credit cards, personal information, or IP, you are managing information. The questions are: How are you managing your information? What controls are in place to protect that information?

Employee, Hacker, Insider, or Outsider

When it comes to risk and risk management, the hardest risk to manage is people. People cause compromises. Whether the compromise is caused by an accident, such as forgetting to reset the default password to the administrator account after a system rebuild or a deliberate attempt to crack passwords to get at some credit card information, a person is ultimately responsible. People have good days and bad days. People have lives other than what we see at work. Some people are spies or operators and although they work for your company, they are also working for your competitor or some foreign government. In his book entitled *Spies among Us*, Ira Winkler (2005) talked about how difficult it is to detect a spy. He described two documents while he was working at the NSA that illustrate the point. Both documents describe an ideal candidate as

- Shows an interest in what coworkers are doing;
- Always volunteers for extra work or assignments;
- Works late hours; and
- Rarely takes a vacation.

One document was written on how to get promoted at NSA, whereas the other was written to be aware of signs that an employee may be a spy or have something to hide. Sometimes your hardest working employee may be a spy or have ulterior motives. These ulterior motives may include stealing information or funds from the organization. It may also be the example of someone trying to get ahead or just keeping up. The point is that you do not know. Even asking may not give you the answer. Consider that someone with psychopathic behaviors may be able to lie sincerely, as was described by Dr. Robert Hare in his books on psychopaths. You may never know.

Ira Winkler (2005) went on to discuss Money, Ideology, Coercion, and Ego (MICE) or the potential motivators for people to commit spying or other anti-social behaviors. Downsizing, rightsizing, transformation—or whatever you want to call cutting jobs—creates more opportunities for people, especially when revenge or the "they owed it to me" factor is included. We all might have our own reasons for being motivated to steal, spy, or damage or destroy; the bottom line is that people's behaviors cannot always be rationalized.

We typically divide the threats and risks into two camps: insiders and outsiders. Insiders have authorized access to the information. Outsiders are not authorized and have no access to the information. There also is the possibility that there is collusion between insiders and outsiders, as described by Winkler (2005) when he discussed spying.

One thing that we are never aware of is the person who takes little pieces of information. Bill Boni coined the term "death by a thousand cuts," which translates into small losses of information accumulate into major losses. Another way of looking at this is to consider "Long Tail" as it relates to selling books. When Chris Anderson (2004) first coined the phrase, he was arguing that products in low demand or having a low volume can collectively make up a market share that rivals or exceeds the current best sellers and blockbusters. The same can be true for information leakage. People often steal small pieces of information, such as a couple of pages at a time, to avoid detection; as an example, take Brian Patrick Regan working for TRW and stealing top-secret documents by printing them out a few pages at a time. We further discuss information leakage and data loss prevention in the section Data Loss Prevention/Information Leakage in this chapter.

Insiders

Insiders are generally employees of the organization. They may also be partners or have an association with the organization. In the Justice Sector we often provided local police with access to JUSTIN and CORNET. We also provided limited access to CORNET to social workers and hospital workers who had a need to know about certain inmates relating to a medical condition or who were released on probation and required social assistance.

The extended family of an organization often encompasses customers and clients. There seems to be an ever-increasing need for people to access their information from government, medical facilities, and any other organization that has their information. In most cases, customer or client information is very limited and people have restricted access only to their own information. In unusual circumstances, that information is exposed to a much wider audience, including hackers, as we witnessed in the AT&T breach of pre-order information for Apple's iPhone 4, in which there have been several mishaps following the first breach where over 100,000 iPad user's confidential information was hacked on June 9, 2010. Since then, several customers have gotten different names when they check their order status. We do not know who our digital customer really is. Names can be forged, changed, and addresses, telephone numbers faked. The cartoon by Peter Steiner in *The New Yorker* (July 5, 1993 issue) sums it up nicely: "On the Internet nobody knows you are a dog." The cartoon shows two dogs, one sitting at a computer. We do not have any assurance that the person placing an order is a valid person or a hacker with a stolen credit card. And social networks create even more opportunities for hackers and misrepresentation.

So one of the first questions you need to ask is who has access to your information? This applies to both physical and logical access.

Janitors have physical access to your systems and work late at night when no one else is there. Is that really a janitor, or a spy, or a hacker? Yes, the company that you hired to do the cleaning has done a background check. He may show a clean record but is really an operative for another organization. Did you check his lifestyle? How about that gambling debt? Is he a cyber warrior and spends considerable time at Poker-on-Line?

We have this trust relationship with people who we hire and the people who we work with. As Ira Winkler (2005) described in his book *Spies among Us*, we are often beguiled by the person next door or that nice person in the office who is always willing to take extra work home. Insiders can be divided into several types: employees, partners, contractors, and outsourced.

Employees Our most trusted people are our employees. They were hired to perform specific tasks and are paid by the organization. In many cases, they signed a confidentiality agreement or swore an oath. We have to trust them. They are given access to our most sensitive and valuable information.

In most cases we are dealing with knowledge workers. Knowledge workers sell their know-how and knowledge to companies. We are blessed by them and cursed by them. We all have had the genius who creates the most complex program, or architecture, or something unique. Then he or she leaves, leaving us to clean up the mess.

We may be working with employees who handle cash. When it comes to electronic funds transfer, it is often difficult to spot the embezzler. In their book, *The Accountants Handbook of Fraud and Commercial Crime*, on fraud and criminal crime, the authors provide some typical examples of fraud committed by employees:

- Officers of a company issuing false financial reports to improve their own performance measures;
- Managers receiving kickbacks from suppliers;
- Employees inflating their expense accounts;
- Employees skimming cash or account receivable lapping; and
- Stock market manipulation and insider trading.

We also know that employees steal customer lists, IP, processes, special set up and configuration information, telephone lists, confidential information, and just about anything that they think may be valuable to them and their next job. A survey in 2009 by Cyber-Ark Software Inc. asked the question about privileged users (administrators): What information would you steal? Interestingly, there was a very long list of information that they would steal, including:

- Privileged password list (42%)
- Financial reports (46%)
- Copy of Research & Development plans (46%)
- Mergers and Acquisitions plans (47%)
- Email server admin account (47%)
- Customer database (47%)
- CEO's password (46%)

The questions that this begs is: How much of this information is already in their possession? What other information do they have access to, and what can they do with that information?

There are no sure-fire ways to prevent this from happening. We establish a set of controls and countermeasures including periodic audits to help reduce our risks of employee theft. One of the easiest things to steal is information. We enable our employees to access this information. They need the information to do their work. In many cases we compartmentalize the information within an organization. We deny access except for a need to know. However, we do not control administrators. If you think about email, it is like sending a postcard in the mail. Anyone who can see it can read it. And we often attach sensitive material to the email or include information in the email itself. How about those marketing plans? Did the administrator see that information and give it to his drinking buddy who works over at your competitor? We talk about our work over coffee at the coffee shop. We discuss our strategy over lunch at the local restaurant. Who hears that information? The old adage from World War II that "loose lips sink ships" applies to our everyday conversations. Ira Winkler (2005) in *Spies among Us*, told of a time when he was asked to penetrate a company and went into a boardroom where there were neatly piled stacks of paper outlining next week's sales plans, including customer information. Apparently it was done the night before so sales reps could have their meeting early in the morning and get on the road quicker. What was to prevent someone from copying the plan?

One of the most important things to remember is that when employees leave, transfer to new areas, or retire, we need to make sure we review their access and stop any access that is no longer required. This is especially true with administrators and power users who may have multiple accounts set up on multiple systems.

Partners   We all have partners in business. While I was working as a consultant for several large consulting firms, we often combined forces with some of our competitors to bid on very large projects. We called it "co-opetition." There was always a dance of different vendors who needed just that certain expertise or product to compete for the business. And the dance will continue as organizations vie for business.

Supply chains like Wal-Mart have embraced just-in-time delivery of goods to reduce their costs. This just-in-time delivery is about information. As the products are consumed off the shelf, Wal-Mart orders more. There is a direct link between the cash register information about a product and the supplier. This tightly couples the supplier with the retailer. There is a lot of competitive information available for competitors of Wal-Mart and their suppliers.

So what controls do you have in place about your information that you share with your partners? Do they have the equivalent or better controls about your information that they get from you?

Contractors   Using contractors is good if you need a specific project completed or to complement your staff. At the Ministry of Attorney General, we had a project manager who did a reasonable job of managing a fairly large deployment project. We eventually replaced him with an internal project manager. The contractor retained a large number of sensitive documents about the project even after his contract was terminated although the contract stipulated that he remove all such information from his systems at the termination of the contract. We only found out about this information some time later due to some other issue he was having and a third party was involved. The third party came into possession of this information and returned it to the ministry. The realization that he had this information—and may have had more sensitive information due to the nature of his work—created the need for a letter from the legal department to him to properly destroy all such information.

Outsourced In some cases we outsource the work, such as security guards and janitors. We depend on the outsource company to bond and indemnify its employees as well as perform complete background checks. Being in the Justice Sector we had more rigor than most organizations for making sure that background checks were completed and passed by us. On more than a few occasions I had to refuse employment to individuals working for our outsource partners. One incident sticks in my mind: A police officer handling the background checks actually called me and told me not to hire a particular person. The person had an affiliation with the Hells Angels and a string of criminal offenses.

We are moving toward more outsourcing as a means of reducing the cost of computing. Cloud computing offers us more capacity and capacity on demand. We start getting out of the IT infrastructure business and give that task to a vendor to manage. Getting these economies of scale will give you lower costs and higher uptimes. It also means you lose control over your information. Physical access to the hardware and software is now at your provider. Logical access to your applications and databases resides with your provider. What assurances do you have that the information is protected?

Insider Threats

So what are the insider threats? Remember that a threat is a potential to do harm. The insider can do harm to an organization in numerous ways. This harm could be created either accidentally or intentionally. From Chapter 6 we need to consider harm in terms of risk, impact, and consequence. From an information perspective, there are three risks.

1. *Disclosure of information:* Information may be disclosed to the wrong person at the wrong time, creating some impact and consequence.
2. *Availability of information:* Information may not be available to the right person at the right time, creating some impact and consequence.
3. *Integrity of information:* Information may be modified in some way to present the wrong information at the wrong time.

Notice that theft of information is not included. I would argue that theft of information is unauthorized disclosure. In some cases, information may be compromised, such as when a laptop with a sensitive sales report is stolen. However, in some of these cases, the information is not the asset of value to the thief. The only time it becomes important is when you know or can discern that the information is being used by someone—hence the impact and consequence. The impact of someone stealing your information could be a loss in reputation. The consequence could be catastrophic and cause the market value to plummet.

I have avoided likelihood or probability when it comes to information because it is a matter of someone is stealing your information now, has already stolen your information, or will steal your information. It is when you can tell if someone is doing something with your information that allows you to do something about it.

Insider Controls

We have discussed the various types of insiders and how they can get your information. The insider is the authorized user. What controls do you have currently that provide you with protection? In our discussion about information security, we discussed ingress and egress controls. Ingress controls include access controls, meaning the controls manage access to your applications, databases, and information. Typically, we deploy access controls such as firewalls, identity management, anti-virus, ACLs, and network and drive shares to control access to our information. We do a good job in most cases. There are exceptions and I think we do not do active monitoring of all these controls to determine what event is going on that may harm our organization. When was the last time your security personnel looked at your identities and determined if the list was up-to-date and had valid authorization to your information? If your organization is like most, a "periodic review" means once a year or when someone leaves. What happens when someone changes jobs and no longer requires access to that asset?

What we do not do a good job of is information leakage. This means egress controls. What information is leaving your organization? What sensitive and valuable information has changed? Was the change authorized? If you have a specific list of words or terms that triggers your data loss prevention software on your network when the data leaves the organization, can you detect when someone makes a deliberate change? What if someone changes "confidential" to "baseball statistics"? Can you detect that change? We further discuss controlled vocabularies and data loss prevention in the sections Data Loss Prevention/ Information Knowledge Leakage (this chapter) and Chapter 16.

Outsiders

Outsiders can be divided into camps: the general public, competitors, government, hackers, organized crime, and terrorists.

General Public   Most users of the Internet fall into this category, and most of these users are benign. Their intention is usually innocent. However, if they manage to get certain information and report it, it gets media attention and you have to manage the storm.

Hackers   Perhaps the most feared group or community on the Internet other than the media are the hackers. There are several groups of hackers: script kiddies, hackers, and crackers. Hackers and crackers can also be further divided into loners, organized crime, government sponsored, and terrorist. Loners are often elite professionals who sell their services to various organizations and individuals and create or develop some if not most of the code that exploits vulnerabilities. Organized crime may have government connections that tolerate their operations in countries in exchange for money or trade secrets. Governments sponsor trained spies who work directly for the government and have political, military or national security agendas. And of course we need to consider terrorist groups who are looking for funding.

We can assume that there are two approaches taken by hackers: targeted attack and random attack. A targeted attack is when your organization or an individual has been selected and the hacker or group is actively working on getting specific information from your organization. A random attack is usually an automated script with a specific exploit that tests many different systems looking for vulnerable systems. We saw such an attack when one of the Justice Sector servers was compromised. The attack originated in China and, according to our logs, the script simply pinged an IP address looking for a specific response. If no response, the script updated the IP address and tried the next IP. When a system responded, the script executed a code to download specific instructions that compromised the system. The script notified its owner and continued. The owner then entered the system and set up further accounts. We found the compromise before any harm could be done and removed the vulnerability.

A targeted attack involves social engineering. Social engineering can be anything from an email requesting that an action be taken, such as go to this address and reenter your bank account information, to very sophisticated emails that appear to be coming from a co-worker trying to get you to open an attachment or go to a Web site. The other aspects of social engineering can be telephone calls where the individual on the other end may pretend to be on the help desk to people asking innocuous questions that give them pieces of information to help them put the bigger picture together.

Customers, Clients, Others   These are our most valuable people, next to our employees. Without the customer, we would not be in business. Even government has clients, although sometimes governments do not recognize that citizens are their clients and take things for granted. It seems that customers and clients want more access to their information that organizations hold. There are a lot of concerns regarding privacy and the management of personal information. Yet you look at social Web sites like Facebook and a lot of people put a lot of information on these sites, perhaps too much information about themselves. Facebook and other social Web sites make it easier for someone to get more information about a person and then use that information against the individual.

Outsider Threats   If we listed all the threats, we would fill a few books. We can look at threats at a high level and put threats into the following categories:

- Inappropriate access
- Information leakage
- Viruses, worms, Trojans (malware)

- Hackers, crackers
- Organized crime, government sponsored, terrorist
- Denial of service

Outsider Controls To protect your organization, you need appropriate measures that are commensurate with the value you are protecting, risks and threats. Avoid FUD to sell controls to senior management. You need to perform a risk assessment to look at your ingress controls as well as any egress controls you may have. You certainly need awareness and education of your users to reduce the threat of social engineering. You also require a way for users to tell someone to take action when something appears to be wrong. Ira Winkler (2005), in *Spies among Us*, told of bypassing guards and getting users to divulge passwords. So when your users are approached by someone claiming to be on the help desk, do they question the validity of the person and the request or just do what is asked?

Most organizations do not have good egress controls. The next section discusses data loss prevention and information leakage. We know that we need some control over information to prevent information leakage. The question is: What solution should you implement?

Data Loss Prevention/Information Knowledge Leakage

In Chapter 16 we discussed how information flows in an organization, just like blood flows in our veins (Figure 17.4). We know that information flows into an organization and gets processed. Then information flows out of an organization in the form of marketing information, reports, and product information.

In best-case scenarios, all information going out of an organization is controlled. That is, someone has strategically determined that the information can be released. However, organizations are made up of individuals and individuals have ethics. Their ethical behavior primarily depends on their situation. That is, their ethical behavior can be influenced by their emotions. The most unpredictable risks are people, and there is a direct correlation between risks, ethical behavior, and emotions. And the risks are that people will cause an information leak that will harm the organization or individuals. This release or leak

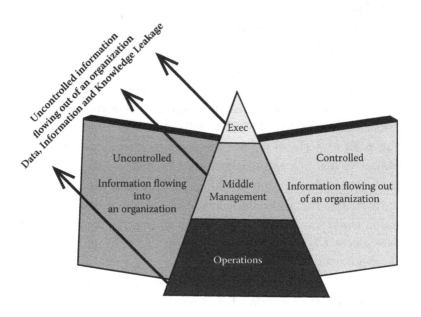

Figure 17.4 Information leakage.

of information is an uncontrolled information flow. The leak can be internal or external. It can be accidental or deliberate.

Internal leaks may be accidental or deliberate. In many ways, internal leaks are usually an informal information flow. For example, an executive or manager accidentally provides a piece of information that adds to the day-to-day conversations, rumor mills, and gossip. The information may or may not be based on facts. It may generate a behavior change such as valuable employees applying to other organizations because they felt threatened or were discomforted by that information. For example, the rumor of a possible merger may send knowledge workers into a frenzy of writing resumes and applying for other jobs. Internal leaks may have unforeseen consequences. These consequences could be damage to reputation, loss of sales or revenue, loss of market share, loss of employees, lowering employee morale, loss of productivity, and even safety issues.

External leaks may be accidental or deliberate. An external leak is an uncontrolled information flow outside the organization that will cause harm. The amount of information flowing out in an uncontrolled flow may not be significant. The content is important. The recipient of the information is important. In his book *Spies among Us*, Ira Winkler (2005) described how operatives garner trust with their insider contacts and gather small amounts of innocuous information at first. The first time someone releases information may be accidental, perhaps over a few drinks. The operative then encourages the insider to get more information and rewards that behavior with gifts. External information leaks can be very damaging to organizations. As the old war poster said, "Loose Lips Sink Ships," referring to the small talk in bars and restaurants in port towns that told enemy agents of upcoming sailings of merchant ships.

The leak may be accidental or deliberate. The differences are: Should disciplinary actions be applied? Can civil actions or criminal charges be applied? As an example, when changes are made to an external-facing application, did the administrator apply all the controls to prevent a security breach from happening? Did someone check the controls? If the administrator was an insider and was providing access to an operative to gain access to credit card information, was the action deliberate or accidental? We all might say deliberate because I painted the scenario as the insider working for an operative. However, in an investigation, you need to prove that the action was deliberate. This goes back to audit logs, communication information, and a lot of other information that must be reviewed. Using the same scenario, the insider may have communicated by email or instant messaging to the operative. Can you find that information?

In a February 2009 report, the Ponemon Institute did a study of data loss risks during downsizing. The study indicated that up to 67% of the respondents used their former companies' confidential, proprietary, or sensitive information to leverage a new job. The reality is that information is collected by employees during their time at an organization. That information is aggregated with existing information that the person already has. These persons are our knowledge workers whom we hire because of their knowledge and expertise. The knowledge is gained through experience and sometimes through exploitation of weaknesses in information security and management. We cannot take tacit knowledge away from our knowledge workers; however, we can prevent data leakage from occurring by making sure our information management practices are sound and our information security is protecting our information assets. One of the important aspects is to make sure you have audit trails. That is, you can tell who did what and when. Data loss prevention is not only about preventing information from being disclosed to unauthorized access; it is also about knowing who accessed the information.

With more people shifting to social networks, there is more uncontrolled information flowing out of an organization. The fact is that there are so many ways to lose control of your information and so many ways for the information to leak out of your organization. We need to understand that there will always be uncontrolled information flow internally and externally. What we want to manage is the level of control that is necessary to reduce the risks associated with information leakage. The decisions that need to be made include

- What level of control do we need?
- What information do we want to control?
- What are the consequences of that control in terms of productivity and employee management?
- How much money do we want to spend versus the harm or consequences if we do nothing?

We need to consider some forms of technologies to help us manage our level of control to reduce information leakage. The other aspect of the technology is educating and auditing users.

If you read any report or any literature from vendors about their data loss prevention or information rights management products, they will tell you that they can prevent information leakage. And in most cases they can, but it does mean different things and in most cases the users have to change the way they are doing things.

Before you can deploy any data loss prevention or information rights protection solutions, you should do the following:

- Identify your sensitive information;
- Classify your information;
- Find your information;
- Develop controlled vocabularies;
- Develop policies, procedures, and guidelines; and
- Train your users.

Solutions such as the DLP products from Symantec offer discovery tools that do a good job of identifying and classifying certain types of information on your network. Symantec and other vendors offer a number of predefined policies based on specific industry requirements, such as PCI compliance that will search and find all credit card information on your network. In speaking with one of the technical experts from Symantec, he indicated that clients who had implemented Symantec's solution were already seeing a return on investment through the improved protection of their sensitive information. This does solve the immediate issue of identifying specific sensitive information; however, I recommend that you formally go through the process of developing and implementing an information management strategy. You will find that there is other information that you will want to protect and prevent from leaking.

We can easily divide technical solutions into two categories:

1. Database solutions
2. Network and end-point solutions

Database Solutions

Database solutions can be divided into structured information and unstructured information:

- *Structured information* means a database and there are some solutions that add extra security around your sensitive data. Oracle Database Vault™ is a good example of a security option for an Oracle database. It has a set of controls that includes
  - Realms that act as a firewall inside an Oracle database; this enables additional controls over privileged user's access.
  - Command rules and factors add controls over who, when, where, and how databases are accessed.
  - Separation of duties enforces a least privilege model on existing databases, such as separating account management from traditional database administration.
- *Unstructured information* usually involves some content management capability. There are a lot of content management solutions available, from Open Source (Alfresco), to Open Text, and Oracle at the high end. Some of them have the capability to further restrict distribution of information using information rights management. Information rights

management extends the content management solution from the vendor by adding additional controls. These controls add protection to the document that extends the protection of the document even if it leaves the organization. Open Text Rights Management is a good example of additional security on the Open Text ECM suite. Rights management extends the controls to

- Prevent distribution of uncontrolled copies of enterprise content.
- Protect content downloaded to end points within the network or distributed outside the network.
- Defined business rules that permit content authors to govern how content is interacted with throughout its life cycle.
- Control viewing, editing, printing, and other actions based on document protection attributes either assigned by the author or assigned as the protection attributes of the repository.

Network and End-Point Solutions

DLP can be deployed as a network or end-point solution. DLP solutions have the ability for deep content inspection based on central policies. Although encryption can be considered a DLP solution, it does not have this capability. DLP solutions generally have the following characteristics/features:

- *Content discovery:* ability to scan stored content for policy violations.
- *File system protection:* monitoring and enforcement of file operations as they occur; can be used to prevent content from being written to portable devices or enable automatic encryption.
- *Network protection:* monitoring and enforcement of network operations.
- *GUI/kernel protection:* to protect against use cases such as cut and paste, print screen.

Most vendors offer complete solutions integrating network and end-point capabilities for DLP.

Network solutions deploy at gateways at logical points on a network where sensitive documents are managed and transported. They are typically dedicated hardware/software servers. Typically, there are a number of components working together to orchestrate DLP. These are policy-based applications that scan traffic for specific words or phrases associated with sensitive information. Depending on the configuration, they can notify users, monitor and report on traffic, or actually prevent information from leaving the network.

End-point solutions deploy as agents that sit on end-point devices such as laptops and workstations. This can be challenging if the end-point management is outsourced. Adding agents that have GUI/kernel protection means integration with the operating system. This may conflict with the terms of the contract for managing workstations. We discovered this as an issue when we deployed file-level encryption at the Ministry of Attorney General. Every time the outsourcer upgraded, we had to scramble to ensure compatibility.

Portable Device Control

There is a third potential solution that is device centric, such as portable device control or USB blocking. I do not include this in Information Right Management or Data Loss Prevention solutions as these are more technology based, dealing with device restrictions. There are technical solutions that prohibit the storage of information on devices like memory sticks, CDs, or DVDs. By the same token, you could also disable your USB ports, DVD devices, and restrict users from downloading any software.

Defining the Risk

Let's first define the risk. Data or information leakage occurs in every organization every day. Information must flow within and external to an organization for it to function. The uncontrolled flow of information is what we want to control. When I was the manager for Infrastructure Security, I managed a team of investigators. We were responsible for investigating incidents such as when documents mysteriously were leaked to the press. In government, there is a lot of collaboration and often a sensitive document may be "touched" by twenty to fifty people, each adding their opinion and expertise to the document. Documents are printed, sent by email, copied, and sometimes just left in open view on someone's desk. I was always reminded of a Paul Simon song except I changed the last few words: "There may be 50 ways to leak your information." Most of the time, we never knew exactly how the information was leaked. We could tell who had access to the information on the server. We could tell who sent and received the information via email. In some cases, we could even tell where it was printed. What we could not tell was who took the information and gave it to the press.

So the risk is that organizational information is being disclosed to unauthorized parties. The consequences vary, depending on the information being disclosed. It also depends on who is getting this information. Let's just say that consequences range from insignificant to catastrophic. We also must consider that some information we would describe as public information (such as name, title, email address, and phone number) is good information to provide. But there is always a flip side. If I am trying to get some market intelligence on your product, can I use that information? Let's use the simple example that I know the name, address, and phone number of the director for research. I also know the engineers who work for that director; after all, you publish that information in a directory. If I know that the director is away (I called and her voice mail told me she is away for two weeks on vacation in Mexico), then I can call the engineers to try to solicit information from them using her name as someone who directed me to them to help me get some information about our new product that I am trying to sell. It is called social engineering, and it is very effective, as human beings we tend to err on the side of helpful. That is good for humanity but bad for security.

The scenario above gives you a sense of how small pieces of information can be used to gather intelligence to attack your organization. In reality, we put a tremendous amount of information up on the Internet that can be used by criminals to gather information about our organization and our employees. A study looked at the year 2008 and indicated that Americans consume about 34 GB of information daily. This includes TV, radio, Internet, email, text messaging, phone, and instant messaging. When we start to understand that we are awash in information and we are now averaging 11.8 hours per day in electronic media, it requires us to pay more attention to what information is being released by our employees. This includes social media such as Twitter, Facebook, Gmail, Hotmail, MSN messaging, text messaging, and phone.

DLP is about preventing information from leaking or being stolen from your organization. There are no single solutions that you can buy to prevent all information from leaving the organization. We also do not want to prevent people from doing their jobs and sharing information. We need to manage our information but we have to be careful about how much management effort we put on our employees. For some critical information, we need to have strict policies, procedures, and the appropriate technologies to manage the information correctly. For other information, we may want to have fewer controls in order to promote collaboration and sharing of information. As an example, during the development of documents for application development, you may want to use a wiki to put your information into, with limited access to those people with a need to know. After the documents are developed and the final copy is completed, you can put the finished documents into a content, document, or records management repository to more tightly control versioning, editing, and distribution. You can limit the printing, copying, or storage of these documents in any other location. That is where information rights management is important.

Deploying DLP Solutions

According to a Data Loss Prevention Report from Aberdeen in 2008, the traditional perimeter-based approach using firewalls and intrusion detection was becoming less effective as mobile workers, social networks, and customer, partner access dissolved the perimeter. In its place, an information-centric approach is emerging. In an information-centric approach, data loss prevention solutions are seen as part of the overall information security architecture and strategy to protect sensitive and valuable information. However, before you rush out to buy a DLP solution, make sure you are solving a specific business problem. Gartner was very forthright in their statement about DLP.

Start with one big business problem and focus on solving it first. DLP is one solution that you must consider in information security for protecting your sensitive information. In most organizations, the most sensitive and valuable information usually comprises less than 10% of all information. That is where DLP needs to focus. Information management will probably solve many of your other information issues.

DLP solutions come in many forms. The objective of implementing a DLP solution is to prevent information from being disclosed to unauthorized parties. Three considerations for DLP are data at rest; data in transit; and data at end points.

Data at rest means documents, files stored in some server or repository. Data in transit means information traveling between two points. Data at end points means the viewing mechanism into your network, such as a laptop or hand-held device. A simple rule for mobile or portable devices such as laptops is that information on the device should be encrypted.

Some mechanisms for DLP include encryption, access controls, labeling, metadata, network devices, and software solutions.

At the Ministry of Attorney General, we deployed encryption for data loss prevention. There were a number of applications for encryption to protect sensitive data. Court Services sheriffs used encryption to protect information for the security of the court buildings. Our biggest user was the Criminal Justice Branch, which encrypted all its information. The encrypted information was stored on standard shared file and print servers. By encrypting their information, it meant that only those persons with encryption keys and authorization could access their information. Not even the administrators of the shared file and print servers could access their information. We used SafeNet's ProtectFile™ as the file encryption software, Entrust client software, and the Canadian federal government PKI for our certificates.

There were lessons learned in deploying encryption that would apply to any DLP technology. The most important lesson was keeping the solution focused on solving a business problem, which was the Criminal Justice Branch's requirement for protecting its sensitive information. Another lesson was dealing with client software issues. When you combine software that must operate at the core operating system level to encrypt and decrypt, you will encounter many problems with new releases from all vendors. We had to deal with Microsoft patches, SafeNet™ updates, and Entrust® upgrades. And then there were the users. We spent a lot of time educating and training users. In actual fact, there were three distinct requirements for support: product; project; and program. Initially it was the project roll-out that we needed to support. After the project was completed, we needed to support the program and the products. The program involved users and registration authorities who issued and revoked certificates.

Deployment of a DLP solution still relies on good information management. As I defined in Chapter 16, you need to identify your critical, valuable, and sensitive information assets. You will need a controlled vocabulary, and you will need to know where your information is located. This includes both structured and unstructured information. You should also look to see if you have already deployed a content management solution. If this is where you keep all your sensitive information, you may want to look at information rights management.

Remember that you need to solve a specific business problem and not boil the ocean. For example, you may want to focus on PCI compliance and look at protecting Personally Identifiable Information (PII). I would be very specific and start with customer PII only as a first step. Here is an outline of some of the steps that you would need to take in deploying a DLP solution:

1. Preparation for deployment: Define your requirements (what you are protecting, what budget you will need, who needs to be involved, risk assessment—if this information was stolen, what would it mean, how best to protect it, Key Performance Indicators (KPIs)—how do we measure success, incident management—what to do if there is a breach [education, awareness disciplinary], scope and scale of deployment).

2. Evaluation of solution: Determine what you need to protect your information. Is this a network/end-point solution, an information rights management solution, or both Request for Proposal (RFP) and Request for Information (RFI), depending on your urgency. Are there contractual obligations such as with an outsourcer? What are your criteria?

3. Integration and testing: How does the solution fit into your environment? How do you get the agents on the systems? Do

you have policies for the agents? Start small, deploy the agents without rules, and then slowly add rules to test each policy.

4. Define processes: Once the agents are deployed, you will want to determine what policies you will enforce and how. This means educating users and advising them of the policies, what constitutes a violation, and what it means to them? It also means working with HR, legal, and managers to define responses to incidents, especially if disciplinary steps will be taken for violations.

5. Management, maintaining, and updating: DLP solutions require constant management. This means monitoring. Most installations of DLP and other technology solutions fail to perform as expected because very little afterthought goes into production management. You also have to consider maintenance and product updates. Policies sometimes go out of date or require changes. Someone has to manage all these.

Paper: Print, Keep, Shred

Paper has been the medium of choice for hundreds of years. Since Gutenberg introduced movable-type printing in 1439, we have become more reliant on paper to convey information. Since the 1950s, paper use has grown more than sixfold. The average office worker in the United States prints about 12,000 sheets of paper per year. Most of this is wasted in drafts, reports, spreadsheets, and other material that the typical office worker may use and throw away immediately. The questions are

- What information is on that paper?
- Where does that paper go?

As the director for Information Security, I would glance at the papers left on printers and copiers to see what information was being left behind. It was not surprising to find a lot of sensitive information, such as personal files, sensitive project plans, network architectural diagrams, directives, and even security plans. It is highly likely that the same thing occurs in every organization. A lot of sensitive information is left on printers and copiers. It could be a phone call, email, instant message, or fellow employee; there are a lot of distractions that could cause the person printing to forget about the printout. Worse yet, someone else picked it up as part of their printout and did not return it until later, if at all. So then the person prints another copy.

What about all those reports that are printed just before the meeting? Whatever the document, there is a lot of paper lying around with some pretty sensitive information. And paper is easy to put into a briefcase or slide in with other papers to transport outside the office. Just like Patrick Regan printed pages of intelligence information and transported pages out in his briefcase.

Where does the paper go after the meeting or when the final version is printed? This is an important question to consider. Having seen many documents left in meeting rooms, on printers, copiers, desks, chairs, and just about anywhere in the office, we know that the paper with that valuable information could be discarded as the next priority sends the people scurrying. Poor management of paper constitutes a risk to information security. Even when we carefully store the paper in a filing cabinet with a lock and key, what happens to the paper when the person leaves? What about those files that have been left there from the predecessor's predecessor? Can those paper files turn into a liability?

So, ideally we would not print documents. This would save a lot of trees. However, paper is still a good medium to convey information. Although viewing information of a screen is getting better, there are still many people who prefer a paper version once the number of pages exceeds some quantity (probably five to seven sheets based on our memory capability). So there are four things to consider when using paper:

1. *Does it need to be printed?* I know; the executive wants a hard copy because, well, she has always read reports from paper. She is an executive and she will have it her way. You know those individuals very well. And they may drop the paper on their assistant's lap after reading it—for filing away in some filing cabinet to never again see the light of day. And how about those reports for the meetings, do we need them? Generally, a review of printed documents will reveal some interesting habits and, more importantly, get you started on understand-

ing paper usage at the office. After the report is printed and the meeting held, what happens to the paper copies?

2. *Do we need to keep it?* For contracts, a signed copy may be the only evidence of agreed obligations and must be kept. At the Ministry of Attorney General, we had everyone sign a computer access form. We kept all the forms in boxes. When we had to vacate the room, we started to look at what we had in the room—boxes and boxes of computer access forms, some dating back to 1995. A lot of the people were no longer with the ministry. The dilemma was about liability. If we destroyed the forms and had to take a person to court over inappropriate use of a computer, did we need the consent form to say that they had read the terms of use? Another choice was to go through all the boxes and remove those people's forms who were no longer with the ministry. The lesson learned was that it was good to get people to read and sign agreements; however, the paper trail became an intense manual process and we decided to take a different approach using electronic forms.

Just remember that paper is not necessarily the best way to keep information. The Ministry of Attorney General has more than a hundred thousand boxes of records kept in off-site facilities. The number of boxes retrieved is around ten per month. The number of boxes is growing at a 10% annual rate. Although records managers will assure you that they can find the records, they are not that searchable by just anyone—unlike a content management solution.

3. *How long do we need to keep it?* We all have friends, acquaintances, or colleagues who are hoarders of information. That is, they keep everything. Organizations cannot keep information forever unless it has value. There are statutory, regulatory, and legal obligations for keeping information. These must be followed. For all other information, especially in paper form, there need to be schedules to get rid of information that no longer has value. Which brings us to the final question …

4. *How are we disposing of printed copies?* Sometimes we need to have many copies of a complex agreement so we can review and discuss. At the end of the discussion, how do we make sure that there is only one official copy? How do we make

sure that any sensitive information that is printed is properly disposed? There are two ways: shredding bins and shredders. A shredding bin is a locked box that is periodically emptied by a bonded and verified contractor or internal resource and taken to a shredder for shredding. A shredder, as it name implies, shreds paper. Most homes now have shredders to prevent identity theft. All organizations should have one or more shredders for sensitive paper document disposal.

18
E-DISCOVERY

One of the biggest problems facing CIOs occurs when litigation hits the organization. This has IT, lawyers, and business folks scrambling to find and preserve information. And the cost of finding, recovering, collecting, and managing the information may run into hundreds of thousands of dollars. A court case involving WestLB produced 650,000 pages of evidence and cost $480,000 just for the specialist firms hired to recover the documents, and it was estimated the legal costs were $200,000 to 300,000 per month. It is very expensive, not to mention the IT personnel involvement and the shift from service delivery to unplanned work. The best approach is to manage unstructured information.

One of the aspects of having people work from home is information on their home computers. From investigations, we have found that through intent or unintentionally, people often have organizational information on their home computers. In one case, we were investigating a disciplinary action against an employee and discovered through other processes that the person had been emailing very sensitive reports to her home email address. The lawyers had to issue a court-ordered seizure of her hard drive to ensure proper disposal of sensitive information. When considering disciplinary actions against employees or dismissal, you need to consider what access they have to valuable or sensitive information and whether they are storing that information on other computers or mobile devices.

Another consideration is social networks. With the tremendous popularity of services such as Facebook, Twitter, and MySpace, we have many more exposures that could end up as information for the courts. In an article entitled "E-discovery gets an F," Briony Smith quoted one of the lawyers at a Symantec webinar:

> "E-discovery has always been an issue for lawyers to handle, but now there's that added complexity with wikis, Facebook, Twitter, and other

new technologies," said George Socha, a litigation attorney who works with the Electronic Discovery Reference Model (EDRM) Project. "A lot of lawyers' eyes roll back into their head and they curl up like possums because they just don't want to deal with it." (2009)

Most of us do not want to deal with other new technologies and we do not know what is on the horizon for newer technologies that may supersede these technologies, much like we are seeing with Generation X and the Baby Boomers whose preferences often dictate what technologies are to be used and what is being supported. These technologies extend the requirement for electronic discovery even further. There have been a number of defamatory cases where people have expressed their anger in a twitter and have been taken to court. An article by Gilliam Shaw (2009) in the *Vancouver Sun* talked about social networkers finding that a few words may lead to trouble. In the article, there is some good legal advice from lawyer Ken Cavalier, who said:

"My recommendation for people who use social networking is be even more careful than you normally would be. If you're talking to your neighbour and you say something about your other neighbour and it's defamatory and they find out about it, they can sue you. When it comes to networking sorts of things, it is like doing it over a megaphone. One of the problems is any time you put anything online, it is out there—you can't recall it," he adds. "There are tons and tons of landmines out there. My advice on social networking is, if you are going to make statements make sure they are pretty innocuous."

More corporations are either enabling their users to use social networks or disabling them. Either way, there are plenty of ways for people to get in trouble and some of this trouble will end up in court. When we talk about e-discovery, there may be a real need to access the information on these social networks, and gaining access to the right information without some other pieces of information creeping into the picture may be challenging. In our investigations we had to be careful about gathering information for "witch hunts," as we referred to the fishing expeditions of managers who may have a personal vendetta against an employee. It is very important that you make sure you have the right authorization when gathering information. Extraneous information may lead to additional lawsuits, and it is better left to the lawyers to determine what information is needed for the courts.

Rules and Obligations

The requirement to disclose information in court cases has not changed. The amount and media associated with the information have changed significantly. Most information is produced and stored electronically. As much as 40% of all information is unstructured information. A lot of what is required in court cases is email; however, you also need to consider some of the other communication mechanisms such as instant messaging, document sharing, and collaboration tools. The BC government upgraded to Microsoft Office 2007 as part of their refresh of the desktops, and one of the benefits was the addition of Microsoft's collaboration tools. The lawyers were concerned that these tools would be subject to court-ordered search of information relating to court cases. We undertook an examination of the proposed practices and made significant recommendations to change the way we managed these tools as well as some of the records management practices for the information being communicated. Make sure you consider all your communication tools when looking at searching, recovering, preserving, and presenting the information pertinent to a court case.

> The U.S. Federal Rules of Civil Procedure provide the rules for duty to disclose and general provisions governing discovery. For example, Rule 26 (a) (ii): "a copy or a description by category and location—of all documents, electronically stored information—along with subjects of that information—that the disclosing party may use to support its claims or defenses."
> The Province of Ontario has released guidelines for the discovery of electronic documents.
> The Sedona Conference, which is a high-level international meeting of professionals in the legal community, has released The Sedona Guidelines: "Best Practice Guidelines & Commentary for Managing Information & Records in the Electronic Age" and established a working group to help manage electronic document retention and production.

Table 18.1   Standards of Proof

KIND	LEVEL OF EVIDENCE	STANDARD
Regulatory, legal		Precautionary principle
Legal—Civil	*	More likely than not
Legal—Civil	**	Clear and convincing
Legal—Criminal	***	Beyond a reasonable doubt
Scientific	****	Irrefutable

Source: From C.G. Miller and D.W. Miller, *Journal of American Physicians and Surgeons,* 2005, 10(3), 70–75.

In Chapter 6, we discussed an approach for dealing with information to make sure you understand what trust you can put in that information. We deal with facts, calculations, estimations, and guesses. In much the same way, the judge or jury is going to review the information presented to them as evidence and depending on how well the lawyer presents the information, they may view it as fact or dismiss it as hearsay. The burden of proof lies with the presenter of the information.

Donald Miller and Clifford Miller (2005) listed five standards of proof, by level of evidence, as given in Table 18.1. We also have other ways of looking at the level of evidence and burden of proof.

Standard of Proof

The amount of evidence that a plaintiff (or a prosecuting attorney in a criminal case) must present at trial in order to win is called the *standard of proof.* Different cases require different standards of proof, depending on what is at stake. The common standards are:

1. "Beyond a reasonable doubt"—used in criminal cases: "The test is one of reasonable doubt. A reasonable doubt is a doubt based upon reason and common sense—the kind of doubt that would make a reasonable person hesitate to act. Proof beyond a reasonable doubt must, therefore, be proof of such a convincing character that you would be willing to rely and act upon it unhesitatingly in the most important of your own affairs. A reasonable doubt exists whenever, after careful and impartial consideration of all the evidence in the case, the jurors do not feel convinced to a moral certainty that a

defendant is guilty of the charge." (Federal Jury Instructions; See Devitt & Blackmar, Section 11.01)

2. "Clear and convincing evidence"—used in fraud cases: The trier of fact must believe that it is highly probable that the facts are true or exist; while it is not necessary to believe to the point of almost certainty, or beyond a reasonable doubt, or that they certainly are true or exist; yet it is not sufficient to believe that it is merely more probable that they are true or exist than it is that they are false or do not exist. (See *Collins Securities Corp v. SEC*, 562 F.2d 820 [D.C. Cir. 1977]; see Gellhorn, p. 270.)

3. "Preponderance of the evidence"—used in civil cases: The trier of fact must believe that it is more probable that the fact is true or exists than it is that it does not exist. (See Gellhorn, p. 270 & Oregon Jury Instructions 22.02.)

4. "Substantial evidence—used in most administrative cases: More than a mere scintilla. It means such relevant evidence as a reasonable mind might accept as adequate to support a conclusion. (See *Richardson v. Perales*, 402 U.S. 389; *Universal Camera Corp. v. NLRB*, 340 U.S. 474. See Gellhorn, pp. 258, 259, 737.)

5. "A mere scintilla of evidence"—used in some old administrative cases: Enough evidence to create a suspicion of the existence of a fact. (See *Universal Camera v. NLRB*.)

The point of relating these standards is to give you a sense of what is required to manage the chain of custody to present the information in the best way to convince the judge or jury that your information is true and properly managed. As discussed previously, having a proper information management strategy and processes is the best approach.

You need to have proper and documented procedures for e-discovery that will allow you to streamline requests and minimize disruption to your staff. This is especially important for email. One of the questions is: How long should you keep emails? It really depends on what the content of the email is. Some emails are decisions and are required as part of the history of how that decision was derived. We discussed records management and the Office of Primary Interest (OPI) in Chapter 16. Because we have different people types and

different styles of managing information, some people keep everything while others try to get rid of everything. There needs to be a
consistent approach that is put into policy and practice and managed
accordingly. It may mean that the OPI is not responsible for the information and you manage all information according to a specified life
cycle. It would be better to have documented procedures regarding
proper disposition of records than none.

E-Discovery Process

One of the key issues of e-discovery is diverting scarce IT resources
from planned work to unplanned work managing e-discovery. As a
matter of fact, there is a significant cost associated with e-discovery
in terms of personnel time involving the business, IT, and legal in
managing evidence. The Electronic Discovery Reference Model
(EDRM) is an excellent model to use to help manage the information. Figure 18.1 depicts this model, and we discuss each state.

In the EDRM, the importance of the process is that it takes a significant volume of information and redacts the information to relevance in
the specific case. Note that the first step is information management.

Information Management

Without some form of information management, you are tasked with
the overwhelming job of finding all relevant information. As we know,
electronic information is growing exponentially in every organization.

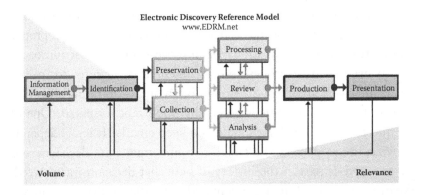

Figure 18.1   E-discovery process.

We discussed information management in Chapter 16 and if you have not started developing an information management strategy, then it may be prudent to start now prior to some litigation that will cost hundreds of thousands of dollars—and perhaps millions—just to get the information together for the case. As a matter of fact, one of the justifications for information management may be litigation, either existing or pending.

Identification: locating potential sources of applicable information and determining its source, location, format, and volume. When I was working at the Department of National Defence in Ottawa, Canada, there was a requirement to find specific information regarding some litigation. To facilitate this search, the top brass ordered a one-day shutdown of the operations to specifically search for this information. This meant that over 80,000 people were doing unplanned work and the cost was significant. If you have to find information that is distributed across the organization in multiple geographic zones, you may not find it all and, as in the case of *Colman v. Morgan Stanley*, be subject to court decisions. Additional information may be found outside your organization, such as within social networks and other organizations, and require extra work in getting the appropriate information.

Collection and Preservation

Gathering and preserving information for further use in e-discovery. When I was working for the GCIO, I was responsible for all investigations involving electronic information. We were often asked to recover emails. The challenge of recovering email is creating the environment to restore the email boxes so you can recover the emails. This becomes more onerous the older the tapes and if you have changed email servers. We also had to sift through the emails using search tools that may not recover relevant information. Typical search tools use words to find the information and these words may not be in an email; however, the subject matter within the email may be pertinent as evidence.

The U.S. Department of Justice developed a proposed standard for the exchange of digital evidence in 2000. Electronic evidence must be able to meet a standard of proof to be viable in a case. Any indication of tampering may render the evidence inadmissible or may give your opponent an opportunity to discredit your evidence. An appropriate environment and a mechanism to demonstrate a chain of custody must be created to manage the evidence. When we investigated security breaches, we often saw IT folks change the evidence in their attempts to determine the cause of the failure.

Analysis, review, and processing: reducing the volume of information through review and analysis. In terms of FOI requests, we would refine the request and redact the information to contain only what was requested. Similarly, the lawyers want to reduce the amount of extraneous information to only what is relevant to the case. It is best not to assume that we know what information is needed as evidence but leave it to the lawyers.

Production

Production refers to delivering the information in appropriate formats and delivery mechanisms. It is interesting to see how much information is being disclosed during any trial. In criminal cases there is a requirement to present the information to the person charged and their legal representative. In the Justice Sector we have had some challenges in presenting the information to certain individuals, and a judge's order made it clear that we must present the information. One such individual actually took apart the laptop that we had given him and destroyed the hard drive, thinking that he had destroyed the evidence against him. If you have to disclose to other parties, then the information must be in an acceptable format.

Presentation

Presentation involves displaying of information before the appropriate audiences, including defense, depositions, hearings, and trials. The best presentation is in native format. However, if the file format is not readable by the adverse party, you may have to convert the files into a readable form. This will create the onerous problem of managing the chain of custody where you need to manage the appropriate controls around preserving electronic information to demonstrate that the information has not changed.

Summary of E-Discovery

The best defense is to have an information management strategy in place, to include how to manage emails. A good reference for guidelines on how to manage information and records is the Sedona Guidelines. Now more than ever, emails, collaboration tools, and even social network information are being targeted as evidence. Judges are becoming very technology savvy and courts are not very favorable to a lack of response when they are asking for information. Although records management personnel may consider some information transitory, the court may determine that information as important. As an example, one of the cases that the BC government lost was based on a doodle on the back of a document that clearly demonstrated to the court and the judge that there was prejudice on the government's part. The award in damages exceeded $100 million.

There is a lot at stake when litigation hits an organization. It involves not only dollars, but careers and people's lives will be disrupted. A search for information will involve a search through offices and perhaps extend into the private lives of individuals. When the Basi-Virk trial was initiated by the BC government investigating inappropriate use of public office, the lawyers gathered boxes of paper information as well as seizing hard drives and email. The judge requested that all emails be turned over to the court as evidence and in some quirk of fate, the emails were deleted as part of operational procedures. The recovery of those emails required a substantial investment in forensic time and materials.

In today's environment with the mobility of communications including Blackberrys, laptops, home systems, servers, routers, and firewalls, there are logs and information everywhere. Even worse, there may be logs or information stored on other systems such as with MSN or Hotmail. Depending on the litigation (or worse, the crime committed), there may be a requirement to produce thousands of pieces of information including logs, hard drives, documents, and emails. Some cases, such as the bombing of an Air India flight, have involved millions of documents, including tapes and videos, all being compiled and reviewed by the lawyers.

When a request for information is initiated, IT is notified. Information that is known is gathered. The search may be very limited in scope or very broad. As in an FOI request, the information may be contained in documents or emails. One of the interesting aspects of email is that it is an electronic conversation between parties. In the BC government, records management viewed a lot of the emails as transitory; that is, if you are not the person sending the email or the OPI, then the email is not a record. However, because email is a replacement for a conversation and may extend for weeks, months, and even years on a topic, it was always good to keep the email so you can refer back to key points in the conversation. This presents a problem when dealing with e-discovery and emails. Who was copied on what email, and what did they do with the email? Did they make comments and send another email to more folks? Is that part of the conversation dealing with the litigation? Should this be included? Are the comments relevant? Does the other party have this information, and can it be used against our position? Email is perhaps one of the hardest requirements of e-discovery at this point in time. We also need to consider other forms of communications such as Instant Messaging, Groove®, Live Meeting®, and OneNote® where people may have put additional information or the information has moved to other parts of the organization or beyond. This is what makes the search so difficult. As discussed, electronic information propagates quickly, and multiple copies of it may exist in multiple locations and in multiple formats. Having a good information management strategy and proper information life-cycle management is very important. This does not mean everything gets destroyed after a certain time. It means having documented procedures and technologies that manage the information.

An important aspect of e-discovery is preservation of evidence. Once you have found the information and recovered the information into some readable format, there is a need to preserve the information to demonstrate that you had control over the information and that it was not changed in any way. There was a time when electronic information was not admissible in court and viewed as hearsay. This has changed with legislation in various countries such as in Canada with the Privacy Information Protection and Electronic Documents Act (PIPEDA). Electronic information is now viewed as evidence and you must show that you have appropriate controls that demonstrate a chain of custody showing that the information has not changed while in your custody. Forensic software such as EnCase® preserves the software in the original format and demonstrates a chain of custody assuming you are following proper procedures. EnCase can be used to capture images of disks but not email. Email is different and the burden of proof of authenticity is with the party presenting the email as evidence.

One of the interesting aspects of email is the ability to spoof or make changes without demonstrating proof that the person who sent the email actually made the change. This is an important part in the preservation of evidence or the chain of custody. We had implemented PKI within the Justice Sector and one aspect of PKI is digital signatures. Signing every email digitally means that there is a very high probability that the person who signed the email was also the author of the email. Much like pen-to-paper signatures, there is still a chance of fraud. Someone may gain custody of my digital key for signing; however, with two-factor authentication, it is much less probable without my knowledge. This also assumes that proper procedures are followed. Why is this important? We know that there is a lot of spam these days and that spam may look legitimate, even coming from someone within your organization authorizing or approving something. We need to demonstrate that the person who sent the email was in fact the person who authored the email.

The use of tools like EnCase will help preserve information and demonstrate that you have an appropriate chain of custody; that is, there is no ambiguity that this is the original document and that it has not been changed.

19
PRIVACY

In any organization there are privacy concerns. Privacy is personal information being disclosed to the wrong person at the wrong time. It could be personnel files, medical records, or customer records. Every organization has personal information. There are rules and various legislation regarding the disclosure of personal information. Inappropriate disclosure of personal information is a risk. Mitigation of the risk and the protection of personal information are security controls. Security controls may be technical, procedural, or physical.

Personal information was defined by the U.S. government in 2007 as PII. The Office of Management and Budget defined PII as

> Information which can be used to distinguish or trace an individual's identity, such as their name, social security number, biometric records, etc. alone or when combined with other personal or identifying information which is linked or linkable to a specific individual, such as date and place of birth, mother's maiden name, etc.*

NIST has developed SP800-122, Guide to Protecting the Confidentiality of Personally Identifiable Information (PII) for protecting personally identifiable information that may be useful when combined with PCI data security standards.

A breach in privacy is usually a breach in security. This means that one or more controls have been compromised. Even when authorized people inadvertently disclose personal information, there is usually a control compromised. Privacy breaches tend to get more visibility. There is not one day that goes by where a privacy breach is not reported. Some of these are laptops containing personal information being stolen or lost. Some are information being leaked; some are personal information being sold. There are so many incidents of personal information being lost, stolen, or leaked that it is now a

---

* http://www.whitehouse.gov/omb/memoranda/fy2007/m07-16.pdf.

common occurrence. The questions are where, when, how much, and how long has it been going on? Employees have been caught stealing customer records and selling these records on the Internet. As indicated previously, there is value in personal information and if you do not protect your personal information, there is a good chance that your organization will end up on the front page of a newspaper or major blogging news.

The OECD developed a set of privacy principles in 1980. These should be reviewed; they will provide a foundation for your privacy policies. A summary of the privacy principles are found in Appendix A or you can look on the OECD Website ("The OECD Guidelines on the Protection of Privacy and Transborder Flows of Personal Data"; www.oecd.org).

If you are collecting personal information, you must conform to a number of laws. In Canada there is the PIPEDA. In California, SB 1386 is the disclosure law requiring businesses to disclose a privacy breach. There are a lot of other laws and acts coming on line and most likely the U.S. Government will pass an overarching law to protect all personal information similar to its federal disclosure law for health-care (HIPAA).

There are privacy seals for your Web site that you can purchase from a number of vendors. A privacy seal is an image that is displayed on a Website. A privacy seal means that your organization has a minimum set of guidelines of how you collect, handle, store, and share personally identifiable information. These are a minimum set of guidelines and there appear to be no penalties attached if your organization fails to comply other than the privacy seal vendor will not reissue their privacy seal.

One final note: There is a protocol for privacy protection on the Web known as the Platform for Privacy Preferences (or P3P). P3P is a generalized vocabulary for describing Web site privacy policies. Please understand that having a P3P rating does not imply that the site will or will not protect the privacy of its visitors. The user must download the policy and read it. If you have a privacy policy regarding the use of personal information, make sure it is clear about what you intend to do with the information.

Privacy is a topic unto itself. With the collection of any personal information comes the responsibility of protecting that information.

This includes any procedures for handling, managing, and storing personal information. If you determine that you must share personal information, you should have a contract or agreement that outlines your requirements and legal obligations to protect the information. One thing to remember is that electronic information is easy to share and it proliferates quickly.

20
POLICIES AND PROCEDURES

In any civilization there are rules. Rules are made because of complexity and the need for consistency. As organizations grow in complexity, there is a need for more rules to handle the complexity and maintain consistency. In most cases, rules are about consistency in behaviors. On the flip side of rules are enforcement and punishment. Making rules is not good without enforcement and punishment for breaking the rules. A simple example is when you are driving a car; you must stop at a stop sign. If you are caught not stopping, an enforcer of the rules (police) will pull you over and give you punishment (a fine). If you do not pay this fine and are caught again, further punishment is given (more fines); and finally, if you do not obey and pay the fines, you can go to jail.

We live in a very complex world. We work in very complex organizations. We communicate over very complex networks. We use very complex tools like computers, smart phones, and applications. And everything is constantly changing. There is a need for consistency in human behavior just like we want consistency in our interaction with computers. That is why we need policies and procedures. Policies and procedures help set the tone for the right behaviors that we expect from our employees.

Policies are not new to organizations. We have volumes of policies for just about any type of behavior, policies on how we want employees to act. As a matter of fact, in large organizations like government, there are so many policies that nobody knows which policy is important and which is not. The bottom line: If a policy is not enforced, it is a meaningless statement.

Good policies and procedures are formal written documents that are carefully managed, reviewed periodically, and updated accordingly. Policies and procedures are a formal declaration of an organization's commitments and practices at a specific time. Policies and procedures provide standards of conduct; that is, they define the expected behavior for whatever actions and activities employees take in operational tasks and business on behalf of the organization. Good policies and procedures provide a legal context in a dispute about behavior in an organization, providing there are written policies and procedures; employees have been informed about the policies and procedures; and policies and procedures are consistently enforced.

Just to be clear, we will define what we mean by the terms *policies* and *procedures*.

- *Policies* are courses or methods of actions deliberately chosen that guide or influence future decisions and behaviors.
- *Procedures* are the standard methods of doing things. Procedures are also the customary manners or ways of conducting business.

So what are the characteristics of good policies and procedures? Considering that the ethical behavior of many people depends on the situation, the better your policies and procedures are written, managed, conveyed, and enforced, the more likely your employees will adhere to them. Characteristics of good policies and procedures include

- Written and documented
- Authoritative (right authority to write, manage, and enforce)
- Defensible (hold up in court)
- Clear and concise
- Easy to find
- Given to all staff
- Changes conveyed quickly to staff
- Policies and procedures are appropriately linked
- Enforced for everyone
- Based on principles
- Managed, reviewed, and updated periodically

Policies must be written by the right authority; that is, if it is related to personnel, the HR department should be writing the policies. Even with technology, HR must be involved. Too often we have policies and procedures written by the technical experts. Keep in mind that policies should be written to define expected behaviors and enforced to demonstrate to employees that adherence to the policies is expected.

If policies are broken, then the policy must be defensible in court. That means the policy is written, authoritative, clear and concise, communicated, and enforced.

Writing Good Policies

The problem with policies is that you can write many. For example, in 2008, the BC government published its Information Security Policy (ISP). The ISP was not well written; it was voluminous (weighing in at 280 pages) and unenforceable. Based on ISO 17799:2005, the policy reiterated and expanded every section of ISO 17799. Most of the policy statements did not have guidelines, authorities, or metrics, so you could not measure if you were in compliance—nor could you ask an authority for advice because none were identified. Even if metrics were present, they did not provide good information to determine how to measure. To gauge compliance with the ISP, the government CIO measured ministries in an annual security health check.

Now combine that with another set of government policies known as the "Core Policy and Procedures Manual," legislation such as the Freedom of Information and Protection of Privacy Act and the Document Disposal Act, and ministry-specific policies and you have confusion. A stated policy in one manual did not necessarily agree with another or with a ministry-specific policy. So what does compliance mean to the employee, and what was enforced? For example, under Section 11.1.4 of the ISP, security controls must be applied to protect data and personal information. The policy goes further to talk about the Freedom of Information and Protection of Privacy Act and the Core Policy and Procedures Manual 12.3.3 and Privacy Impact Assessment. So which document is the authority? It gets even more interesting when you start to look at ministry-specific policies and other policies within government that probably make some mention of protecting data and personal information. And we want our employees to be in compliance with policy.

The ISP goes on even further in the policy to look at metrics and enforcement, and the policy states that the metrics used to measure compliance are the percentages of new information systems that have completed Privacy Impact Assessments and the number of Privacy Impact Assessments reviewed or updated. Why are these metrics? The policy statement deals with both data and personal information. If we were focused on personal information, would a better metric not be the number of privacy breaches? How about measuring the number of security breaches? After all, we are talking about appropriate security controls to protect data and personal information, so we should measure the controls to determine if the security control is performing in accordance with what we set out in the business requirements.

If you look at your own organization, how many policies are there? If you are a small organization, you probably have a few policies that are fairly simple and everyone knows them. Most likely, it evolves around the company. As the organization becomes larger, there are more people, the complexity increases, and there are more policies. Each function starts to interpret its requirements and develop policies. Each technical expert interprets the requirements and writes a policy. Does it make sense for your information security analyst to write your information security policies? Let's go back to the reason for having policies: to guide people in future decisions and behaviors. The objective is to write policies that are clear, concise, authoritative, enforceable, and easy to communicate that guide employees in making good decisions that conform to business and social norms within the organization.

Most technical people cannot write good policies. As identified above, writing an information security policy based on ISO 17799 is not a good thing from a policy perspective. However, technical people will think it is a great idea because that is what they know. Enter the human element: the policy must be easy to read and interpret to guide people in making the right decisions. The policy must also be able to be interpreted correctly in a court of law to make sure that the policy is defensible.

I remember working with the Canadian government CIO at the Treasury Board, writing the certificate policies for their PKI. There was a working committee of at least twenty people. I think half were lawyers and the other half were subject matter experts, with me being a subject matter expert. There were tremendous arguments among the lawyers over simple words like *must*, *shall*, *should*, and *will* as they applied to some policy statement. Using must and should as examples, must means obligation whereas should suggests an obligation. In a legal sense, should is a weaker obligation and can be interpreted differently by the viewer. The lawyers were quite clear in their requirements for certain policy statements. They did not want any liability on the part of the government. Most technical people will not understand or interpret policies in terms of liabilities. Some technical people can write well and write decent policy. However, in my experience, many technical people do not want to write reports, document procedures, or write policies.

It is obvious that you need subject matter experts to write good policies. You need legal opinion. HR is an important aspect of policies because policies are about influencing behavior. You need business engaged because the *raison d'être* is the business. You need senior management involved because they set the direction of the organization. And you need a good writer or perhaps a policy analyst. This should be a standing team or committee that has formal meetings, has an appropriate lead or chair, and should write all policies for the organization. This will give you consistency and reduce redundancy and confusion by have a single interlinked policy. Subject matter experts should be brought in as appropriate to help understand different areas of policies that need to be written.

Some simple things to help write good policy:

- Select words carefully, especially words like shall, should, or may. These words will make the difference between compulsory compliance and guidance.
- Use fewer words, such as "this policy is ...."
- Keep it general because a policy cannot take precise account of all possible situations. The policy should be principle based.
- Keep it helpful so the person reading the policy knows who it is written for, how it applies, and any conditions or restrictions.

Writing good policy is difficult. I have seen lots of bad policies written, but the biggest failure is the failure to communicate policy.

Communicating Policy

Once you have written a good policy, the next most important step is to communicate the policy. We have heard it before, when the crisis hits, you should have read the policies. So are your policies easy to find? Are they linked to other policies as necessary to provide the reader with enough information to interpret the policy correctly? Have you told people about the policies? How about when policies have changed?

Policies are living and breathing documents. Things change and policies must be updated to reflect the change. Most policies were written prior to social networks. Have you updated your policies to reflect how, why, and what people can do regarding social networks? While I was with the Justice Sector, I saw the inevitability of social networking coming to the workplace. I initiated discussions with the lines of business to garner their support and to enable them to set direction on how the Justice Sector wanted to proceed by setting the appropriate policies in place. Some sectors within the Justice Sector wanted complete disabling of access to social networks, whereas other areas were open about their employees using Facebook and other social media. I also knew that the Public Service Agency was looking seriously at using social networks to attract more talent to the BC government. We already were using some aspects of social networks for communications and I wanted to be ahead of the adoption curve. We needed to write some policies that positioned the business in adopting social networks at their pace and within their tolerance for risk. Once the policies were written, then we needed to communicate these new policies to the employees.

In communicating policies, you need to consider the ability of your audience to receive the message, understand the message, and have a person and a place to go to for answers to questions.

Enforcing Policy

There are more policies that are unenforced than policies that are enforced. And there is a lack of consistency in the enforcement. This will get organizations in legal and labor trouble. My spouse always mentions to me how some executives ignore specific policies when they want to get something done. Is this good or bad? Or is it bad policies? Policies should never get in the way of getting organizational work done. However, we do need the bureaucracy to manage consistency. So the dilemma becomes: What are good policies that should be enforced, and what are bad policies that should be rewritten or abandoned altogether?

For example, under the ISP policy 7.5.5, inactive sessions must be shut down after a defined period of time. In this case, the BC government set the period of inactivity at fifteen minutes. I do not know how many times I walked by my boss's office and saw his system open, usually in email, with some sensitive information being displayed. If the CIO is not going to follow this policy, then is the policy a good one? From an information security perspective, you should lock your workstation when you leave for extended periods. This could mean locking the door to your office or locking your computer so that you need to reauthorize. However, if your boss could not be convinced to lock his workstation, then why would anyone else? In other words, if you have a policy that is worth enforcing, then everyone must be in compliance ... including the boss. The boss should lead when it comes to policy compliance.

If you have just released new policies, then you must follow up by monitoring compliance with the policies. This means doing an audit of the behavior that the policy is attempting to change. In the case of a large number of policies being released at the same time, I suggest that you pick one or two and focus your efforts on making sure these are enforced through audit, reminders, and remediation. There is nothing that gets people's attention than when someone is disciplined for not following policy. Word of mouth slinks faster through the grapevine than through formal channels.

Writing Good Procedures

In his book entitled *Practical Intelligence*, Karl Albrecht (2007) wrote about thinking styles. He used the example of software developers at IBM who were creating electronic typewriters with display screens. The designers wrote operator manuals to help operators use the new typewriters. They were frustrated to learn that most of the operators never opened the manuals but continued to learn by trial and error.

The experts were at a loss to understand why the operators did not read the manuals. One of the designers interviewed operators and, while interviewing one of the operators in training, tried to explain some basic concepts of the typewriter to the operator. The operator did not want to know the basic concepts; the operator only wanted to know how to do the procedures.

The designers, all of whom were highly educated and accustomed to reading detailed technical material, had designed the manuals for themselves. The operators were not as highly trained and did not want to spend time reading detailed technical material. The difference in learning patterns was significant. Technical experts start with the big picture and work toward specifics. Their learning style is one that craves information, whereas operators start from specific cases and work toward a general understanding.

This is about learning styles—how people learn to do some procedure. Technical experts tend to be deductive learners; that is, moving from the general to the specific. Nontechnical experts tend to be inductive learners; that is, moving from the specific to the general. The experience of trying to teach a procedure to someone who has a different thinking style (deductive or inductive) can often be frustrating. Writing good procedures is about thinking how people process information. Because the audience might process information using deductive or inductive logic, it will require the writer to write procedures in a way to enable users to quickly find the information they need about the procedure. That means writing a procedure that has two entry points: the general and the specific. Ideally written procedures would have a top-level page that allows navigation for a very specific question, to giving a high-level understanding about the procedure. This would cover both information processing styles.

Following Procedures

In the IT world, it is often the super-administrators who do not follow the procedures. These are the professionals who can fix most of the problems most of the time. They may be the most valuable people on your team. However, if they are not following proper procedures, then they may be causing more problems than solving them. In *The Visible Ops Handbook*, Behr, Kim, and Spafford (2004–2005) talked about 80% of system failures being caused by human error. This usually has resulted from some undocumented fixes that later turned out to be a problem. Somebody did not follow procedures. Going back to the chapter on "Process Management" (Chapter 11), one of the key principles of good process management is good documented procedures. Even then, failure to follow procedures can lead to major problems.

For example, within the Justice Sector we used PKI to protect our information as well as give us two-factor authentication for certain applications. We found that many of the upgrades to our PKI applications required a specific sequence of updates to the various software packages. Failure to follow these procedures meant that the applications would fail to initialize correctly. This meant that users could not log on or use their tokens to get access to their information. And the procedures were performed overnight so we would wake up wondering if the upgrades were successful. In those few cases where the technician decided not to follow procedures, we had some catastrophic failures and the help-desk phones were ringing off the wall.

Much like employees should be in compliance with policies, they should also follow procedures. We will always know that human error will cause failures. We can minimize these failures by following procedures. Failure to follow procedures should be handled through disciplinary actions to set the example.

Next-Generation Policies and Procedures

Have you ever tried to find a specific policy? I was speaking with one of the information security analysts from the BC government and she spent about half an hour trying to find a specific policy to answer a question from a Ministry Information Security Officer. She told me that she had knowledge about who wrote that specific policy and when it was created, so she could search appropriate directories and find the information. And it still it took her a half an hour and she knew exactly what she was looking for and where to look. Now imagine that you have 30,000 people looking for policies and procedures and they do not know where to begin to look or how to find what they are looking for. In most organizations, policies and procedures are written by functional areas and maintained by the functional areas. That means you have to know where to look to find specific policies. And the policies tend to be written differently based on the different skill sets and expertise of the individuals writing the policies and procedures.

So how do you write the next generation of policies and procedures to make it easy for your employees to find the necessary information to make better decisions? Here are some suggestions to help you write your next generation of policies and procedures:

1. *Governance:* Create a central team for policy development with the mandate to manage all policies (get control of your policies). Develop the process for approvals of policies and procedures.
2. *Review:* Find and review all policies (if it is not important, it will not show up).
3. *Set standards:* Develop controlled vocabularies for policies to get consistency.
4. *Use the Web:* The Web has hyperlinks, hypertext, XML, and other capabilities to create and manage your policies; stop using Word and PDF.
5. *Use metadata:* Find, develop, and implement tagging to maximize interconnecting of policies as well as the ability to have separate policies that deal with a specific subject matter like HR, information security, privacy, etc.
6. *Rewrite:* Rewrite your policies using standards, metadata, controlled vocabularies, and the Web.
7. *Test:* Test your new policies.
8. *Vet:* Vet your new policies (develop procedures for suggesting, testing, vetting, and releasing your policies).
9. *Inform everyone:* Communicate the new policies to everyone.
10. *Enforce your policies:* Make sure that enforcement includes everyone.

In the end, it is not the responsibility of the CIO to get a handle on all the policies; however, the more consistency the CIO can bring to the table and the more value in setting up standards to make adherence to policy easier, the more the CIO is positioned as a leader. Remember that policies and procedures are about behavior changes to enforce good and consistent behavior for employees. It reduces risks.

Procedures are a little more focused than policies. However, you can still develop controlled vocabularies, metadata, standards, and have governance over how they are written. The same governance structure for policies should be used to set standards, controlled vocabularies, and manage the processes for approvals.

21

PLANNING FOR BIG FAILURES OR BUSINESS CONTINUITY

We know it's inevitable—there will always be those failures in our systems, fires, earthquakes, floods, or some natural or manmade disaster that causes our systems to become unavailable. We have to consider what we do and how we respond. This means business continuity planning. There are several things to consider: the severity of the situation, safety, essential services availability, building, people, and emergency services. Most of the time the situation is not severe. However, in the event of regional disasters such as Hurricane Katrina when the situation is extremely severe and wide scale—when there are no essential services such as electricity, water, telephone, Internet—safety is the primary concern. People's priorities shift from their job to survival and concerns for their family.

Organizations have to consider the situation when depending on people to maintain operations. In extremely severe situations, the safety of their people and their families must be the highest priority. As we have learned from countless stories, people will abandon their posts to make sure their loved ones are safe. After they feel that their family is safe, they will return.

There are a number of factors to consider when looking at operations and business continuity. One of the first considerations is the cost of downtime. For essential services such as fire, ambulance, emergency services, and police, the cost of downtime is measured in lives. Can these services operate without the ability to coordinate and dispatch? Having been personally involved in emergency services, the answer is yes, but at reduced efficiency and effectiveness. You also must consider that you may be sending emergency crews into situations where they cannot get help themselves if essential services like communications are or become unavailable. When the police in Victoria (British Columbia, Canada) upgraded their radio dispatch system to a new system called Capital Region Emergency Services Telecom (CREST), they found that there were certain situations where the communications failed or were garbled, thus putting police officers' lives at risk. Although it was fixed, there was a period of time that the officers were very concerned with the communications.

For most CIOs the concern is the flow of information for maintaining organization operations. This means that systems are available, critical applications are operational, networks are available, and endpoints can connect. Remember the discussion about the user experience where any one of the many components could be unavailable and to the user the system was down? When you consider the complexity of our systems today, especially as we move toward full Web 2.0 and the next-generation applications, there is a need to consider what are critical applications, systems, and network to enable people to access your information when needed. Does that mean as close to 100% uptime on your critical infrastructure as possible? When we consider a three-tiered architecture with firewalls, routers, and switches, what does that mean?

When I was managing infrastructure security for the BC government, we were responsible for incident management when a virus or worm infected our systems. We had more events prior to installing the intrusion prevention systems at the gateways. One particular event occurred in 2004 with a new strain of a virus called Sasser, where we were being infected at a tremendous rate and the virus was mutating as we watched. I remember standing in a room with a number of workstations and watching as the virus infected each one. We humans could not move fast enough to stop this virus from spreading. That is when the realization that we really needed automated defenses sunk in. We also needed some contingency planning when this type of incident started to shut down our capabilities to deliver IT services.

I have been advocating escalation procedures when an incident turns ugly and starts to have an impact on business. In an environment with 30,000+ workstations, a few hundred workstations rendered inoperable is not statistically huge. However, when a few thousand workstations are infected with a virus, we start to see a business impact in terms of productivity losses. People cannot use their tools. People cannot access their calendars. The noise on the network from the virus becomes significant and starts degrading network performance.

Application performance starts degrading. At what point do you turn an incident into full-blown business continuity or disaster recovery?

When looking at business continuity or disaster recovery planning, you do not often see escalation procedures. Business continuity or disaster recovery is usually remediation of a major disruption of services. In the event of minor disruptions of services where there is minimal impact on the business, most of the planning, remediation, and management of the event is covered in daily operations. However, problem escalation should not be left to technical operations.

While I was a field engineer with Digital Equipment, we had very well-established escalation procedures to remediate problems. These were based on standard levels of services and after fours hours, you were required to call in if the problem was not resolved and report on the situation. After eight hours, the call was automatically escalated to the next level of service operations or, in our case, a district engineer was notified and was assigned to the call. After sixteen hours, the regional engineer was notified and assigned to the call. At some point in time, the call was escalated to corporate support. This took the decision about whether to call in or not out of the hands of the technical person. As a field engineer, I was always trying to resolve problems quickly and was very proud of my ability to troubleshoot any problem. However, there was a culture that recognized that the customer was more important than professional pride, and that downtime represented money to the customer. The escalation process was there to prevent professional pride from getting in the way of making sure that the system was doing what the customer needed and paid for in terms of buying the equipment and the maintenance service.

In today's environment, I have seen too many cowboys in IT. You know who I mean: the technical star who can fix anything. As I pointed out in the process chapter (Chapter 11), you need to continue to reward individual behaviors that create value yet balance the behavior with good procedures and documentation to mitigate failures. Having documented procedures that take the decision pressure off the technical resources is a way of dealing with technical stars who feel that given just one more hour they can resolve the problem. It focuses the attention on solving the problem as a team with proper management authority. It opens up communications to the executives who can make informed decisions about the impact on the business based on good reporting of the event.

So, in a nutshell, here are the things you should consider when looking at business continuity management. First you have to consider whether your organization should outsource IT to a third party who can guarantee uptime. If we consider that IT is a utility service, then should your organization be providing the infrastructure necessary to run your business? Otherwise, you need to consider the operational time that the business needs access to their information. Is the business a 24/7 operation? Does downtime mean significant loss in revenue? Loss of life or limb? The business impact and consequences of an outage must be the deciding factor. In a large organization, the prioritization of what is mission critical and what is business critical is made by the executive. In business it is fairly clear-cut that anything that impacts revenue is mission critical. In government, it becomes less clear. The impact of a loss in revenue must be weighed against loss of life and public safety.

- *Mission critical:* means that a loss or downtime could result in a catastrophic failure. From an IT perspective, this could mean the organization might fail to survive if information is unavailable for even a short period of time.
- *Business critical:* means that a loss or downtime could result in a major failure. From an IT perspective, this could mean that the organization will survive but a business line might suffer a significant loss if information is unavailable for a period of time.

If you decide that the application and infrastructure are mission critical, then you need to consider redundancy to maintain resilience. A lot of planning goes into making the servers, databases, and applications redundant but, interestingly enough, the planning often fails to add redundancy to the network. Going back to our user experience, any system, network, application, workstation, or database failure that breaks the link from users to the information they need to do their job is considered an IT failure by the user.

Business Resilience and Redundancy

Information must be available to your organization 24/7. This is mission critical. Downtime will result in a catastrophic failure, either in direct financial cost or the potential for loss of life and limb. Examples include banking, nuclear power plants, and emergency services. For companies, downtime has been calculated in the thousands of dollars per second or there is the potential risk to public safety, such as chemical plants where the release of chemicals could cause the death of thousands (e.g., the Bhopal disaster in 1984 at the Union Carbide India Limited pesticide plant in Bhopal, India, which resulted in the exposure of more than 500,000 people to a leak of methyl isocyanate gas).

Our dependency on Supervisory Control and Data Acquisition (SCADA), which is becoming increasingly computerized and linked to networks, means a higher reliance on computers to never fail or have appropriate failover mechanisms to prevent failure. An example of a massive power outage was the Northeast Blackout of 2003 that affected approximately 55 million people in the northeastern United States and Canada. The power failure was traced to a software bug in FirstEnergy Corporation's energy management system that prevented an alarm from tripping and alerting operators to the failure of a power line.

The decision to have built-in redundancy to maintain business operations is not made lightly. There is a significant cost to redundancy, and failover testing must be done to make sure that the systems are in sync, information is not lost, and operations are not affected. Most worldwide businesses operate multiple locations with built-in safeguards to prevent operational failures from exposing the business to disruption. One of the aspects that must be considered is the Internet. The Internet provides access to most organizations with public-facing services. How the organization is connected to the Internet can be critical in maintaining these services. One of the exposures that is exploited by criminals is Internet services when the criminals can attack these services using a denial-of-service. A denial-of-service attack (also called a distributed denial-of-service, DDOS) occurs when a large number of bogus communications requests overwhelm the system responding to the requests so it cannot respond to legitimate requests for service. There are preventive methods to deal with denial-of-service and these should be considered in any planning for Internet-facing services.

A business impact assessment or a risk assessment should be done to consider the best approach to business resilience. Key considerations are operational requirements for information. If the information is mission critical and the result might be a catastrophic failure of the business or a loss of life, then redundancy or outsourcing may be a good approach to mitigating that failure.

Business Continuity Management

When I was responsible for business continuity at the Justice Sector of the BC government, my business continuity expert continued coming to me and telling me two key points about business continuity: (1) planning and (2) exercising the plan. Her goals were to ensure that plans were in place and that the ministries had exercised the plans. These are great goals for anyone who needs to ensure that their organization has the ability to survive a disaster.

Disasters come in many forms. Disasters can be natural, manmade, accidental, deliberate, or a chain of small events that lead to a catastrophic failure. In any situation there is a magnitude or scale of the disaster. In a large event such as an earthquake, the priority would be the safety of people and their families. Most communications would be down. Buildings would be deemed unsafe until inspected by the proper authorities. Basic survival would be the order of the day. We have seen the devastation of earthquakes, such as Haiti in 2010 where a magnitude 7 earthquake shook the island and caused widespread devastation.

I know from our planning that the facilities were considered at risk. We planned that in the event that one of our buildings was rendered unsafe through a fire or other event, that we could set up an operations center in another building using a boardroom with the appropriate wiring, workstations, and network connections. We also planned on allowing people to work from home. There were lists of essential positions with names of the people assigned. I insisted that there be positions with a list of potential names versus just the names of people. In any process for mid-sized or large organizations, there still is a tendency to assign a person rather than a position. We know that Bill is the right person as the assigned database analyst who is always there to fix the database problems. However, if Bill is on holidays or has just won the lottery, we cannot depend on Bill in the event of an emergency.

Business continuity takes planning and it must be written in a document. Everyone involved must have a copy. It could be a written document such as a binder or a soft copy that could be on a memory stick. Once you have a written plan, you need to exercise the plan. It can be done on paper first to minimize cost. However, it should be done as a live exercise at least annually. There is nothing like staging an event to help people fuddle through an event to get a feel for the processes and for dealing with an event prior to a real event happening. When the real event hits, people react differently. Unless you have adequate training, people will panic and the results may be catastrophic.

22

LIABILITIES MANAGEMENT

Section Summary

The CIO must manage liabilities. This means good information security to prevent the wrong person from getting the wrong information at the wrong time. It also means good information management because decisions are made with information, and enabling the right information to be available at the right time to the right person will make better decisions. There are three areas of concern:

1. *Personal information:* loss, theft, or disclosure of personal information such as credit card, medical record, credit history, and confidential information about people.
2. *Intellectual property:* loss, theft, or disclosure of intellectual property such as defense information, trademark secrets, industrial secrets, and case information.
3. *Decision information:* key decisions made using the wrong information to cause business failure, loss of life, loss of reputation, or have an impact on finances or safety.

The loss, theft, or inappropriate disclosure of information is a risk. It means that the wrong person has access to your valuable information. As a CIO, you are responsible for electronic information. This means you must have the appropriate safeguards in place and the capabilities necessary to manage your information. Information security and management are two very important means of protecting and managing your electronic information. The level of protection and management must be commensurate with the value of the information. For example, you cannot prevent the information from being printed by an authorized person and leaving the custody of the organization. You can put in place egress monitoring that audits the printing or even prevent the printing of certain documents using digital rights management; however, unless the information has very high value, the cost of such monitoring could be prohibitive. When people take work home, trying to be more productive, you do not know whether that effort will cause an issue later on. For example, the police found 1,400 sensitive documents containing personal information inside the home of a government worker. These documents were printed records. It was clearly a security breach and questions about authorization and document and records management remain. You should have clear policies and procedures about working on sensitive information, including access from home or taking work home.

You must have good information security. A large security breach can cost millions of dollars. A security breach involving the theft of IP can cost billions and even be a risk to national security. Active monitoring of your most valuable information is good information security. Periodic auditing of your access controls is a must. There are too many cases of unauthorized access by people who have been let go from the organization, and these are only the ones that have been published. A data loss prevention strategy is a must. Information protection is now a boardroom consideration as we continue to connect systems together on the Internet. If your board members are not involved in decisions about information protection, then you need to inform them of the issues and how you plan on mitigating these issues.

A privacy breach is a security breach. If you do not have good security technologies, processes, and people, you will have more breaches. Breaches, loss of IP, and theft of personal information are the risks that you must consider regarding information protection: appropriate controls must be in place and continuously monitored. Controls include good policies that help set expectations about appropriate employee behavior. Procedures enforce good policies and continue to ensure that people follow documented procedures. One of the most important aspects of good information protection is continuous monitoring and enforcement. Even if you cannot afford to continuously monitor everything, there should be some periodic reviews of audit logs to determine if inappropriate actions have been taken. Audit logs give forensic evidence of who did what and when.

When the lawyers come knocking, you must be ready. E-discovery is really about document or information management. The better your practices, policies, and technology for managing information, the less expensive the cost and, more than likely, the better prepared your lawyers will be. When someone sues, you are in a defensive position. You must provide all the necessary information to defend your position. This means emails, documents, videos, and maybe instant messages, Livelink®, and any other relevant information. If you do not have a good information retention and disposition program, you may be in trouble. In a court case, the BC government had to find relevant emails for the case. The problem was that the backup tapes that were supposed to be kept for the case were destroyed. It took a concentrated and expensive effort to recover most of the emails from backup hard drives and other locations.

Decisions are made based on the information presented. If you do not manage your information, decisions will be made based on the information available. This may mean poorer decisions and dollars spent on the wrong things. We all have examples of decisions that were made and more information becoming available that overturned the previous decision. Unfortunately, the change in decision may come after a lot of money has been spent.

Security breaches cost money. Security breaches often have an impact on service delivery. In the BC government, several critical servers were compromised through a known vulnerability. The servers were removed entirely from service, thus compromising public safety. The servers had to be rebuilt. There was an investigation involving a number of people. The police were involved because hackers compromised the servers. The cost to public safety cannot be estimated. The service was unavailable for a period of time. You should measure information security based on its impact on service delivery.

PART IV

PUTTING IT
ALL TOGETHER

Risk management is about reducing your risks. Reducing risks means reducing impacts on your business. If you are measuring based on outcomes, key metrics will be measuring the impact on service delivery, not server uptime. You must develop a roll-up strategy so that each person feels responsible for contributing to a key metric. Isolating metrics at a very high level does not give people at all levels a sense of pride and ownership in the success of good service delivery and the protection of your organization's valuable information. When asked what he was doing, the janitor at NASA during the race to put a man on the moon said he was helping put a man on the moon. The point is that he was committed to the program and had a sense of pride and urgency. We need that pride and commitment for our service delivery, management, and protection of our valuable information assets.

As a CIO, you must deliver information to the business when needed: the right information to the right person at the right time. Information flows in an organization. Information comes into an organization in an uncontrolled flow and should be released in a controlled flow. Unfortunately, information is leaked, both accidentally and deliberately, in an uncontrolled manner through a wide variety of sources. Because information is the lifeblood of an organization, it must be managed, protected, and delivered appropriately. An information strategy must be in place to manage, protect, and deliver information. That is,

- *Information delivery:* right information to the right person at the right time.
- *Information protection:* controlling access and release of information, knowing who did what and when.
- *Information management:* organized and managed according to value and an established life cycle, making information findable.

An information strategy should include good policies and procedures. Policies should be in place to influence behavior and inform people about the policies. Policies must be enforced. Procedures must be documented and followed. Any risks to an information strategy must be identified, assessed, categorized, and mitigated appropriately through good risk assessment techniques. These should form a risk management strategy.

A risk management strategy must include requirements such as service delivery, compliance, information security, information management, availability, and risks to confidentiality and integrity of information. The pressure to produce reporting for regulatory compliance is becoming greater and if you do not have an overall strategy for managing this reporting, a fragmented approach will cost more money, more staff time, and lost productivity.

So why a risk management strategy? According to a survey by Crowe Horwath of CFOs across North America, fully 65% said the biggest challenge facing them was managing risk across the entire company; 40% of CFOs said that technology factors were substantial causes of concern at their companies in the next year. They identified four areas that were most critical in reducing business risk:

1. Improving production and operating processes
2. More timely and accurate financial forecasting
3. Better inventory planning
4. Better information security/privacy

A Ponemon Institute study in the United Kingdom in 2010 interviewed CEOs and other C-level executives. The study looked at data protection and organizational goals that depend on data protection. CEOs indicated that good data protection improved customer trust and loyalty, as well as maintaining reputation and brand. These were positive aspects of good data protection. Data protection also increased the value of the organization by reducing the risk of a data breach, increasing brand and market image and improving data or information flow in the organization.

Data protection is one aspect of information flowing through an organization. In an ideal organization, information that is released to customers, partners, and the public is controlled. That controlled release must consider information management and information delivery. The policies, procedures, and controls used to deliver, manage, and protect information must limit the exposure of organizations to data or information leakage. Information leakage can be accidental or deliberate. The objective of good policies, procedures, and controls is to reduce accidental leakage. At the same time, good policies, procedures, and controls will ensure that if the leakage is deliberate, then we can catch the perpetrators of the leak. Good policies, procedures, and controls form the basis of good risk management.

In most organizations, risk is managed in silos. Each business area manages risk in accordance with its needs. This includes IM/IT and even within IM/IT shops, risk is not managed as an overall strategy.

There are lots of pressures being put on the CIO. These pressures include

- A limited budget: We are being asked to do more with less money; we have to manage our budgets more carefully.
- Delivery of information so that people can do their jobs.
- An increasing dependency on computers.
- Legal and regulatory requirements, including more compliance requirements and more reporting.
- Continuous escalation of criminal activities targeting your most valuable information and your people.
- People risks, including competencies, skills, losing valuable employees and their knowledge, fraud, and theft.
- Litigation defense and the management of information to ensure you have the information necessary to defend your organization.
- Management of information, including emails, documents, media in many formats, and the volume of the information, including version control, distribution, multiple copies, multiple formats.

And now the expectation is that CIOs will deliver opportunity capacity, that is, allowing the business to exploit IM/IT to its maximum capacity. CIOs are now being measured on their ability to be ahead of technology changes and offer services to the business that can be a competitive advantage.

All these add up to not enough people or enough budget to manage everything. CIOs are under the gun to make sure that information is delivered to the right person at the right time to get the job done while preventing the wrong information from going to the wrong person at the wrong time. This means a balance between managing service delivery and managing liabilities. An overall risk management strategy is the only way a CIO can manage both.

23

DESIGNING A RISK MANAGEMENT STRATEGY

Not every organization has an enterprise risk management strategy. More likely, risk management is being managed at the business unit level. In the Crowe Horwath-sponsored survey of CFOs (www.crowehorwath.com), the biggest challenge that CFOs identified was managing risk across the organization. The survey identified that 40% of CFOs said that technology factors were a high concern for business performance disruption. Technology factors are associated with information and communication systems.

The CIO needs to understand how risks are managed within the organization. If there is an enterprise risk management strategy, then the CIO must look at the technology factors and the risks associated with technology in the organization and how it fits with the enterprise risk management strategy. If risk is managed at the business unit level, then the CIO should be looking at a risk management strategy for information—that is, making sure the right information gets to the right person at the right time while denying the wrong information to the wrong person at the wrong time. The CIO must manage risks for both service delivery and liabilities relating to information.

At a high level, a risk management strategy should be designed to include the following:

1. Assessment of external factors: includes market, budget, news, industry, competitors, suppliers, politics, and financial.
2. Identification of the organization structure: organization structure often dictates how risks are managed.
3. Identification of assets and a valuation for each asset: information is often not classified and protected commensurate with the value of the information.

4. Identification of business units and their objectives and what success looks like for each objective.
5. Identification of risks associated with each objective: developing scenarios for each risk will help in understanding the impact if the risk is realized.
6. Identification of government, legal, and compliance requirements and the impact of not being in compliance. Sometimes the cost of noncompliance is lower than the cost of compliance.
7. Analysis of risks and identification of common or similar risks: this may create a common risk mitigation strategy that is more cost effective than managing a common risk separately.
8. Identification of the risk culture and risk management profiles of the organization, business units, and individuals: will help in understanding how people manage risks. Risk takers will take more risks and spend less on risk mitigation, while risk avoiders will take fewer risks and allocate more on risk mitigation.
9. Development of a governance structure for risk management.
10. Development of a risk management strategy for service delivery, making sure the right information is available to the right person at the right time.
11. Development of a risk management strategy for liabilities, making sure the wrong information does not get to the wrong person at the wrong time.
12. Consolidation of both strategies and report risks and mitigation efforts to executives, allowing them to make key decisions about what risks to accept, mitigate, or transfer.
13. Maintenance and management of risk management as a program.

External Factors

External factors may have a major influence on risk. If your company is in the news regarding a credit card security breach, then your stock prices will be impacted. If a competitor is having financial trouble, your products may be in more demand. It is prudent to assess external factors and consider their impact. Developing scenarios around the risks that are derived will help shape the risk management strategy.

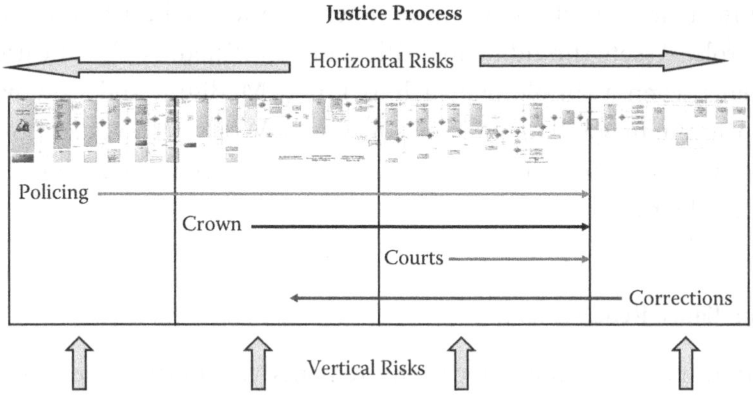

Justice Process

Figure 23.1 Justice process horizontal and vertical risks.

Organization Structure

Understand the organization's structure. Organizations are very different in how they are structured and have both dependencies and interdependencies. Organizations have vertical risks (business unit or product line specific) and horizontal or enterprise risks. Information technology is an example of a horizontal risk. Figure 23.1 reveals that within the Justice Criminal Process, each part has both vertical risks and horizontal risks. A vertical risk associated with Corrections is that a criminal may escape custody. That risk is not shared by any other entity within the Justice community in the same way. A vertical risk for the Crown is that the information may not be complete from the police to prosecute the case.

Part of the discovery surrounding the organization structure is to determine business objectives. Each business unit has objectives that are set corporately and some locally. These business objectives have associated risks that may inhibit the business unit from reaching its objectives. Identifying the structure, business lines, objectives, and risks will help determine horizontal or enterprise risks, vertical risks, and sometimes common risks that will provide for an overall risk management strategy.

Identify Assets

Identify what assets are valuable. Information has a life cycle and does not always retain value. The identification and classification of information will allow you to determine where best to put your controls. Assets should be identified and classified. A classification schema, even a simple one such as High, Medium, and Low will help you manage your information assets. Work with your records administrators to help look at the life cycle of information and asset valuation.

Compliance Requirements

Determine what compliance requirements you must meet in your organization. These may be SOX, HIPAA, PCI, or local, state, and federal requirements. If your organization is international, make sure you take into consideration any requirements for country laws and regulations.

Risk Management Profiles

Determining the Risk Management Profile (RMP) of individuals is an important part of risk management. People manage risks differently and their RMP will determine their level of comfort with taking risks and their degree of competence in making risky decisions. Determining the RMP provides a level of confidence that you can assign a person to the appropriate role and assign proper responsibilities. Different risk management philosophies will often dictate the risk culture of the organization.

Risk Culture

The risk culture of an organization and units within an organization can differ. If you aggregate the individual risk management profiles of an organization, you may be able to determine a pattern that will describe a risk culture. Overall there may be a risk culture for the entire organization but individual areas within the organization may have different cultures, especially considering international organizations and the culture of the country. Take sales or marketing as an example; people are more risk takers. Or accounting and auditing; the RMP should be one of risk management or risk avoidance.

Governance

A governance structure must be set up to manage risks. Typically there are two groups or committees: the executive committee that sets business strategy and the working committee that executes the business strategy.

Risk Management Strategy for Service Delivery

Service delivery, or making sure the right information gets to the right person at the right time, should be measured at the business level or outcomes. If you consider service delivery a product of your organization, then you must manage the product. This includes the processes and projects related to the product. The bottom line is that if you are not measuring your outputs to contribute to business outcomes, you are not measuring anything useful. I think that measuring the impact of IM/IT on service delivery is the best metric. As previously discussed, the measurement of the user's experience is overlooked and the CIO should focus on that metric to measure how well his or her services are being delivered. Your risk management program should focus on managing the risks associated with service delivery. Typically that means the availability of systems.

Risk Management Strategy for Liabilities

Managing liability risks is important to the success of any organization. If your resources are tied up in managing security breaches, they cannot be working on improving or maintaining service delivery. A security breach requires a reaction and is unplanned work. The size and scope of the breach dictates the number of resources required. Liabilities risk management must include technologies, processes, and policies for information security, information management, and privacy. Education and awareness is an important aspect of proactive management of risks.

Consolidated Risk Management Strategy

Once you have developed risk management strategies for both service delivery and liabilities, you need to consolidate them into a risk management program to avoid overlapping policies and procedures and assign appropriate roles and responsibilities. The risk management program should start at the top. Business objectives or outcomes should be identified. The top three or four business objectives of each business area should be identified. Risks or impediments to meet these objectives should be identified. Aggregate and analyze risks to determine if there are overlaps and common areas of risk. Identify any risks associated with IM/IT and prioritize according to a risk assessment. Make sure you include any requirements for compliance with regulatory, legal, or industry requirements.

A risk management framework is a good way to input all variables into a single framework with other associated documents providing the details. A framework outlines key objectives, requirements, principles, policies, procedures, and reporting. An outline of a risk management framework is provided below.

Risk Management Framework: Outline

- *Executive Summary:* Provides a one- to two-page summary of the framework for executives.
- *Objectives:* Provides the objectives of the risk management program relating to business outcomes, including the protection of information assets and the management of risks associated with service delivery.
- *Requirements:* Defines the requirements for risk management by business function and consolidating common requirements. A separate document may be appropriate to manage the details of business function requirements to protect any sensitive information. The requirements should detail what information assets you are protecting.
- *Governance:* Having an executive sponsor and the appropriate level of involvement of the right mix of people is important. Ideally, the Chief Financial Officer or the Chief Executive Officer would be the sponsor. Governance also means the policies, procedures, and guidelines to help people in the organization manage risks.
- *Principles:* Combine the different principles such as risk management, information security, and information

management, as well as any other corporate or ethical principles, and place here.

- *Policies:* Outlines the different policies, such as information security and HR. Separate documents should be referred to in the framework; do not put all the policies into the framework.
- *Procedures:* Refer to procedures documents in the framework. Operational, security, and incident response procedures should be separate documents.
- *Architecture:* The framework should provide a high-level architecture of the enterprise based on a standard such as the Zachman Framework (Enterprise Architecture Framework). Similarly, the protection strategy should be based on something like SABSA. Make sure these are high level and the details are in separate documents.
- *Standards:* Any corporate-endorsed standards should be documented here. Again, this should be a reference to other documents that details the standards.
- *Reporting:* What metrics are being reported? The framework should provide an outline of the reports, including frequency.

A key aspect of consolidating risk management strategies is reporting. The most important report is an impact on service delivery. In Part II and Part III, we discussed reporting the impact on service delivery from an information services perspective and the impact of service delivery from a security perspective. We want to measure the outcome impact of both. This means rolling up outputs into a common outcome that we can report to executives; that is, the overall IM/IT impact on service delivery, including both the downtime of information services as measured in terms of service delivery and the impact of security caused-outages as measured in terms of service delivery plus any costs associated with lost or stolen information.

Maintain Risk Management Program

Assign a person to be responsible for risk management program. Make sure you have appropriate measures in place for that person. A risk management program is a process and must be continuously reviewed and updated. The program should be well documented.

Using a framework will allow you flexibility in managing the overall program yet make changes to the details as operations, applications, and procedures evolve.

Resourcing a Risk Management Program

Questions that will be asked include the following:

- How many people and what budget do I need for a risk management program?
- What are the skills that I should be looking for in risk personnel?
- Do I need auditors?

It depends. The risk management function can range from a simple reporting function through to a full-scale department with a number of staff who review, consolidate, analyze, and report risks. For the CIO, a starting point may be reporting on project risks.

Often, risk management starts with Information Security. Most CIOs are very concerned with liabilities, that is, someone stealing personal information or IP. If your organization is engaged in PCI compliance, that may be a good starting point to expand the opportunity to other areas.

Risk management is being practiced in many aspects in most organizations. What is typically missing are dedicated people and the reporting of risks. Whether you add this task to existing personnel or create a new position, risk management is important. Failure to recognize the importance of risk management and the consolidation of risk management and treatments will continue to manifest in breaches, inefficiencies, and silos.

24

FORWARD-LOOKING
RISK MANAGEMENT

Another way of looking at information risk management is to take a forward-looking view. Using the financial market as an example, because they manage portfolios, in their book entitled *Seeing Tomorrow*, Ron Dembo and Andrew Freeman (1998) defined four elements they consider for forward-looking risk management:

1. *Time horizon:* Over what period of time are we considering our exposure to risks?
2. *Scenarios:* What events could unfold in the future, and how would they affect the value of our investments?
3. *Risk measure:* What is the unit we are using to gauge our exposure to risk?
4. *Benchmarks:* What are the points of comparison against which we can measure our performance?

Time horizon. When managing our business, we have defined budgets and using a forward-looking approach will help us define where we should focus our attention to mitigate risks. Typically, our time horizon is one year. Our budget cycle normally is one year and we may have projects that extend over several years (we expect project managers to manage the risks of their projects, but who is managing the entire portfolio?). Projects should be incorporated as well as processes, as described previously.

Scenarios. What events could occur that may cause changes to our current projects, processes, and even the products? In the 1980s, IBM was pondering the future of the personal computer. Market forecast was estimating about 275,000 personal computers in use in about a decade. We all know how wrong that forecast was and how it impacted IBM and the whole digital age, including the Internet. Within my own experience in 1995, the Department of National

337

Defence (DND) in Ottawa initiated the Defence Information Network (DIN). I was the project manager and developed the functional concepts as well as the business case. Another "competing" project was the Electronic Document and Records Management System (EDRMS). The person responsible had written a paper that described the Internet as a passing fad. We dismissed the paper and continued to develop the DIN, which I must say is an integral part of the communication systems within the DND. The point is that events can change history, much as the Internet has changed our lives. We are now dealing with social networks such as Facebook and Twitter. What is the next new Internet capability that will be introduced? The convergence of technology, such as digital cameras, could not have been predicted by the experts. Polaroid was a dominant force in cameras and now is a minor player in the digital camera market. When we think of digital cameras, we think of Canon, Olympus, Nikon, Sony, and maybe Panasonic—not Polaroid.

Risk Measure. How do we want to measure risk? Is it monetary? Time? Public safety? Lives? Environment? We may need different gauges for different reasons. When we look at the value of information, we need to determine the risks associated with incorrect information (wrong information), availability (wrong time), and theft (wrong person). The liability aspects of managing information are key factors in measuring risks. This will determine the mitigation strategies. An example is financial losses from downtime are significant enough to justify redundancy not only within the data center but also having several data centers distributed around the world (like Google, for example).

Benchmarks. Are there benchmarks that we can use to measure against? Do we use standards like COBIT or ITIL or focus on similar organizations in our industry? We must be careful about what we are comparing ourselves to in order to get the right benchmark. When we look at our internal processes, do we compare ourselves with others in the same industry? If our peers are not up to our standard, do we look elsewhere to make sure we are continuously improving? If we have achieved Level 4 in our process maturity, as defined by Watts Humphrey in his Process Maturity Levels, is that sufficient to maintain? We really need to determine what process level is most cost effective for our organization; Level 3 may be the best based on a cost analysis and ROI.

These four elements—time horizon, scenarios, risk measure, and benchmarks—are useful in providing forward-looking risk management. Although we cannot predict a black swan and its impact, we can assess some of our operational risks using forward-looking risk management. This can be accomplished by reviewing the products, processes, and projects to determine alignment with budget and expectations. Let's face it, the more complexity and uncertainty, the higher the risks. These two factors—complexity and uncertainty— were predominant factors in determining project risks when I developed a method for measuring if a project was risky and what controls should be applied to reduce the risks (see Appendix B). To make sure you are on track, you need to look at next year to know you are doing the right things to meet business objectives. So a yearly review of your products, processes, and projects should keep you aligned. Questions to ask include

- What are the major market, environmental, social, political, technology changes or innovations that might impact our products, processes, and projects?
- What products are being offered?
- Are my processes aligned to deliver the information necessary for those products?
- Are my projects aligned to support the delivery of information for those products?

There may be events in your life that you can neither prepare for nor predict. Okay, we can prepare for a lot of things using business continuity management, or some refer to it as business resilience. In any event, there is a certain amount of preparation that can be done to minimize the impact as much as possible. There is a term for an improbable event and that is a *black swan* (see Chapter 25).

25

PREPARING FOR A "BLACK SWAN"

A "black swan" is a highly improbable event. Nassim Nicholas Taleb (2007), in his book entitled *The Black Swan*, described it as follows:

A BLACK SWAN is a highly improbable event with three principle characteristics: It is unpredictable; it carries a massive impact; and, after the fact we concoct an explanation that makes it appear less random, and more predicable, than it was.

Leonard Mlodinow (2008), in his book entitled *The Drunkard's Walk*, described how randomness rules our lives. We often think we are in control of events when there are so many factors that enter into each day. The "butterfly effect" is a phrase that describes Chaos Theory. In 1972, Philip Merilees concocted "Does the flap of a butterfly's wings in Brazil set off a tornado in Texas?" The point of all this is to tell you that there are events outside your control and these events may have an effect on your operations. A little bit of forward-looking risk management may give you insight into predicting some events that may have an impact on your organization; however, there are events that do change things significantly like 9/11 and the 2008 market meltdown.

An article by Elise Stolte in the *Montreal Gazette* (September 5, 2009) described a perfect example of how a random event caused the complete disruption of research work in the high Arctic. A University of Alberta researcher had to be airlifted and cancel her research after a pilot with an eco-tourism agency left cardboard boxes of bacon and sausages on the tundra near their camp. The smell of the bacon attracted wolves that gorged themselves on the bacon and then did not want to leave. The researcher, fearing for her own safety, fled and could not complete her studies. The leaving of packages of bacon and the coincidence that wolves were nearby caused the termination of the research. These events could not have been predicted by the researcher and were completely out of her control. You may not have Arctic wolves circling your camp but there are random events that can have an impact on service delivery.

The objective is not to prepare for every potential event. Rather, the objective is to have processes in place that can handle most of the events. An incident response process is important. Whether it is a security breach or a system outage, there should be a consistent approach taken to deal with such events. Different skills are required for different events and, depending on the size and scope of the event, will dictate communications, command and control requirements, and the extent of the response.

26
Conclusion

Risk management starts with a commitment from the top. Executives must buy into making risk management a priority. Risks must be managed at all levels. Risks may be isolated events that have a local impact or they may be events that impact the entire organization. The butterfly effect may cause dynasties to fall.

Risk management is not easy. Implementing a risk management program is even more difficult. This book is not meant to be prescriptive about how you should implement risk management. One size does not fit all organizations. There are some underlying principles, concepts, and practices that should be incorporated into every organization. Every organization should have a risk management strategy. There are common risks that must be addressed. One of them concerns information and information technology. Because information technology is now the way we manage information, we need to adopt an enterprise risk management approach.

Enterprise risk management is not a panacea. Risks are managed at all levels, and the recognition that there are both horizontal risks and vertical risks implies that a single risk management strategy cannot be applied to all risks. We must recognize that there are intersections between vertical risks and horizontal risks that may be more effective using an enterprise risk management approach; similar risks in vertical business areas that will enable a similar approach to managing risks.

CIOs are responsible for making sure that information is available to the right person at the right time to effect good outcomes. This means

- *Information delivery:* making sure that information is available, either structured or unstructured.
- *Information management:* making sure the right applications are there to allow information to be found, analyzed, manipulated, and managed.

- *Information protection:* making sure the right controls are in place to protect the integrity and confidentiality of, as well as allowing or denying access to the information

Information is the lifeblood of any organization. Executives, managers, and knowledge workers all need good information. The demand for information is only increasing, putting pressure on the CIO to be more effective in managing resources and budgets. Not only is the demand for good information increasing, but the volume of information is increasing exponentially. CIOs must deal with increased volumes and demands that are being placed on their organizations. Realigning the organization with the focus on information is imperative.

Information flows into an organization in an uncontrolled manner and should be released in a controlled manner. Unfortunately, there are individuals who accidentally or deliberately release information in an uncontrolled manner, referred to as data or information leakage. In some cases this is because we are dealing with magnitudes of complexity in technologies, applications, and organizations, our interfaces to the world creating significant uncertainties. These uncertainties add risks to the organization. The risks are to reputation, brand, customer trust, loyalties, and operations. The cost of a security breach continues to rise. With each breach reported there are new requirements for compliance. PCI, privacy, SOX, and a host of other compliance requirements are moving from the auditors to the boardroom. These risks are causing a rethink of how information is managed and protected. The damage caused by the loss of intellectual property is staggering. The U.S. government reports that it costs U.S. companies billions of dollars each year.

The CIO is responsible for making sure the right information gets to the right person at the right time so they can do their job. The CIO is also responsible for making sure that the wrong information does not get to the wrong person at the wrong time, thus creating liability. It is a balancing act: focus on one and the other suffers. If there is no risk management at the top, the CIO must create an information risk management program that manages the risks to information delivery, management, and protection.

Organizations are measured in outcomes. Outcomes are defined as the delivery of products, services, and support that sustain and grow the organization. We must not confuse output metrics with outcome metrics. Output metrics such as uptime contribute to outcomes. Risk management needs to focus on both vertical risks and horizontal risks. Good risk managers look for the intersection and interdependencies of risks. Risks are not static, and relying on historical data is not the best approach to good risk management. You need to look and understand trends, markets, economics, and—most of all—people. People cause most of the failures, and good risk management looks at how we can mitigate these failures by providing the right controls. This includes good policies and procedures.

A good risk management program can start small and be expanded as needed. At the end of the day, we manage risks as individuals. Our risk management philosophy dictates that some of us will take spectacular risks depending on the rewards. Others will take a very conservative approach. Once we start looking at risks from an organization perspective, we can then start managing risks better.

Appendix A: OECD Privacy Principles

Collection Limitation Principle

There should be limits to the collection of personal data and any such data should be obtained by lawful and fair means and, where appropriate, with the knowledge or consent of the data subject.

Data Quality Principle

Personal data should be relevant to the purposes for which they are to be used, and, to the extent necessary for those purposes, should be accurate, complete, and kept up-to-date.

Purpose Specification Principle

The purposes for which personal data are collected should be specified not later than at the time of data collection and the subsequent use limited to the fulfilment of those purposes or such others as are not incompatible with those purposes and as are specified on each occasion of change of purpose.

Use Limitation Principle

Personal data should not be disclosed, made available or otherwise used for purposes other than those specified in accordance with the Purpose Specific Principle except:

a) With the consent of the data subject; or
b) By the authority of law.

Security Safeguards Principle

Personal data should be protected by reasonable security safeguards against such risks as loss or unauthorised access, destruction, use, modification or disclosure of data.

Openness Principle

There should be a general policy of openness about developments, practices and policies with respect to personal data. Means should be readily available of establishing the existence and nature of personal data, and the main purposes of their use, as well as the identity and usual residence of the data controller.

Individual Participation Principle

An individual should have the right:

a) To obtain from a data controller, or otherwise, confirmation of whether or not the data controller has data relating to him;
b) To have communicated to him, data relating to him
   • Within a reasonable time;
   • At a charge, if any, that is not excessive;
   • In a reasonable manner; and
   • In a form that is readily intelligible to him;
c) To be given reasons if a request made under subparagraphs (a) and (b) is denied, and to be able to challenge such denial; and
d) To challenge data relating to him and, if the challenge is success-ful to have the data erased, rectified, completed or amended.

Accountability Principle

A data controller should be accountable for complying with measures which give effect to the principles stated above.

(*Source:* From OECP privacy principles; www.oecd.org.)

Appendix B: Project Profiling Risk Assessment

PROJECT RISK	VERY LOW	LOW	MODERATE	HIGH	VERY HIGH
1. The objective of the project is well defined and aligned with the business and program delivery	1. Known deliverable, possible contractual or legislative requirement	2. Known deliverable, some minor changes to existing business process expected	3. Moderate changes to existing business processes and the deliverable/outcome is fairly well understood	4. Significant changes to existing business processes required	5. New and unknown business requirements are being implemented
2. The scope of the project is well defined	1. Scope is well defined and will not change	2. Scope is defined and there may be small changes	3. Scope is reasonably defined and there may be moderate changes	4. Scope is not well defined and there may be major changes	5. Scope is not well defined, and the outcomes are not certain; it is anticipated that there will be up to a 50% change in the scope
3. The impact of the project is well defined	1. Group within a business or division critical	2. Larger group, unit, or division critical	3. Business (branch) critical	4. Mission critical	5. Life/limb or public safety critical
4. The cost of the project is known and sized appropriately	1. Less than $50,000	2. $50,000–$100,000	3. $100,000–$250,000	4. $250,000–$500,0000	5. $500,000+

	1	2	3	4	5
5. The technology being used for the project is well defined	1. Existing technology used, well understood; local and in-house expertise	2. Existing technology used, new way of deploying; well understood; local and in-house expertise	3. Some new technology used, no major changes; fairly well understood; some local and in-house expertise	4. New technology used, major changes; not well understood; have not done this before; limited local or in-house expertise	5. New architecture and new technology, very little if any expertise in-house or local
6. The schedule of the project is well defined and appropriate for the size and scope of the project	1. Less than 3 months	2. 3 months to 6 months	3. 6 months to 12 months	4. 12 months to 18 months	5. More than 18 months
7. Stakeholders of the project are known, support and understand the project	1. One management sponsor; small community of interest	2. One executive sponsor and management approval	3. Two executive sponsors from different program areas	4. Multiple executive sponsors from different program areas same business function	5. Multiple executive sponsors, multiple partners, high potential for conflicting objectives
8. All dependencies have been identified and are known	1. None	2. Limited dependencies, well insulated from other projects	3. Moderate dependencies have been identified and there is loose coupling with other projects and/or technologies	4. Significant dependencies are identified and there is coupling with other projects and/or technologies	5. Tightly coupled with other projects, technologies, and partners

Continued

PROJECT RISK	VERY LOW	LOW	MODERATE	HIGH	VERY HIGH
9. Resourcing for the project, including an appropriate project manager, has been identified and assigned	1. 1 or 2 resources are required and already assigned	2. 3 to 5 Resources are required and assigned	3. 6 to 10 Resources are required and some have been assigned; contracting with one or more vendors	4. 11 to 15 Resources are required, some are unknown, few are assigned; contracting with one or more vendors	5. 16 or more Resources are required, many are unknown; contracting to multiple vendors, few are assigned
10. The project visibility is known and understood	1. The outcome of the project is very localized and will affect only a few people	2. The outcome of the project is specific to a targeted group of people and will not affect the public	3. The outcome of the project has a moderate effect on the business and program delivery	4. The outcome of the project has a major impact on the business and program delivery. There may be some impact on the public; mostly internal to government	5. The outcome of the project will affect many people including the public. It is highly publicized and/or has legislative changes

Appendix C: Risk Impact Scales

This is a simple risk impact scale that can be used to help individuals put the impact of a breach in confidentiality, integrity, or availability into scope. It gives two aspects to the impact: financial and a descriptor. The scale is logarithmic and provides magnitude or exponential levels of impact. The value of x is a numeric value that can be assigned based on the size of the organization or the amount of revenue. The dollar value of x should be of sufficient dollar value as to represent a catastrophic failure to the executive. In other words, if the breach will result in a major or catastrophic loss, then we need to consider mitigation.

IMPACT RISK	INSIGNIFICANT 10x	MINOR 100x	MODERATE 1,000x	MAJOR 10,000x	CATASTROPHIC 100,000x
Privacy	The consequences are dealt with by routine operations	The consequences are dealt with by routine operations and could have impacts that could require nominal defensive action	The consequences will result in a privacy breach and will require remedial action but falls within normal operational parameters	The consequences will result in a privacy breach and will require remedial action and falls outside of normal operations requiring extraordinary intervention	The consequences will result in a privacy breach and will require remedial action and will cause the organization significant problems requiring significant actions
Reputation	The consequences will not result in any reputation loss	The consequences will not result in loss of reputation but could have impacts that require nominal defensive action	The consequences may result in minor reputation loss and will require remedial action that falls within normal operating procedures	The consequences will result in reputation loss and will require remedial action that will require extraordinary intervention	The consequences will result in reputation loss and will require remedial action and will cause significant problems requiring significant actions
Productivity	The consequences are dealt with by routine operations	The consequences will result in loss of productivity and will require intervention	The consequences may result in minor productivity loss and will require remedial action that falls within normal operating procedures	The consequences will result in productivity loss and will require remedial action that will require extraordinary intervention	The consequences will result in productivity loss and will require remedial action and will cause significant problems requiring significant actions

	Monetary loss would be negligible	Monetary loss would be minor	Monetary loss would be medium	Monetary loss would be major	Monetary loss would be disasterous
Direct financial loss					
Legal	The consequences do not result in legal actions	The consequences will not have legal action but will require actions to remediate	The consequences will result in legal actions and will require remedial action but falls within normal operational parameters	The consequences will result in legal actions and will require remedial actions. This falls outside of normal operations and will require extraordinary intervention	The consequences will result in legal actions and will require significant actions
Life/limb	The consequences will not affect life and limb	The consequences may have an effect on life and limb but are part of operational procedures	The consequences will have an effect on life and limb and may result in damage. This still falls within normal operational parameters	The consequences will have loss of life or limb and will require extraordinary intervention	The consequences will have a loss of life or limb and will require significant actions
Safety	The consequences are dealt with by routine operations	The consequences have minor effects on safety and are dealt with by normal operations	The consequences have an effect on safety and result in actional that is still within normal operational parameters	The consequences have a direct impact on safety and will require extraordinary intervention	The consequences will impact safety and will require significant actions

Note: x = dollar value that is commensurate with the value of the organization. Example 1) Corporation is valued at $250 million; x could be $100. Example 2) Corporation is valued at $10 billion; x could be $5,000.

Appendix D: Classification Schema

LEVEL	DEFINITION	EXAMPLES
High	Could reasonably be expected **to cause extremely serious personal or enterprise injury**, including any combination of: • Extremely significant financial loss, • Loss of life or public safety, • Loss of confidence in the government, • Social hardship, or • Major political or economic impact.	**Confidentiality** examples include: • Information on a police informant or witness protection subject, • Cabinet confidence, • Exploration data in a mineral or oil industry, • Information relating to a sex offender, and • Information relating to the case files of a major crime. **Availability** examples include: • Crisis communication during emergencies, • Essential police communications information, and • Emergency health information services.

Continued

LEVEL	DEFINITION	EXAMPLES
		Integrity examples include: • Information systems used for testing food or water supplies that could result in loss of life or severe illness, • Information systems related to emergency health care, • Law enforcement information, • Extremely large financial transaction transfers, and • Extended loss of service resulting in the need to institute manual processes.
Medium	Could reasonably be expected **to cause serious personal or enterprise injury**, including any combination of: • Loss of competitive advantage, • Loss of confidence in the government program, • Significant financial loss, • Legal action, or • Damage to partnerships, relationships, and reputation.	**Confidentiality** examples include: • Compromise of personal medical or health information, • Information on a completed tax return form, • Information describing personal finances, • Eligibility information for social benefits, and • Disclosure of trade secrets or intellectual property. **Availability** examples include: • Payments of benefits to Canadians, and • Financial and management information systems. **Integrity** examples include: • Information assets related to food or water supply that would not meet expected standards of quality and would not cause illness, • Information assets related to non-emergency health care, • Financial transaction transfers and payments, and • Information that could be used for criminal purposes (e.g., false identity or impersonation).

LEVEL	DEFINITION	EXAMPLES
Low	Could reasonably be expected **to cause significant injury to individuals or enterprises**, including any combination of: • Limited financial losses, • Limited impact in service level, or • Performance embarrassment and inconvenience.	**Confidentiality** examples include: • Basic or "tombstone" personal information, • Status of government evaluation of a company product, and • Unauthorized release of the job applicant's names. **Availability** examples include: • Denial of service resulting in status of social assistance application not being available. **Integrity** examples include: • Information assets relating to administrative information such as volume and type of customer orders, and • Operational procedure assets relating to non-critical activities.
Unclassified	Will **not result in injury** to individuals, governments, or private sector institutions and **financial loss would be insignificant.**	The type of information, if lost, changed, or denied **would not result in injury to an individual or government organization**. **Confidentiality** examples include: • Information of public knowledge that can be found on most government Web sites and would include such information as the government telephone books, advertisements for job opportunities in the various ministries, government-wide initiatives such as Government-On-Line, public health information, job classification level, and range of pay scale. **Availability** examples include: • Certain delay to access the information is tolerable. **Integrity** examples include: • Internal information of an organization with no legal effect.

Source: Public Sector Security Classification Guideline; www.im.gov.ab.ca/imtopics/pdf/PublicSectorSecurityClassGuide.pdf

Bibliography

Albrecht, K. *Practical Intelligence: The Art and Science of Common Sense.* Jossey-Bass, San Francisco, CA, 2007.

American National Standards Institute. Guidelines for the Construction, Format and Management of Monolingual Controlled Vocabularies, 2005. American National Standards Institute, ANSI/NISO Z39.19-2005, www.niso.org.

Amy, D. The Importance of a Print Management Strategy, 2008. Convergence Consulting Inc. www.convergenceconsulting.biz.

ARMA. Developing a Records Retention Program, 1986. ARMA, www.arma.org.

Ayres, I. *Super Crunchers.* Bantam, New York, 2007.

Babiak, P. and Hare, R. *Snakes in Suits.* Collins Business, New York, 2006.

Bakan, J. *The Corporation.* Penguin Books, Toronto, Canada, 2004.

Beasley, M.S., Joseph V., Carcello, J.V., Hermanson, D.R., and Neal, T.L. Fraudulent Financial Reporting 1998–2007. COSO, May 2010.

Becker, J. Five Ways Continuous Control Monitoring (CCM) Is Supporting Risk-Management Programs, June 2010. www.Complianceweek.com.

Behr, K., Kim, G., and Spafford, G. *The Visible Ops Handbook.* Information Technology Process Institute, Eugene, OR, 2004–2005.

Bernoulli, D. Exposition of a new theory on the measurement of risk. *Econometrica,* 22(1), 23–36, January 1954.

Brink, D. *Data Loss Prevention.* Aberdeen Group, Boston, MA, May 2008.

Brink, D. The Case for SIEM. Aberdeen Group. Boston, MA, May 18, 2005.

Bryan, L.L. and Joyce, C. The 21st century organization. *McKinsey Quarterly,* July 28, 2009.

Buntine, W., Perttu, S., and Tirri, H. Building and maintaining web taxono-mies. *Proceedings of the XML Finland 2002 Conference* (pp. 54–65), HIIT Publications, Finland, 2002.

Canadian Bar Association. Guidelines for the Discovery of Electronic Documents in Ontario. www.cba.org.

Canadian Institute of Actuaries. *A New Approach for Managing Operational Risk.* Canadian Institute of Actuaries, Ottowa, Ontario, Canada, 2009.

Canadian Institute of Chartered Accountants. *Audit Implications of EDI.* The Canadian Institute of Chartered Accountants, Toronto, Ontario, Canada, 1996.

Canadian Institute of Chartered Accountants. *Audit Implications of Electronic Document Management.* The Canadian Institute of Chartered Accountants, Toronto, Ontario, Canada,1996.

Caralli, R.A. Managing for Enterprise Security. Carnegie Mellon University, Pittsburgh, PA, December 2004.

Cavoukian, A., and Tapscott, D. *Who Knows.* Vintage, Canada, 1995.

Colgan, J.J. GARP: Principle of Disposition, June 30, 2010. ARMA, www.arma.org.

Cramm, S. *Circa 2015: The CIO of the future.* Valudance, 2008.

Cross, S. and Taylor, L. *Global Enterprise Risk Management Survey 10.* AON Corporation, 2010.

Crump, G. Deduplication: The New Math, June 14, 2010, www.analytics.infor-mationweek.com.

Cyber-Ark. Trust, Security & Passwords Survey Research Brief. Cyber-Ark Software, Inc. www.cyber-ark.com. June 10, 2009.

D'Aveni, R. *Hypercompetition.* Free Press, New York, 1994.

Dazo, R., and Yeager, B. *Enterprise Content Management: From Strategy to Solution. Dynamic Content Software,* 2010. Strategies Consulting Service, www.infotrends.com.

Dembo, R.S. and Freeman, A. *Seeing Tomorrow.* McClelland & Stewart Inc., Toronto, Ontario, Canada, 1998.

Dewhurst, M., Guthridge, M., and Mohr, E. Motivating people: Getting beyond the money. *McKinsey Quarterly,* November 2009.

Dravis, F. Enterprise Information Management. Strategy, Best Practices and Technologies on Your Path to Success, 2008. Baseline Consulting, www.baseline-consulting.com.

Edvinsson, L. and Malone, M.S. *Intellectual Capital.* Harper Business, New York, 1997.

Federal Bureau of Investigation. Digital evidence: Standards and principles. U.S. Department of Justice, *Forensic Science Communications,* 2(2), April 2000.

Feldman, E., Gilson, S., and Villalonga, B. *When Do Analysts Add Value? Evidence from Corporate Spinoffs.* Harvard Business School, Boston, MA, 2010.

FIPS Standards for Security Categorization of Federal Information and Information Systems. 199. February 2004.

FIPS PUB 200. Minimum Security Requirements for Federal Information and Information Systems. NIST, March 9, 2006, http://.crsc.nist.gov/ publications.

FISMA. Federal Information Security Management Act of 2002. U.S. Government.

Flynn, N. *The e-Policy Handbook*. Amacom. American Management Association, New York, 2001.

Frid, R. The Frid Factor: A Practical Guide to Building a Knowledge Management Program, 2002, www.cikm.com.

Frid, R. Knowledge-Enabled Business Management. Canadian Institute of Knowledge Management, October 9, 2003, www.cikm.com.

Gahtan, A.M., Kratz, M.P.J., and Mann, J.E. *Internet Law. Carswell, Scarborough, U.K.*, 1998.

Gentile, M., Collette, R., and August, T. *The CISO Handbook*. Auerbach Publications, New York, 2006.

Gibson, W. *Neuromancer*. Ace Books, New York, 1984.

Glassey, O. Method and instruments for modeling integrated knowledge. *Knowledge and Process Management*, 15, 247–257, 2008.

Goldsmith, R.F. e-guide. *Software Requirements Management*, 2010, www.searchsoftwarequality.com. www.searchwindevelopment.com.

Group 2. Wal-Mart Case Study ó RFID and Supply Chain Management, November 30, 200530/11/2005, mason.gmu.edu/~ryellapr/walmart.doc.

Gunn, G. Ethics at the Top: Your Most Effective Control. KPMG. January 20, 2010.

Gutmann, P. Why Biometrics and RFID Are Not a Panacea. University of Aukland, New Zealand.

H.R. 2458-48. 2002.

Hare, R.D. *Without Conscience*. Guilford Press, New York, 1993.

Harris, J. *Blindsided*. Captstone Publishing, Oxford, U.K., 2002.

Hartley, M., and Critchley, B. Canadian Firm's Lawsuit Halts Some Microsoft Word Sales in U.S. Canwest News Service. August 13, 2009.

Hartman, G. *Risk Is a Four Letter Word*. Stoddart Publishing, Toronto, Ontario, Canada, 1994.

Hexter, E.S. and Bayer, D.S. Building Risk Awareness into Performance: Integrating ERM and Performance Management. The Conference Board, 2008, www.conference-board.org.

Hillson, D. Integrated Risk Management as a Framework for Organisational Success, 2006. *2006 PMI Global Congress Proceedings*, www.risk-doctor.com.

Homer-Dixon, T. *The Ingenuity Gap*. Alfred A. Knopf, New York, 2000.

Horn, R. *Mapping Hypertext*. The Lexington Institute, Lexington, MA, 1989.

Hubbard, D.W. *How to Measure Anything*. Wiley, New York, 2007.

Hubbard, D.W. *The Failure of Risk Management*. Wiley, New York, 2009.

Humphrey, W.S. *Managing the Software Process*. Addison-Wesley, Boston, MA, 1995.

IBM. Closing the Data Privacy Gap: Protecting Sensitive Data in Non-Production Environments. IBM, March 2009, www.ibm.com.

IBM. Top 5 IT Budget Killers. IBM, July 2008, http:www.techrepublic.com/whitepapers/dmi-db2-ebook-top-5-it-budget-killers/2315981.

Informatica. Archiving best practices. *Informatica,* April 2009, http://www.techrepublic.com/whitepapers/archiving-best-practices-9-steps-to-successful-information-lifecycle-management/963479.

Information Systems Security Association. Generally Accepted Information Security Principles (GAISP 3.0). Information Systems Security Association, 2003, www.issa.org.

InQuira. *10 Knowledge Management Mistakes Others Have Made.* InQuira Inc., San Bruno, CA, 2009, http://www.inquira.com/pdf/10-mistakes-ebooks.pdf?elq=c2198c9d890c464ca2e15516ac01d659.

Internet Security Alliance. The Financial Management of Cyber Risk, 2010, www.isalliance.org and www.ansi.org.

ISA-ANSI. The Financial Management of Cyber Risk, 2010, www.isalliance and org. www.ansi.org.

ISACA. IS Auditing Procedure P1. IS Risk Assessment Measurement, April 1, 2002, www.isaca.org.

ISACA. The Risk IT Framework. ISACA. Rolling Meadows, IL, 2009.

IT Process Institute. Change, Configuration, and Release: What's Really Driving Top Performance, Eugene, OR, 2007, www.itpi.org.

IT Process Institute. Process Maturity Matters: The Key to Unlocking the Power of IT Controls, Eugene, OR, 2007, www.itpi.org.

IT Process Institute. Reframing IT Audit and Control Resource Decisions, Eugene, OR, 2006, www.itpi.org.

JISC. Records Management Infokit. JISC infoNet, Newcastle upon Tyne, U.K., 2007, http://www.jiscinfonet.ac.uk/infokits/records-management.

Julien, R. and Marks, J.T. *Avoiding the Black Swan: Barriers to Improving Risk Management.* Crowe Horwath, South Bend, IN, 2009.

Kabay, M.E. Using social psychology to implement security policies. In *Computer Security Handbook, 4th edition* (Chapter 35). John Wiley & Sons, New York, 2002.

Kahn, R.A. and Blair, B.T. *Information Nation.* Wiley Publishing, New York, 2009.

Karbaliotis, C. E-Discovery and Electronic Document Retention in Canada Using Symantec Enterprise Vault. Symantec Technologies, Mountain View, CA, 2007.

Kelly, K. The next 5000 days of the web. *2007 EG Conference,* Monterey, CA, 2007.

KellySears. Risk Profiling Toolkit. Developing a Corporate Risk Profile for Your Organization. KellySears Consulting Group. http://www.kellysears.ca/resources.htm.

Knowledge Wharton. Re-thinking Risk Management: Why the Mindset Matters More than the Model. Knowledge Wharton, April 15, 2009, http://knowledge.wharton.upenn.edu/article.cfm?articleid=2205.

Kulwal, M. Integrating Risk Management with Business Strategy. SAS, 2010, http://twitter.com/manojkulwal.

Land, G. Creativity and Innovation: The Natural Way. *Collaborate99*. November 1999.

Landoll, D. J. *The Security Risk Assessment Handbook*. Auerbach Publications, New York, 2006.

Laserfiche. Document Management Overview. Laserfiche, 2007, www.laserfiche.com.

Le Clair, C., and Moore, C. *Dynamic Case Management – An Old Idea Catches New Fire*. Forrester Research. Cambridge, MA, December 28, 2009.

Levine, R., Locke, C., Searls, D., and Weinberger, D. *The Cluetrain Manifesto*. Perseus Books, Inc., New York, 2000.

Libicki, M.C. Cyberdeterrence and Cyberwar. RAND Corporation, Santa Monica, CA, 2009, www.rand.org.

Lippis III, N.J. A Rational Approach to Data Loss Prevention, December 2008, http://lippisreport.com.

Little, T., Greene, F., Phillips, T., Pilger, R., and Poldervaart, R. Adaptive agility: Managing complexity and uncertainty. *IEEE Agile Development Conference*, pp. 63–70, June 6, 2004.

Lombardi. Getting Started with BPM. An Introduction to Business Process Management, 2000–2008, www.lombardi.com.

Lumension. Demystifying IT Risk to Achieve Greater Security and Compliance. Lumension, November 2009, www.lumension.com.

MacCormack, A., Baldwin, C., and Rusnak, J. *The Architecture of Complex Systems: Do Core-Periphery Structures Dominate?* Harvard Business School. Cambridge, MA, 2010.

Mark, A. and Snowden, D. *Researching Practice or Practicing Research: Innovating Methods in Healthcare—The Contribution of Cynefin*. Innovations in Healthcare. Palgrave McMillan, Reading, U.K., 2006.

Mathew, G. Data Loss Prevention Requirements Roadmap, April 2009, www.ca.com.

Mayer, J.H., and Schaper, M. *Data to Dollars: Supporting Top Management with Next-Generation Executive Information Systems*. Mckinsey & Company, New York, 2010.

McAfee. McAfee Virtual Crime Report, 2009, www.mcafee.com.

McCallister, E., Grance, T., and Scarfone, K. Guide to Protecting the Confidentiality of Personally Identifiable Information (PII), January 2009, NIST Special Publication 800-122 (DRAFT).

McCuaig, B. Developing the Appropriate Risk Appetite for Your ERM Program. Paisley GRC Solutions, 2010, www.paisley.thomsonreuters.com.

McCuaig, B. Fundamentals of GRC: Mastering Risk Assessment, 2009, www.paisley.com.

McCue, C. *Data Mining and Predictive Analysis*. Elsevier, Amsterdam, 2007.

Miller, D.W., and Miller, C.G. On evidence, medical and legal. *Journal of American Physicians and Surgeons*, 10(3), 70–75, 2005.

Miller, G.A. The magical number seven, *The Psychological Review*, 63, 81–97, 1956.

Milne, K. Optimizing Application Lifecycle Management, 2008, www.itpi. org.

Milne, K., and Bowles, A. How IT Governance Drives Improved Performance 2009, www.itpi.org.

Milne, K., and Orlov, L.M. Know Thy Self: Improving an IT Organization's Ability to Drive Business Success, 2008, www.itpi.org.

Minto, B. *The Minto Pyramid Principle.* Minto Books International, Inc. London, U.K., 2007.

Mlodinow, L. *The Drunkard's Walk.* Pantheon Books, New York, 2008.

Mogull, R. Best Practices for Endpoint Data Loss Prevention. Securosis. Sponsored by Symantec, 2010, http://securosis.com.

National Archives. Managing Information Risk. Information Policy Team. Office of Public Sector Information, Kew, Richmond, Surrey TW9 4DU. 2008.

NIST. Guide for Applying the Risk Management Framework to Federal Information Systems. NIST SP 800-37 revision 1, February 2010.

NIST. Managing Risk from Information Systems. NIST SP 800-39. April 2008.

NIST. Recommended Security Controls for Federal Information Systems and Organizations. NIST SP 800-53 revision 3, August 2009.

Novell. Novell File Reporter. Administration Guide. Novell, January 2010, www.novell.com.

OECD. OECD Principles of Corporate Governance. Organization for Economic Co-operation and Development. Paris, France, 2004.

Open Text. Seven Best Practices for your Enterprise Content Management Implementation. Open Text, 2010, www.opentext.com.

Paloalto Networks. *The Application Usage and Risk Report, 5th edition.* Palo Alto Networks, Spring 2010.

Perrow, C. *Complex organizations.* McGraw-Hill, New York. 1986.

Perry, J.M. Hearing on Credit Card Data Processing: How Secure Is It? Statement of Cardsystems Solutions before United States House of Representatives. July 21, 2005.

Peterson, G. Security Architecture Blueprint. Artec Group, Ft. Worth, TX, 2006.

Pfeffer, J., and Sutton, R.I. *Hard Facts.* Harvard Business School Press, Cambridge, MA, 2006.

Ponemon Institute. 2009 PCI DSS Compliance Survey. Sponsored by Imperva, September 24, 2009, http://www.ponemon.org

Ponemon Institute. Business Case for Data Protection. Sponsored by IBM, March 2010, http://www.ponemon.org.

Ponemon Institute. Data Loss Risks during Downsizing: As Employees Exit, So Does Corporate Data. Sponsored by Symantec, February 23, 2009, http://www.ponemon.org.

Ponemon Institute. Data Security in Development & Testing. Sponsored by Micro Focus. July 31, 2009.

Ponemon, L. *Cost of Data Breach.* Ponemon Institute, Traverse City, MI, 2006.

Proctor, P.E., and Ouellet, E. Magic Quadrant for Content-Aware Data Loss Prevention. Gartner RAS. Core research note G00200788. June 2010.

Province of British Columbia. Information Security Policy version 1.2. Office of the Government Chief Information Officer. March 2008.

PSCIOC. Public Sector Security Classification Guideline. Public Sector CIO Council. June 2004.

RedSeal. FISMA, Continuous Monitoring and Real-Time Risk Management. RedSeal. San Mateo, CA, 2009.

RIMS. Risk Maturity Model for Enterprise Risk Management. Risk and Insurance Management Society, 2008, www.rims.org.

Roberts, R., and Sikes, J. *IT in the New Normal.* McKinsey & Company, New York, 2009.

Roxburgh, C. The use and abuse of scenarios. *McKinsey Quarterly,* November 2009, www.mckinsey.com.

RSA. 6 Best Practices for Preventing Enterprise Data Loss. RSA – The security division of EMC. 2007–2009.

SAS. Best Practices in Reporting Meeting the Goal of an Enterprise Risk Management Platform. SAS Institute. 2008.

Schneier, B. The Psychology of Security, January 21, 2008, www.schneier.com/essay-155.html.

SearchSecurity.com. *Governance, Risk, Compliance Policy Management: Methods and Tools,* 2009, www.searchcompliance.com. www.searchsecurity.com.

SearchSecurity.com. *Online Fraud: Mitigation and Detection to Reduce the Threat of Online Crime,* 2009. e-book, www.SearchSecurity.com.

Sedona Guidelines. Best Practice Guidelines & Commentary for Managing Information and Records in the Electronic Age. The Sedona Conference, 2nd edition. Sedona, AZ, November 2007.

Shah, M., and Littlefield, M. Managing Risks in Asset Intensive Operations. Aberdeen Group. Boston, MA, 2009.

Sharma, R.S., Chia, M., Choo, V. and Samuel, E. Using a taxonomy for knowledge audits: Some field experiences. *Journal of Knowledge Management Practice,* 11(1), March 2010.

Sharma, R.S., Foo, S., and Morales-Arroyo, M. Developing Corporate Taxonomies for Knowledge Auditability. Knowledge Organisation, Nanyang Technological University, Singapore, 2008.

Shaw, G. Twitter can be a legal minefield: Watch what you say. *Vancouver Sun,* Vancouver, BC, October 17, 2009.

Sherwood, J., Clark, A., and Lynas, D. Enterprise Security Architecture, 1995–2009, SABSA. www.sabsa.org.

Sierra Systems. *CORNET Keeps Track of All Provincial Offenders, Both in Custody and Out of Custody.* Sierra Systems, 2006.

Simon, G. Managing Risk and Uncertainty. An Executive's Guide to Integrated Business Planning, 2009, www.fsn.co.uk and www.oracle,com.

Smith, B. E-discovery gets an F. *Computerworld Canada.* March 24, 2009.

Snowden, D. The paradox of story. *Journal of Strategy and Scenario Planning,* 1(5), 16–20, November 1999.

Stoneburner, G., Goguen, A., and Feringa, A. Risk Management Guide for Information Technology Systems. NIST. SP 800-30. July 2002.

Stultz, R.M. Six ways companies mismanage risk. *Harvard Business Review*, March 2009, www.hbr.org.

Sullivan, D. *The Shortcut Guide to Prioritizing Security Spending*. IBM, 2009.

Symons, C. *Measuring the Business Value of IT*. Forrester Research, Boston, MA, September 25, 2006.

Taleb, N.N. *The Black Swan*. Random House, New York, 2007.

Tbeileh, K. *Oracle Database Vault*. Oracle, Redwood Shore, CA, July 2009.

Thomas, L. Records Management: Who Is Taking Responsibility? Aim, 2009, www.aiim.org.

Tolson, B. The Know-IT-All's Guide to eDiscovery. Mimosa Systems, 2009, www.mimosasystems.com.

University of California Santa Cruz. Guide to Writing Policy and Procedures, October 28, 1994, www.ucsc.edu.

University of Exeter School of Psychology. The Psychology of Scams: Provoking and Committing Errors of Judgement. Office of Fair Trading, May 2009, http://www.oft.gov.uk/shared_oft/reports/consumer_protection/oft1070.pdf.

U.S. Department of Energy. IT Security Architecture. U.S. Department of Energy, February 2007.

Verizon Business RISK Team. 2009 Data Breach Investigations Supplemental Report. Verizon, 2009, http://securityblog.verizonbusiness.com.

Verizon. 2009 Data Breach Investigation Report. Verizon Business Risk Team. 2009.

Vivisimo. Restricted Access. Entering the World of Secure Search. Vivisimo, 2010. www.vivisimo.com.

Walker, D. Review of Corporate Governance in UK Banks and Other Financial Industry Entities. Final Recommendations, November 26, 2009, http://www.hm-treasury.gov.uk/walker_review_information.htm.

Weber, M. *Economy and Society*. University of California Press, Berkeley, CA, 1978.

Westerman, G. *IT Risk Management: From IT Necessity to Strategic Business Value. Center for Information Systems Research*, Massachusetts Institute of Technology, Cambridge, MA, 2006.

Winkler, I. *Spies among Us*. Wiley Publishing, Indianapolis, IN, 2005.

World Economic Forum. Global Risks 2010. A Global Risk Network Report. World Economic Forum, January 2010, www.weforum.org.

Wysocki, R.K. *Effective Project Management*. Wiley, New York, 2003.

Zeltser, L. Emerging Internet Security Threats in 2009, 2009, www.SearchSecurity.com.

Index